CHILD LABOUR AND HUMAN RIGHTS

A Social Dimension

CHILD LABOUR AND HUMAN RIGHTS

A Social Dimension

Dr Lata Kaushal

MD Publications Pvt Ltd
New Delhi
www.mdppl.com

Published by :

MD Publications Pvt Ltd
"MD House", 11, Darya Ganj,
New Delhi - 110 002
Phone : +91-11-41563325 (Customer Service)
+91-11-41562846 (Editorial)
E-mail (orders): order@mdppl.com
Website: www.mdppl.com

ISBN: 978-81-7533-219-5

Published and Printed by Mr. Pranav Gupta on behalf of **MD Publications Pvt Ltd** at Mohit Enterprises, Delhi.

PREFACE

Children constitute part of the labour force in virtually every country. An estimated 246 million people between the ages of 5 and 17 work in the agricultural, industrial, and craft sectors worldwide. Approximately 180 million of these children work under the worst forms of child labour as defined by the International Labour Organization (2002). In spite of conventions and protocols designed to eradicate the worst forms of child labour, international human rights violations concerning children in the workplace persist.

The term child labour is used for employment of children below a certain age, which is considered illegal by law and custom. The stipulated age varies from country to country and government to government. Child labour is a world phenomenon which is considered exploitative and inhuman by many international organizations.

There is no denying the facts that children being defenceless and voiceless have suffered throughout the ages at the hand of society, community and parents. Millions of children, for example, are physically or sexually abused or economically exploited by those who are presumed to bestow them security and love.Around the world, hundreds of millions of children are working. Far too many are denied an education and work in dangerous and unhealthy conditions that expose them to lasting physical and psychological harm.

Child labour is not an easy issue to resolve; while it seems noble to immediately withdraw investments and cooperation with firms and factories that employ child labour it may do more harm than good. Many of these children are from very poor families and work to pay for their family and/or their education. Depriving them of this income has led to some children seeking different, lower paid work, and even prostitution in some cases. Other ways with schemes to help children would likely be needed so that this labour can be phased out.

Children are the blooming flowers in the garden of society. They are the most valuable assets of the nation as "Children of today are the potential citizens of tomorrow". The quality of life, they relish today would categorically determine the quality of life of future population of the nation. The children have rights like other human beings, to be respected with regard to their integrity, dignity, interests and opinions. But significantly enough, children are deprived of even the basic human rights due to them, as they ought to be in any civilised society.

I am very grateful to Mr. Pranav Gupta, Director of MD Publications Pvt Ltd, New Delhi, for his cooperation and support for this book.

Dr Lata Kaushal

Contents

1

Child Labour in India
An Introduction

According to a recent estimate of the International Labour Organization(ILO), more than 120 million children between the ages of 5-14 are employed as full time labourers around the world. A good number of such children labour in the most hazardous and dangerous industries. In India itself, it is estimated that there are at least 44 million child labourers in the age group of 5-14. More than eighty per cent of child labourers in India are employed in the agricultural and non-formal sectors and many are bonded labourers. Most of them are either illiterate or dropped out of school after two or three years. Child labour in India is a grave and extensive problem. Children under the age of 14 are forced to work in glass-blowing, fireworks, and most commonly, carpet-making factories. While the Government of India reports about 20 million children labourers, other non-governmental organizations estimate the number to be closer to 50 million. Most prevalent in the northern part of India, the exploitation of child labour has become an accepted practice, and is viewed by the local population as necessary to overcome the extreme poverty in the region.

Child labour is one of the main components of the carpet industry. Factories pay children extremely low wages, for which adults refuse to work, while forcing the youngsters to slave under perilous and unhygienic labour conditions. Many of these children are migrant workers, the majority coming from northern India, who are sent away by their families to earn an income sent directly home.

Thus, children are forced to endure the despicable conditions of the carpet factories, as their families depend on their wages. The situation of the children at the factories is desperate. Most work around 12 hours a day, with only small breaks for meals. Ill-nourished, the children are very often fed only minimal staples. The vast majority of migrant child workers who cannot return home at night sleep alongside of their loom, further inviting sickness and poor health.

Taking aggressive action to eliminate this problem is difficult in a nation where 75 per cent of the population lives in rural areas, most often stricken by poverty. Children are viewed as a form of economic security in this desolate setting, necessary to help supplement their families' income. Parents often sacrifice their children's education, as offspring are often expected to uphold their roles as wage-earning members of their clan.

The Indian Government has taken some steps to alleviate this monumental problem. In 1989, India invoked a law that made the employment of children under age 14 illegal, except in family-owned factories. However, this law is rarely followed, and does not apply to the employment of family members. Thus, factories often circumvent the law through claims of hiring distant family. Also, in rural areas, there are few enforcement mechanisms, and punishment for factories violating the mandate is minimal, if not nonexistent.

Legal action taken against the proliferation of child labour often produces few results. Laws against such abuses have little effect in a nation where this abhorred practice is accepted as being necessary for poor families to earn an income. Thus, an extensive reform process is necessary to eliminate the proliferation of child labour abuses in India which strives to end the desperate poverty in the nation. Changing the structure of the workforce and hiring the high number of currently unemployed adults in greatly improved work conditions is only the first step in this lengthy process. New labour standards and wages must be adopted and medical examinations and minimum nutrition requirements must be established in India. Establishing schools and eliminating the rampant illiteracy that plagues the country would work to preserve structural changes. However, these changes cannot be accomplished immediately. Pressure from the international community, especially the United States Government, is absolutely necessary to bring about change in India.

It is imperative for the U.S. Congress and the Clinton administration to pay more attention to the exploitation of children in India as well as other areas in South and Southeast Asia. Currently, Germany has instigated a pilot program that places a stamp on all imported carpets that are child labour free, thus urging consumers to buy these products. Because of the high price range of these carpets, similar programs can and should be given serious consideration in the United States.

The Child Labour Deterrence Act of 1993, which is still under consideration, prohibits importing to the U.S. any product made, whole or in part, by children under 15 who are employed in industry. While this aspect of the bill may be effective, the United States needs to take action regarding child labour abuses, specifically targeted at India. Mr. Speaker, I call on every Member of Congress to pay more attention to this little-recognized problem. We must acknowledge the fact that we cannot continue to sustain the exploitation of children by purchasing carpets woven by the hands of children.

Child Labour

Child labour is not child work. Child work can be beneficial and can enhance a child's physical, mental, spiritual, moral or social development without interfering with schooling, recreation and rest. Helping parents in their household activities and business after school in their free time also contributes positively to the development of the child. When such work is truly part of the socialisation process and a means of transmitting skills from parents to child, it is not child labour. Through such work children can increase their status as family members and citizens and gain confidence and self-esteem.

Child labour, however, is the opposite of child work. Child labour hampers the normal physical, intellectual, emotional and moral development of a child. Children who are in the growing process can permanently distort or disable their bodies when they carry heavy loads or are forced to adopt unnatural positions at work for long hours. Children are less resistant to diseases and suffer more readily from chemical hazards and radiation than adults. UNICEF classifies the hazards of child labour into three categories, namely (i) physical; (ii) cognitive; and (iii) emotional, social and moral.

I. Physical Hazards: There are jobs that are hazardous in themselves and affect child labourers immediately. They affect the overall health, coordination, strength, vision and hearing of children. One study indicates that hard physical labour over a period of years stunts a child's physical stature by up to 30 per cent of their biological potential . Working in mines, quarries, construction sites, and carrying heavy loads are some of the activities that put children directly at risk physically. Jobs in the glass and brassware industry in India, where children are exposed to high temperatures while rotating the wheel furnace and use heavy and sharp tools, are clearly physically hazardous to them.

II. Cognitive Hazards: Education helps a child to develop cognitively, emotionally and socially, and needless to say, education is often gravely reduced by child labour. Cognitive development includes literacy, numeracy and the acquisition of knowledge necessary to normal life. Work may take so much of a child's time that it becomes impossible for them to attend school; even if they do attend, they may be too tired to be attentive and follow the lessons.

III. Emotional, Social and Moral Hazards: There are jobs that may jeopardise a child's psychological and social growth more than physical growth. For example, a domestic job can involve relatively 'light' work. However, long hours of work, and the physical, psychological and sexual abuse to which the child domestic labourers are exposed make the work hazardous. Studies show that several domestic servants in India on average work for twenty hours a day with small intervals. According to a UNICEF survey, about 90 per cent of employers of domestic workers in India preferred children of 12 to 15 years of age. This is mostly because they can be easily dominated and obliged to work for long hours and can be paid less than what would have to be paid to an adult worker. Moral hazards generally refer dangers arising for children in activities in which they are used for illegal activities, such as trafficking of drugs, the sex trade, and for the production of pornographic materials.

Child Labour and its Hazards in India

Researchers give a range of incidence of child labour in India from about 14 million to about 100 million. Some studies show every fourth child in the age group of 5-15 is employed. It is estimated that over 20% of the country's GNP is contributed by child labour. The figures released by the non-governmental agencies are much higher than those of the State. UNICEF cites figures from various resources that put child labour in India at between seventy-five to ninety million. For some observers, the exact number of child labourers in India could be as high as 150 million.

In brief, India is the largest producer of child labour and illiteracy on this earth. According to at least one study, a quarter of the world's total number of child labourers are in India and every third household in that country has a child at work. Children in India are employed in almost all the activities of the non-formal sector. However, most of them are employed in the agricultural sector or in jobs closely related to agriculture, as is the pattern in many developing countries. A unique factor in India is that a significant number of these children are bonded labourers.

I. Bonded Child Labour: Slave labour or bonded labour is one of the worst forms of labour not only for children but also for adults. In India, bonded labour has been illegal since 1976 when Parliament enacted the Bonded Labour System (Abolition) Act. However, the practice is still widespread. Even conservative estimates suggest that there are at least 10 million adult bonded labourers in India. 89 per cent of adults in debt bondage belong to scheduled castes and tribes and 89 per cent of those who control them are agricultural landlords. Most of the work carried out by bonded labourers is hard manual labour in the fields or brick kilns. Children or adults are bonded in order to pay off debts that they or members of their families have incurred. They toil all their lives and endure physical attacks that often amount to torture.

There are thousands of bonded child labourers in India. They are also mostly the children of parents who belong to scheduled castes and tribes. Young children are sold to employers by their parents to pay back small loans that they have borrowed. Such children are made to work for many hours a day over several years. According to one study, there are about 10 million bonded child labourers working as house servants in Indian families. Varandani recently estimated that there were nearly 55 million children in India working as bonded labourers in agriculture, mining, brick-kilns, construction work, fishing activities, carpet weaving, fireworks, matches, glass moldings, bidi-making (cigarettes), gem-cutting and polishing work, electroplating, dyeing, washing and domestic work. About 20 per cent of these bonded child labourers were sold to cover some small debts obtained by their parents, usually for some social celebration like a wedding in the family.

One of the most notorious forms of bonded-labour is found in the carpet industry of India. A study undertaken in Kashmir shows that over 80 per cent of child labourers in carpet making work as bonded labourers. These young labourers, many of them 8 or 9 years old, are made to work for 20 hours a day without a break. They have to crouch on their toes from dawn to dusk which stunts their physical growth. Some of the children start to work when they are only 5-6 years of age, and by the time they are 20 they are burnt out. They are physically, mentally and emotionally exhausted so that they are no longer able to work and are doomed to unemployment even in cases when employment is available. The vicious cycle restarts when they want their children to work for them.

II. The Agricultural Sector: A recent ILO report states that in some developing countries nearly one third of the agricultural workforce is comprised of children. According to a survey of 1989, about 82 per cent of the 6.1 million fully economically active children in Bangladesh worked in agriculture. Similarly, in India about 80 per cent of child labourers are employed in agriculture and allied occupations. Studies also reveal that about 86 per cent of bonded labour is found in India's agricultural sector.

III. Street Work: There are thousands of children who live and work in the city streets of India. According to a study conducted among the street children in the city of Chennai (Madras), about 90% of them live with their parents in the streets. The same study also revealed that the largest group of street children in Chennai work as coolies (22%). About 10.4% of them work in hotels (small restaurants and snack bars), 9.6% do rag picking, 8% pull rickshaws, and 7.1% sell flowers. A smaller per centage of children are employed in other areas of work, including prostitution (0.3%). They work for 10-12 hours a day and at the end of the day what they earn is barely enough for their survival. About 32% of them receive less than 100 rupees (about 2.5 U.S. dollars) per month as wages.

Contrary to the general conception that many street children are delinquents, the study revealed that only 6.6% of the total sample had served time in juvenile homes or correctional institutions. Studies in a few other Indian cities showed that the majority of the street children were doing rag picking for their living. Usually, these children are unable to submit references or pay deposits to their employers to obtain any work. They choose rag picking as it is the most convenient way of earning something for their living that does not require much experience and investment. Scavenging is the work that faces children with the most extreme risk. As many of them work with bare feet, they get cuts; they are also exposed to extreme weather conditions, sunstroke, pneumonia, influenza and malaria. They have to carry heavy loads, which stunts their physical growth. They face digestive disorders and food poisoning as they eat thrown away or left over food.

A recent study conducted in Delhi found they were at risk of catching Aids, as they may accidentally come into contact with infected needles deposited in the refuse. Since animals scavenge in the same heaps of refuse, dog bites are quite common among these children. The local police and even the municipal cleaners create great difficulties for the street children in India. For any petty thefts, they are the first ones to be accused by the police. The local municipal cleaners, in turn, demand money and labour from them. If the children refuse to comply, they are threatened with the police, who will compel them to pay even more. A memorandum presented at a 'street children's rally' in Bangalore alleged that the police extorted about half the earnings of the rag pickers as commission. The children also had to pay some staff members of the municipality to ease the way for rag picking.

Child Labour in the Manufacturing Sector of India

Firozabad, an administrative unit in Agra district of Uttar Pradesh is the home of glass bangle and glassware industry in India. It is estimated that about 50,000 children below the age of 14 work in this industry. This is one of the highest concentrations of child labour in the world. According to forecasts, if the child labour were eliminated, production in the glass and bangle industry would go down by 25 per cent. Children are used in all the various phases of bangle making and glass blowing. About 85 per cent of them are employed in carrying molten glass on a seven-foot iron rod called *labya* from the furnace to the adult worker and back to the furnace. They sit in front of furnaces where the temperature is said to be 700 degrees centigrade.

Children, as they are small in stature have, to go close to the fire when they collect molten glass from the furnace. In her field research in the glass industry in India, Dr. Burra Neera notes that the children's faces were only about six to eight inches away from furnaces that were burning at 1500-1800 centigrade. As they work with fire in these factories, accidents are also common. When children carry molded glasses up and down, pieces fall on the floor and unless the children are very careful they can get burn injuries quite easily. In the long-term, the continuous exposure to high temperature harms their health permanently.

For more than seven decades, thousands of children have been working in the match factories at Sivakasi in Tamil Nadu. The total labour force in this industry is estimated to be 200,000, with about 35 per cent being children. Some of these children are bonded child labourers.

Factory owners send their vehicles to collect these children from villages. Many of them start their day as early as 4 a.m. and some even work until 10 p.m. At times they are made to work for 14 hours a day for a few more rupees on their wages; observers state that they work even during national holidays. Children are generally paid on a piece-rate basis. Payment for a piece is very low and thus they are indirectly forced to work faster and longer.

Respiratory diseases, eye infection, and exposure to chemical agents are the major health hazards in the match and fireworks industries. Researchers accuse the employers of not taking any precaution for fire safety in such workshops where even a small crack could start a fire. They found several children with burn scars on their hands, thighs and legs and 80 per cent of the children interviewed in such workshops reported cases of accidents. The Indian government has recognised that Sivakasi is an area with a high concentration of child labour and tries to implement some rehabilitative programmes there. However, child labour is still very much alive in this sector. Any attempt to remove child labour is met with stiff resistance by the interested parties. One study suggests that it would cost the employers Rs.32.8 million per annum if the children were to be replaced by adult workers. Unless and until the government acts with firmness, there is little possibility of 'redeeming' these children.

An ILO study estimates that there could be 420,000 child labourers in India employed in the carpet industry. According to some NGOs, between 1979 and 1993 the value of export earnings in the hand-knotted carpet industry in India grew tenfold. They also claim that the number of children working at the looms has increased from 100,000 in 1975 to 300,000 in 1990. The Indian 'carpet belt' is found mostly in Uttar Pradesh stretching over a vast area. There are usually about 20 or so loom sheds in each village. Some children work as bonded labourers; others are kidnapped from their poverty-stricken home villages, including villages in Bihar, the neighbouring state. Since the carpet industry is labour-intensive, entrepreneurs try to reduce labour costs by employing child labour.

Under the pretext of getting practice, children are introduced into the sector as early as the age of five. Though initially the children find it difficult to sit in the particular posture required for weaving, they gradually adapt to it. There is a new awareness at present in the international media about child labour exploitation in the South Asian carpet industry. This is partly due to 12 year-old Iqbal Masi, a bonded carpet weaver in Pakistan who was later killed for his anti-child labour campaign. At present, genuine efforts are made by some humanitarian agencies in the carpet importing nations to reduce or eliminate child labour in the sector.

According to the researcher Burra Neera, about 40,000-45,000 children are employed in the brass industry in India. Children in the brass industry are employed in different sectors. Molding is one of the activities, which is very hazardous and dangerous both to adults and children. More than 15000 children are employed in this sector. If the child is a new recruit, he is given the work of rotating the wheel that fans the underground furnace. Other children in the molding section must heat the oblong ingot on top of the furnace, break it into small pieces with a hammer and then melt the required amount of brass. When the molten brass is ready, they have to pass the graphite crucible with the raw material to an adult worker holding it with long tongs. Sometimes they themselves have to pour the brass into the moulds and replace the crucible into the furnace.

At times, children have to rotate the fan, remove the crucible and replace it in the furnace. They also may be asked to grind a hot black mixture into a fine powder with their hands and help the adult worker to remove the hot molded metal from the moulds. These activities have to be done continuously and children in the molding section would always be engaged in one or other of these activities. They may not receive any breaks in a ten-hour working day, even though a slight distraction or lapse of concentration may cause the child life-long injuries. The temperature in the furnace is about 1100 centigrade. If a drop of molten metal falls on the child's foot, it will create an immediate hole.

Neera observes in her study that the life span of children employed in the brass industry is quite brief. During her fieldwork she visited about 600 box furnace workshops, and noticed that all molders were less than 30 years of age. She was told that children who work in such workshops either do not survive as adults or become too ill to work. Tuberculosis seems to be an unavoidable consequence for child labourers in the brass industry. Even though these children work sacrificing their own lives for the brass industrialists, what they get in return is very little. In her research Burra Neera noticed that no child under 14 was paid more than 200 rupees per month, irrespective of the type and duration of the work.

The lock industry is mostly concentrated in the Aligarh district of Uttar Pradesh. Studies reveal that more than 60 per cent of the workers in this sector are children under 14 years of age. Children do polishing, electroplating, spray painting and working on hand presses. They cut different components of locks for nearly 12-14 hours a day with hand presses. Exhaustion causes accidents; many lose the tips of their fingers, which get caught in the machines. The most hazardous job for children in the lock industry is polishing.

The boys who do polishing stand close to the buffing machines. The buffing machines that run on electric power have emery powder coated on bobs. While polishing the locks, they inhale emery powder with metal dust and almost all polishers suffer from respiratory disorders and tuberculosis. In the small units, about 70 per cent of the polishers are children. Similarly, electroplating is another extremely hazardous process in which more than 70 per cent of workers are children below the age of 14 years.

Children work with naked hands in dangerous chemicals such as potassium cyanide, sodium phosphate, sodium silicate, hydroelectric acid, sulphuric acid, sodium hydroxide, chromic acid, barium hydroxide, etc. Children, besides being affected by the usual consequences of chemical substances, are also at risk of shocks as these substances also produce electricity and the floors are usually wet. The children have their hands in these solutions for the better part of the twelve-hour-day. Some cases of electrocution have been due to illegal electric connections obtained by some of these units from streetlights. About 50 per cent of the workforce in the spray-painting sector of the lock industry is comprised of children.

While at work, these children inhale large quantities of paint and paint thinners, leading to severe chest disorders. They suffer from breathlessness, fever, tuberculosis, bronchitis, asthma, and pneumoconiosis and from such symptoms and diseases. Work in the lock industry is dangerous and very hazardous for all employees, but is especially so for children. Thus, in India children do all kinds activities, from household work to brick making, from stone breaking to selling in shops and on streets, from bike repairing to garbage collecting and rag-picking. Most children work on farms and plantations or houses, far from the media scrutiny and the reach of a labour inspector.

There is no product that has not been scented by the sweat of a child labourer. India today has earned the dubious distinction of having the highest child labour force in the world. Every year in June, the world community celebrates Anti-Child Labour Day. And in increasing combination, various specialised agencies and non-government organisations (NGOs) have in recent years placed child labour, especially its worst forms, high among their concerns. They also have begun to achieve some discernible progress. But not nearly enough. According to the International Labour Organisation's (ILO) latest – though imperfect global estimate, approximately 246 million children between the age of five and 15 are engaged in "child labour".

The ILO further guesses that seven in 10 of them are in agriculture, followed by service businesses (22 per cent) and industry (nine per cent). Asia-Pacific claims the greatest share of child workers (122 million), then sub-Saharan Africa (49 million). In India, the government itself in its most recent account estimates that 12.6 million children under the age of 14 are at work in various occupations including hazardous occupations. NGO estimates put the number of children employed in domestic work and roadside eateries alone at two million. Centre of Concern for Child Labour, a Delhi based NGO estimated that there are nearly 70 million school-age going children in India who are out of schools. So the total number of working children in India is much higher than the government estimates. Child workers are engaged primarily in agriculture and allied activities in rural areas and in a variety of industries and informal sector activities in the urban areas.

The most exploitative form of chid labour includes child prostitution and forced and bonded labour, which is found in some parts of the country. The situation of girl child labourers in the country would call for particular attention. Children today often labour under extremely hazardous conditions, handling poisonous chemicals, inhaling noxious fumes, hauling excessive weights. They are usually overworked, underfed and underpaid- if they are paid at all. They toil so that their families can survive. The painful voices of working children can be heard the world over and India is no exception.

Seema is barely nine-year-old but from morning till evening she is engaged in the fields of a cotton seed farm that process high tech cotton seeds genetically engineered to contain a natural pesticide. To get the seeds to breed true, the farmers have to cross-pollinate the plants, a laborious task that keeps a peak of a dozen workers busy for several months on just one acre. And to make a profit, the farmers have to use cheap labour. That means using kids like Seema. It is estimated that every year nearly 420,000 labourers under the age of 18 are employed in cotton seed farms in four states- Andhra Pradesh, Karnataka, Maharashtra and Gujarat- across India. Of that total 54 per cent were under the age of 14 and illegally employed. The MV Foundation, an NGO in Andhra Pradesh backed by the Dutch non-profit Hivos campaigned against this practice.

With growing export, new areas of employing child labour are emerging. Garment units, embroidery units are now increasingly in news for violating child labours laws. In Rajasthan, the stone quarries employ under-age workers. Further north, in the state of Uttar Pradesh, hand-knotted carpets are made and sent to showrooms in America informs NGO Rugmark. Child labour is rampant here. Child labour has emerged as an increasingly important issue in the national context reflecting heightened sensitivity to the problem at all levels within the country. Important legislation on child labour includes the Child Labour (Prohibition and Regulation) Act of 1986 prohibiting the employment of children below 14 years of age in specified hazardous occupations and processes.

Along with this, the December 1996 Supreme Court judgments directs the withdrawal of children from hazardous occupation and the creation of a welfare fund for them, besides regulating working conditions in non hazardous occupations. Government policy has also been pro active in the area of child labour since the mid 1980 with the formulation of national policy on Child Labour in August 1987 and subsequent implementation of National

Child Labour Projects. The objective being of reducing the incident of child labour in high concentration areas through improved enforcement, rehabilitating and more integrated provisions of services. Child labour is banned in 13 industrial sectors and 52 types of work listed in the Child Labour (Prohibition) Act.

These sectors will not be able to employ children between 14 and 18 years if the law is amended. A 2006 amendment brought domestic work, work in the hospitality industry, under the ambit of the Act. But NGOs have been saying that despite the under-14 ban, thousands of children are still employed in hazardous industries listed in the Act, thanks to poor implementation of the existing legislation. Save the children's research on child domestic labour shows that 74 per cent of children in domestic work are between the ages of 12 and 16. This leaves a crucial gap in bringing a huge number of working children (aged between 14 and 18) under the protection of this Act.

Thousands of children work in roadside food stalls. Although India banned children under 14 from working as domestic servants or in food stalls, millions are continue to be employed, a study said. About 200,000 children below the age of 14 years are estimated to be working as domestic servants and in teashops, restaurants, spas, hotels, resorts and other recreational centres - the areas from where they were banned in 2006.

Current child legislation is not effective. Save the Children' said that in Delhi alone, close to a million children are still employed at homes or in food stalls. Another 40,000 work in the southern city of Hyderabad and 50,000 more work in Calcutta. The study said that in Delhi 99 per cent of child domestic workers are girls and in a large number of cases they are open to sexual abuse. Many parents say crippling poverty forces them to send their children, sometimes as young as five or six, to work in other people's homes or in factories.

The Constitution of India and successive governments have targeted elimination of child labour and promoted universalisation of education. This task is not easy and the effectiveness of child labour elimination programme must be measured by real change in the situation of children and or by the number of projects funded and networks created or by the research, advocacy educational campaigns or workshops and seminar held or legislations introduced. As Kailash Satyarthi, chairperson of the Global March Against Child Labour, has put it, "The real measure of success is the difference being made in the lives of vulnerable children."

It is important to acknowledge here that since the adoption of the 1989 CRC and particularly the 1999 ILO Convention (No 182) concerning the 'prohibition and immediate elimination of the worst forms of child labour' a commitment to the abolition of child labour as human rights imperative has taken hold and begun to spread. There are number of NGOs working in this field. But whether all this NGOs activity has altered the situation of working children for better is not clear.

Today most NGOs demand for legislation calling for compulsory primary education as a necessary prerequisite for child labour elimination. Reflecting on my own work for two and half decades in this field, I would not privilege education over income substitutions or generation scheme nor would I ignore critical issue in the quality and type of education being offered. Education is part of the child labour solution, but it is not *the* solution.

The issue of poverty and need do not simply go away because a child is enrolled in the school. The project relevant to education is that, without systematic redress of income poverty concerns, there is continuing financial pressure on poor families. While this may seem to be stating obvious, it is something that often is sidelines in child labour prevention and elimination programme. Advocates tend to focus on and privilege the application of legal instruments that relate to education but education legislation does not begin to address underlying economic causality. The moral high grounders claim that state provided education is the solution to child labour. There are number of activists that have been articulating for some time, insisting on one message to government, all children have the right to a full time education.

The first and key policy tenet in human rights (for children) approach to preventing and eliminating child labour is that achievement of quality universal primary education and elimination of poverty are interlinked in complex relationship. Successful sustainable elimination of child labour must face up to the connection between economic poverty and education. The question of child labour elimination is no longer whether or even how to cease the exploitation of children but *how quickly*. The ground reality suggests that while it is good to be developing international and national standards, laws and programmes to combat child labour (particularly the worst forms) until and unless one comes to moral and political grips, with the reality of poverty and with the divide between rich and the poor, the struggle against child labour will fizzle out.

One must, in other words, take holistic approach to child labour and not see it as a discrete problem that can be tackled without reference to the broader socio economic setting, in which it is rooted. The real social change takes places slowly. Millions of children in today's world undergo the worst forms of child labour which includes Child Slavery, Child prostitution, Child Trafficking, Child Soldiers. In modern era of material and technological advancement, children in almost every country are being callously exploited. The official figure of child labourers world wide is 13 million. But the actual number is much higher. Of the estimated 250 million children between the ages of 5 and 14 who are economically active, some 50 million to 60 million between the ages of 5 and 11 are engaged in intolerable forms of labour.

Among the 10 to 14year-old children the working rate is 41.3 per cent in Kenya, 31.4 per cent in Senegal, 30.1 per cent in Bangladesh, 25.8 per cent in Nigeria, 24 per cent in Turkey, 17.7 per cent in Pakistan, 16.1 per cent in Brazil, 14.4 per cent in India, 11.6 per cent in China. ILO estimated that 250 million children between 5 and 14 work for a living, and over 50 million children under age twelve work in hazardous circumstances. United Nations estimate that there were 20 million bonded child labourers worldwide. Based on reliable estimates, at least 700,000 persons to 2 million, especially girls and children, are trafficked each year across international borders. Research suggests that the age of the children involved is decreasing. Most are poor children between the ages of 13 and 18, although there is evidence that very young children even babies, are also caught up in this horrific trade. They come from all parts of the world. Some one million children enter the sex trade, exploited by people or circumstances.

At any one time, more than 300,000 children under 18 - girls and boys - are fighting as soldiers with government armed forces and armed opposition groups in more than 30 countries worldwide. ILO estimates that domestic work is the largest employment category of girls under age 16 in the world. India has the dubious distinction of being the nation with the largest number of child labourers in the world. The child labours endure miserable and difficult lives. They earn little and struggle to make enough to feed themselves and their families. They do not go to school; more than half of them are unable to learn the barest skills of literacy. Poverty is one of the main reasons behind this phenomenon. The unrelenting poverty forces the parents to push their young children in all forms of hazardous occupations. Child labour is a source of income for poor families. They provide help in household enterprises or of household chores in order to free adult household members for economic activity elsewhere.

In some cases, the study found that a child's income accounted for between 34 and 37 per cent of the total household income. In India the emergence of child labour is also because of unsustainable systems of landholding in agricultural areas and caste system in the rural areas. Bonded labour refers to the phenomenon of children working in conditions of servitude in order to pay their debts. The debt that binds them to their employer is incurred not by the children themselves but by their parent. The creditors cum employers offer these loans to destitute parents in an effort to secure the labour of these children. The arrangements between the parents and contracting agents are usually informal and unwritten. The number of years required to pay off such a loan is indeterminate.

The lower castes such as *dalits* and tribal make them vulnerable groups for exploitation. The environmental degradation and lack of employment avenues in the rural areas also cause people to migrate to big cities. On arrival in overcrowded cities the disintegration of family units takes place through alcoholism, unemployment or disillusionment of better life etc.

This in turn leads to emergence of street children and child workers who are forced by their circumstances to work from the early age. The girls are forced to work as sex -workers or beggars. A large number of girls end up working as domestic workers on low wages and unhealthy living conditions. Sometimes children are abandoned by their parents or sold to factory owners.

The last two decades have seen tremendous growth of export based industries and mass production factories utilizing low technologies. They try to maintain competitive positions through low wages and low labour standards. The child labourers exactly suit their requirements. They use all means to lure the parents into giving their children on pretext of providing education and good life. In India majority of children work in industries, such as cracker making, diamond polishing, glass, brass-ware, carpet weaving, bangle making, lock making and mica cutting to name a few. 15% of the 100,000 children work in the carpet industry of Uttar Pradesh. 70-80% of the 8,000 to 50,000 children work in the glass industry in Ferozabad. In the unorganized sector child labour is paid by piece-by-piece rates that result in even longer hours for very low pay. Inadequate schools, a lack of schools, or even the expense of schooling leaves some children with little else to do but work. The attitudes of parents also contribute to child labour; some parents feel that children should work in order to develop skills useful in the job market, instead of taking advantage of a formal education.

From the time of its independence, India has committed itself to be against child labour. Article 24 of the Indian constitution clearly states that "No child below the age of fourteen years shall be employed to work in any factory or mine or employed in any hazardous employment" The Bonded Labour System Act of 1976 fulfills the Indian Constitution's directive of ending forced labour A Plethora of additional protective legislation has been put in place. There are distinct laws governing child labour in factories in commercial establishments, on plantations and in apprenticeships.

There are laws governing the use of migrant labour and contract labour. A recent law The Child Labour (Prohibition and Regulation law) of 1986 designates a child as a person who has not completed their 14th year of age. It purports to regulate the hours and the conditions of child workers and to prohibit child workers in certain enumerated hazardous industries. However there is neither blanket prohibition on the use of child labour, nor any universal minimum age set for child workers.

All of the policies that the Indian government has in place are in accordance with the Constitution of India, and all support the eradication of Child Labour. The problem of child labour still remains even though all of these policies are existent. Enforcement is the key aspect that is lacking in the government's efforts.

Child labour is a global problem. If child labour is to be eradicated, the governments and agencies and those responsible for enforcement need to start doing their jobs. The most important thing is to increase awareness and keep discussing ways and means to check this problem. We have to decide whether we are going to take up the problem head-on and fight it any way we can or leave it to the adults who might not be there when things go out of hand. This has only highlighted the plight of millions of children who are employed in various activities often as bonded labourers in India. It does not discuss the question of solving or reducing this problem.

Often, child labour is considered to be a "necessary evil" in poor countries such as India for the maintenance of the family. In that context, some consider it virtuous to give a job to a child. In fact, some academics and activists campaign not for the reduction of child labour but only for a reduction in the exploitation of children. However, the question has to be asked whether it is justifiable to allow children from poor families to undergo physical, cognitive, emotional and moral hazards because they must help their families. Is the joy of childhood reserved only for some, privileged, children?

2

Children's Rights

"A child is any human being below the age of eighteen years, unless under the law applicable to the child, majority is attained earlier."

Children's rights are the human rights of children with particular attention to the rights of special protection and care afforded to the young, including their right to association with both biological parents, human identity as well as the basic needs for food, universal state-paid education, health care and criminal laws appropriate for the age and development of the child.

Interpretations of children's rights range from allowing children the capacity for autonomous action to the enforcement of children being physically, mentally and emotionally free from abuse. Other definitions include the rights to care and nurturing.

According to Cornell University, a child is a person, not a *subperson,* and the parent has absolute interest and possession of the child. The term "child" does not necessarily mean minor but can include adult children as well as adult nondependent children. There are no definitions of other terms used to describe young people such as "adolescents", "teenagers," or "youth" in international law. The field of children's rights spans the fields of law, politics, religion, and morality.

Rationale

As minors by law children do not have autonomy or the right to make decisions on their own for themselves. Instead their adult caregivers, including parents, social workers, teachers, youth workers and others, are vested with that authority depending on the circumstance the child is in. As applied to children these legal apparatuses are termed as "repressive state apparatuses", a concept which was originally coined by Louis Althusser. Research has found that because of these legal structures children themselves feel powerless and with little control over their own lives, and believe that the power of this structure, as opposed to their age or developmental ability, causes them to be vulnerable.

Structures such as government policy have been found to mask the ways adults abuse and exploit children, resulting in child poverty, lack of educational opportunities, and child labour. Research has also identified children as a minority group towards whom society needs to reconsider the way it behaves. Researchers have identified children as needing to be recognized as participants in society whose rights and responsibilities need to be recognized at all ages. Consensus on defining children's rights has become clearer in the last twenty years. A 1973 publication by Hillary Clinton (then an attorney) stated that children's rights were a "slogan in need of a definition".

According to some researchers, the notion of children's rights is still not well defined, with at least one proposing that there is no singularly accepted definition or theory of the rights held by children. Children's rights law is defined as the point where the law intersects with a child's life. That includes juvenile delinquency, due process for children involved in the criminal justice system, appropriate representation, and effective rehabilitative services; care and protection for children in state care; ensuring education for all children regardless of their origin, race, gender, disabilities, or abilities, and; health care and advocacy.

Types of Rights

Children's rights are defined in numerous ways, including a wide spectrum of civil, cultural, economic, social and political rights. Rights tend to be of two general types: those advocating for children as autonomous persons under the law and those placing a claim on society for protection from harms perpetrated on children because of their dependency. These have been labeled as the right of empowerment and as the right to protection. One Canadian organization categorizes children's rights into three categories:

- *Provision:* Children have the right to an adequate standard of living, health care, education and services, and to play. These include a balanced diet, a warm bed to sleep in, and access to schooling.
- *Protection:* Children have the right to protection from abuse, neglect, exploitation and discrimination. This includes the right to safe places for children to play; constructive child rearing behaviour, and acknowledgment of the evolving capacities of children.
- *Participation:* Children have the right to participate in communities and have programs and services for themselves. This includes children's involvement in libraries and community programs, youth voice activities, and involving children as decision-makers.

In a similar fashion, the Child Rights Information Network, or CRIN for short, categorizes rights into two groups:

- Economic, social and cultural rights, related to the conditions necessary to meet basic human needs such as food, shelter, education, health care, and gainful employment. Included are rights to education, adequate housing, food, water, the highest attainable standard of health, the right to work and rights at work, as well as the cultural rights of minorities and indigenous peoples.

- Environmental, cultural and developmental rights, which are sometimes called "third generation rights," and including the right to live in safe and healthy environments and that groups of people have the right to cultural, political, and economic development.

Amnesty International openly advocates four particular children's rights, including the end to juvenile incarceration without parole, an end to the recruitment of military use of children, ending the death penalty for people under 21, and raising awareness of human rights in the classroom.

Human Rights Watch, an international advocacy organization, includes child labour, juvenile justice, orphans and abandoned children, refugees, street children and corporal punishment.

Scholarly study generally focuses children's rights by identifying individual rights. The following rights "allow children to grow up healthy and free":

- Freedom of speech
- Freedom of thought
- Freedom from fear
- Freedom of choice and the right to make decisions
- Ownership over one's body

A Canadian organization identifies several other issues affecting children's rights, including fetal rights, infanticide, child abandonment, child identity rights, paternity fraud, paternity testing, age of consent, shaken baby syndrome, genital mutilation, bullying, corporal punishment, parental alienation, children's rights in family law, youth suicide, anorexia nervosa, ADHD, smoking, and childhood pregnancy. Other issues affecting children's rights include the sale of children, child prostitution and child pornography.

Children's Rights and Youth Rights

"In the majority of jurisdictions, for instance, children are not allowed to vote, to marry, to buy alcohol, to have sex, or to engage in paid employment." Within the youth rights movement, it is believed that the key difference between *children's* rights and *youth* rights is that children's rights supporters generally advocate the establishment and enforcement of protection for children and youths, while youth rights (a far smaller movement) generally advocates the expansion of freedom for children and/or youths and of rights such as suffrage. They should be allowed to go to the toilet when needing to during school times, as it can cause serious damage later on in life.

Child's Right to be Parented by Biological Parents

The U.N. Convention on the Rights of the Child supports the right of a child to be parented by his/her biological parents) unless the parent(s) is/are either neglectful or abusive to the child in which case the state must protect the child from the parent by means of removing the child or monitoring the parents' actions. The society of the child with the biological parent(s)is commonly identified as an essential child right. This includes the notion that children should not be denied relationships and benefits provided by the relationships and upbringing afforded by their biological parents. The only exception is unless the government must interfere for the purpose of protecting a child from parental abuse or neglect.

These cases are generally addressed by an immediate judicial review with the caveat that "all interested parties shall be given an opportunity to participate in the proceedings and make their views known". Parents affect the lives of children in a unique way, and as such their role in children's rights has to be distinguished in a particular way. Particular issues in the child-parent relationship include child neglect, child abuse, freedom of choice, corporal punishment and child custody. There have been theories offered that provide parents with rights-based practices that resolve the tension between "commonsense parenting" and children's rights.

The issue is particularly relevant in legal proceedings affect the potential emancipation of minors, and in cases where children sue their parents. A child's rights to a relationship with both their parents is increasingly recognized as an important factor for determining the best interests of the child in divorce and child custody proceedings. Some governments have enacted laws creating a rebuttable presumption that shared parenting is in the best interests of children.

Movement

The 1796 publication of Thomas Spence's *The Rights of Infants* is among the earliest English-language assertions of the rights of children. Throughout the 1900s children's rights activists organized for homeless children's rights and public education. The 1927 publication of *The Child's Right to Respect* by Janusz Korczak strengthened the literature surrounding the field, and today dozens of international organizations are working around the world to promote children's rights.

Opposition

The opposition to children's rights far outdates any current trend in society, with recorded statements against the rights of children dating to the 1200s and earlier. Opponents to children's rights believe that young people need to be protected from the adult centric world, including the decisions and responsibilities of that world. In the dominate adult society, childhood is idealized as a time of innocence, a time free of responsibility and conflict, and a time dominated by play. The majority of opposition stems from concerns related to national sovereignty, states' rights, the parent-child relationship. Financial constraints and the "undercurrent of traditional values in opposition to children's rights" are cited, as well. The concept of children's rights has received little attention in the United States.

International Law

The Universal Declaration of Human Rights is seen as a basis for all international legal standards for children's rights today. There are several conventions and laws that address children's rights around the world. A number of current and historical documents affect those rights, including the 1923 Declaration of the Rights of the Child, drafted by Eglantyne Jebb and her sister Dorothy Buxton in London, England in 1919, endorsed by the League of Nations and adopted by the United Nations in 1946. It later served as the basis for the Convention on the Rights of the Child.

Convention on the Rights of the Child

The United Nations' 1989 Convention on the Rights of the Child, or CRC, is the first legally binding international instrument to incorporate the full range of human rights—civil, cultural, economic, political and social rights. Its implementation is monitored by the Committee on the Rights of the Child.

National governments that ratify it commit themselves to protecting and ensuring children's rights, and agree to hold themselves accountable for this commitment before the international community. The CRC, along with international criminal accountability mechanisms such as the International Criminal Court, the Yugoslavia and Rwanda Tribunals, and the Special Court for Sierra Leone, is said to have significantly increased the profile of children's rights worldwide.

Enforcement

A variety of enforcement organizations and mechanisms exist to ensure children's rights and the successful implementation of the Union. They include the Child Rights Caucus for the United Nations General Assembly Special Session on Children. It was set up to promote full implementation and compliance with the Convention on the Rights of the Child, and to ensure that child rights were given priority during the UN General Assembly Special Session on Children and its Preparatory process. The United Nations Human Rights Council was created "with the hope that it could be more objective, credible and efficient in denouncing human rights violations worldwide than the highly politicised Commission on Human Rights."

The NGO Group for the Convention on the Rights of the Child is a coalition of international non-governmental organisations originally formed in 1983 to facilitate the implementation of the United Nations Convention on the Rights of the Child. Many countries around the world have children's rights ombuds people or children's commissioners whose official, governmental duty is to represent the interests of the public by investigating and addressing complaints reported by individual citizens regarding children's rights. Children's ombuds people can also work for a corporation, a newspaper, an NGO, or even for the general public.

United States Law

Children are generally afforded the basic rights embodied by the Constitution, as enshrined by the Fourteenth Amendment to the United States Constitution. The Equal Protection Clause of that amendment is to apply to children, born within a marriage or not, but excludes children not yet born. This was reinforced by the landmark US Supreme Court decision of *In re Gault*. In this trial 15-

year-old Gerald Gault of Arizona was taken into custody by local police after being accused of making an obscene telephone call. He was detained and committed to the Arizona State Industrial School until he reached the age of 21 for making an obscene phone call to an adult neighbour.

In an 8-1 decision, the Court ruled that in hearings which could result in commitment to an institution, people under the age of 18 have the right to notice and counsel, to question witnesses, and to protection against self-incrimination. The Court found that the procedures used in Gault's hearing met none of these requirements. There are other concerns in the United States regarding children's rights. The American Academy of Adoption Attorneys is concerned with children's rights to a safe, supportive and stable family structure. Their position on children's rights in adoption cases states that, "children have a constitutionally based liberty interest in the protection of their established families, rights which are at least equal to, and we believe outweigh, the rights of others who would claim a 'possessory' interest in these children." Other issues raised in American children's rights advocacy include children's rights to inheritance in same-sex marriages and particular rights for youth.

Children's Rights Movement

The Children's Rights Movement is a historical and modern movement committed to the acknowledgment, expansion, and/or regression of the rights of children around the world. While the historical definition of child has varied, the United Nations Convention on the Rights of the Child explains, "A child is any human being below the age of eighteen years, unless under the law applicable to the child, majority is attained earlier." There are no definitions of other terms used to describe young people such as "adolescents", "teenagers" or "youth" in international law.

Thomas Spence's *The Rights of Infants* (1796) is an early English-language assertion of the natural rights of children. In the USA, the Children's Rights Movement was born in the 1800s with the orphan train. In the big cities, when a child's parents died, the child frequently had to go to work to support him or herself. Boys generally became factory or coal workers, and girls became prostitutes or saloon girls, or else went to work in a sweet shop. All of these jobs paid only starvation wages.

In 1852, Massachusetts required children to attend school. In 1853, Charles Brace founded the *Children's Aid Society*, which worked hard to take street children in. The following year, the children were placed on a train headed for the West, where they were adopted, and often given work. By 1929, the orphan train stopped running altogether, but its principles lived on. The *National Child Labour Committee*, an organization dedicated to the abolition of all child labour, was formed in the 1890s. It managed to pass one law, which was struck down by the Supreme Court two years later for violating a child's right to contract his work. In 1924, Congress attempted to pass a constitutional amendment that would authorize a national child labour law. This measure was blocked, and the bill was eventually dropped.

It took the Great Depression to end child labour nationwide; adults had become so desperate for jobs that they would work for the same wage as children. In 1938, President Franklin D. Roosevelt signed the Fair Labour Standards Act which, amongst other things, placed limits on many forms of child labour. Now that child labour had been effectively eradicated in parts of the world, the movement turned to other things, but it again stalled when World War II broke out and children and women began to enter the work force once more. With millions of adults at war, the children were needed to help keep the country running. In Europe, children served as couriers, intelligence collectors, and other underground resistance workers in opposition to Hitler's regime.

Present

In the early twentieth century, moves began to promote the idea of children's rights as distinct from those of adults and as requiring explicit recognition. The Polish educationalist Janusz Korczak wrote of the rights of children in his book *How to Love a Child;* a later book was entitled *The Child's Right to Respect*. In 1917, following the Russian Revolution, the Moscow branch of the organization Proletkult produced a Declaration of Children's Rights. However, the first effective attempt to promote children's rights was the Declaration of the Rights of the Child, drafted by Eglantyne Jebb in 1923 and adopted by the League of Nations in 1924. This was accepted by the United Nations on its formation and updated in 1959, and replaced with a more extensive UN Convention on the Rights of the Child in 1989.

From the formation of the United Nations in the 1940s and extending to present day, the Children's Rights Movement has become global in focus. While the situation of children in the United States has become grave, children around the world have increasingly become engaged in illegal, forced child labour, genital mutilation, military service, and sex trafficking. Several international organizations have rallied to the assistance of children. They include Save the Children, Free the Children, and the Children's Defense Fund. The Child Rights Information Network, or CRIN, formed in 1983, is the group of 1,600 non-governmental organizations from around the world which advocate for the implementation of the Convention on the Rights of the Child. Organization's report on their countries' progress towards implementation, as do governments that have ratified the Convention. Every 5 years reporting to the United Nations Committee on the

Rights of the Child is required for governments.

While there is a long history of children's rights in the U.S., scholars contend that there is no "golden age". Many children's rights advocates in the U.S. today advocate for a smaller agenda than their international peers. Groups predominately focus on child abuse and neglect, child fatalities, foster care, youth aging out of foster care, preventing foster care placement, and adoption. A longstanding movement promoting youth rights in the United States has made substantial gains in the past.

Anti-Children's Rights propagandists often raise the specter of Rights without Responsibilities. The Children's Rights Movement assert that it is rather the case that children have rights which adults, states and government have a responsibility to uphold. The UK maintains a position that UNCRC is not legally enforceable and is hence 'aspirational' only - albeit a 2003 ECHR ruling states: "The human rights of children and the standards to which all governments must aspire in realizing these rights for all children are set out in the Convention on the Rights of the Child." 18 years after ratification, the four Children's Commissioners in the devolved administrations have united in calling for adoption of the Convention into domestic legislation, making children's rights legally enforceable.

Ombudsmanship

Several countries have created an institute of children's rights ombudsman, most notably Sweden, Finland and Ukraine, which is first country worldwide to install children at that post. In Ukraine Ivan Cherevko and Julia Kruk became first children's rights ombudsman in late 2005.

Convention on the Rights of the Child

The United Nations Convention on the Rights of the Child has outlined a standard premise for the children's rights movement and has been ratified by all but two nations

- the United States and Somalia. Somalia's inability to sign the Convention is attributed to their lack of governmental structure. The current US administration has opposed ratifying the Convention because of "serious political and legal concerns that it conflicts with U.S. policies on the central role of parents, sovereignty, and state and local law."

Convention on the Rights of the Child

The United Nations Convention on the Rights of the Child, often referred to as CRC or UNCRC, is an international convention setting out the civil, political, economic, social and cultural rights of children. Nations that ratify this international convention are bound to it by international law. Compliance is monitored by the United Nations Committee on the Rights of the Child which is composed of members from countries around the world. Once a year, the Committee submits a report to the Third Committee of the United Nations General Assembly, which also hears a statement from the CRC Chair, and the Assembly adopts a Resolution on the Rights of the Child.

Governments of countries that have ratified the Convention are required to report to, and appear before, the United Nations Committee on the Rights of the Child periodically to be examined on their progress with regards to the advancement of the implementation of the Convention and the status of child rights in their country. Their reports and the committee's written views and concerns are available on the committee's website.

The United Nations General Assembly adopted the Convention and opened it for signature on 20 November 1989 (the 30th anniversary of its Declaration of the Rights of the Child). It came into force on 2 September 1990, after it was ratified by the required number of nations. As of December 2008, 193 countries have ratified it, including every member of the United Nations except the United States and Somalia.

Two optional protocols were adopted on 25 May 2000. The first one restricts the involvement of children in military conflicts, and the second one prohibits the sale of children, child prostitution and child pornography.

Both protocols have been ratified by more than 120 states. The Convention generally defines a child as any person under the age of 18, unless an earlier age of majority is recognized by a country's law. The Convention deals with the child-specific needs and rights. It requires that states act in the best interests of the child. This approach is different from the common law approach found in many countries that had previously treated children and wives as possessions or chattels, ownership of which was often argued over in family disputes.

In many jurisdictions, properly implementing the Convention requires an overhaul of child custody and guardianship laws, or, at the very least, a creative approach within the existing laws. The Convention acknowledges that every child has certain basic rights, including the right to life, his or her own name and identity, to be raised by his or her parents within a family or cultural grouping and have a relationship with both parents, even if they are separated. The Convention obliges states to allow parents to exercise their parental responsibilities.

The Convention also acknowledges that children have the right to express their opinions and to have those opinions heard and acted upon when appropriate, to be protected from abuse or exploitation, to have their privacy protected and requires that their lives not be subject to excessive interference.

The Convention also obliges signatory states to provide separate legal representation for a child in any judicial dispute concerning their care and asks that the child's viewpoint be heard in such cases. The Convention forbids capital punishment for children.

State Parties and Signatories

As of December 2008, 193 countries have ratified it, including every member of the United Nations except the United States and Somalia.

Canada

Canada has ratified the Convention but has not fully implemented the Convention in Canadian domestic laws. A nonprofit organization called the Canadian Children's Rights Council promotes awareness of the CRC in Canadian media, and provides resources on their website pertaining to the Convention.

Youth criminal laws in Canada underwent major changes resulting in the Youth Criminal Justice Act (YCJA) which went into effect on 1 April 2003. In 1989, the Canadian House of Commons voted unanimously to pass a non-binding resolution to end child poverty by the year 2000. However, the child poverty rate did not change between 1989 and 2000; 16% of Canadian children still live in poverty.

India

In India, there is no outright ban on child labour, and the practice is generally permitted in most industries except those deemed "hazardous". Although a law in October 2006 banned child labour in hotels, restaurants, and as domestic servants, there continues to be high demand for children as hired help in the home.

Current estimates as to the number of child labourers in the country range from the government's conservative estimate of 12 million children under 14 years of age to the much higher estimates of children's rights activists, which hover around 60 million. Little is being done to address the problem since the economy is booming and the nuclear family is spreading, thereby increasing demand for child labourers. Under the auspices of the UNICEF financed Udisha initiative the Government of India is specifying the outline of a means of change and improvement in child care.

Ireland

The Republic of Ireland signed the Convention on the Rights of the Child on 30 September 1990 and ratified it, without reservation, on 21 September 1992. In response to criticisms expressed in the 1998 review by the UN Committee on the Rights of the Child in Geneva, the Irish government established the office of Ombudsman for Children and drew up a national children's strategy. In 2006, following concerns expressed by the committee that the wording of the Irish Constitution does not allow the State to intervene in cases of abuse other than in very exceptional cases, the Irish government undertook to amend the constitution to make a more explicit commitment to children's rights.

New Zealand

New Zealand ratified the Convention 6 April 1993 with reservations concerning the right to distinguish between persons according to the nature of their authority to be in New Zealand, the need for legislative action on economic exploitation - which it argued was adequately protected by existing law, and the provisions for the separation of juvenile offenders from adult offenders. In 1994, the Court of Appeal dismissed the suggestion that the Minister for Immigration and his department were at liberty to ignore the convention, arguing that this would imply that the country's adherence was 'at least partly window-dressing'.

Saudi Arabia

Saudi Arabia ratified the Convention in 1996, with a reservation 'with respect to all such articles as are in conflict with the provisions of Islamic law' and considers it to be a valid source of domestic law. The Committee on the Rights of the Child, which reviewed Saudi Arabia's treatment of children under the Convention in January 2005, strongly condemned the government for its practice of imposing the death penalty on juveniles, calling it "a serious violation of the fundamental rights".

The committee said it was "deeply alarmed" over the discretionary power judges hold to treat juveniles as adults: In its 2004 report the Saudi Arabia government had stated that it "never imposes capital punishment on persons... below the age of 18". However the government delegation later acknowledged that a judge could impose the death penalty whenever he decided that the convicted person had reached his or her majority, regardless of the person's actual age at the time of the crime or at the time of the scheduled execution.

United Kingdom

The United Kingdom ratified the Convention on 16 December 1991, with several declarations and reservations, and made its first report to the Committee on the Rights of the Child in January 1995. Concerns raised by the Committee included the growth in child poverty and inequality, the extent of violence towards children, the use of custody for young offenders, the low age of criminal responsibility, and the lack of opportunities for children and young people to express views. The 2002 report of the Committee expressed similar concerns, including the welfare of children in custody, unequal treatment of asylum seekers, and the negative impact of poverty on children's rights. There was much attention in the media to the criticism of UK parent's rights to hit their children as 'a serious violation of the dignity of the child'. In September 2008 the UK government decided to give up its reservations and agree to the Convention in full.

United States

The United States government played an active role in the drafting of the Convention and signed it on 16 February 1995, but has not ratified it. Opposition to the Convention is in part due to what are seen as potential conflicts with the constitution and because of opposition by some political and religious conservatives.

The two reasons often given for the US Senate not ratifying the Convention were that the State of Texas allows children to be given the death penalty, which the Convention would not allow, and that it would undermine parents' rights. The Heritage Foundation sees the conflict as an issue of national control over domestic policy. President Barack Obama has described the failure to ratify the Convention as 'embarrassing' and has promised to review this. The US has signed and ratified both of the optional protocols to the Convention.

Optional Protocols

Two optional protocols were adopted by the UN General Assembly on 25 May 2000. The Optional Protocol on the Involvement of Children in Armed Conflict requires governments to ensure that children under the age of eighteen are not recruited compulsorily into their armed forces, and calls on governments to do everything feasible to ensure that members of their armed forces who are under eighteen years of age do not take part in hostilities. This protocol entered into force on 12 July 2002; as of December 2008, 123 states are party to the protocol and another 30 states have signed but not yet ratified it. The Optional Protocol on the Sale of Children, Child Prostitution and Child Pornography requires states to prohibit the sale of children, child prostitution and child pornography. It entered into force on 18 January 2002; as of December 2008, 129 states are party to the protocol and another 32 states have signed but not yet ratified it.

Declaration of the Rights of the Child

The Declaration of the Rights of the Child is the name given to a series of related children's rights proclamations. The first was drafted by Eglantyne Jebb and adopted by the International Save the Children Union, Geneva, on 23 February 1923 and endorsed by the League of Nations General Assembly on 26 November 1924 as the World Child Welfare Charter. The original document, in the archives of the city of Geneva, carries the signatures of various international delegates, including Jebb, Janusz Korczak, and Gustave Ador, a former President of the Swiss Confederation.

The SCIU merged into the International Union of Child Welfare by 1946, and this group pressed the newly formed United Nations to continue to work for war-scarred children and for adoption of the World Child Welfare Charter. On 20 November 1959 the United Nations General Assembly adopted a much expanded version as its own Declaration of the Rights of the Child, with ten principles in place of the original five. This date has been adopted as the Universal Children's Day.

The initial 1923 document consisted of the following stipulations:

- The child must be given the means requisite for its normal development, both materially and spiritually.
- The child that is hungry must be fed, the child that is sick must be nursed, the child that is backward must be helped, the delinquent child must be reclaimed, and the orphan and the waif must be sheltered and succoured.
- The child must be the first to receive relief in times of distress.
- The child must be put in a position to earn a livelihood, and must be protected against every form of exploitation.

- The child must be brought up in the consciousness that its talents must be devoted to the service of its fellow men.

The Convention concerning the Prohibition and Immediate Action for the Elimination of the Worst Forms of Child Labour, known in short as the Worst Forms of Child Labour Convention, was adopted by the International Labour Organization (ILO) in 1999 as ILO Convention No 182. By ratifying this Convention No. 182, a country commits itself to taking immediate action to prohibit and eliminate the worst forms of child labour. The Convention is enjoying the fastest pace of ratifications in the ILO's history since 1919.

The ILO's International Programme on the Elimination of Child Labour (IPEC) is responsible for assisting countries in this regard as well as monitoring compliance. One of the methods used by IPEC to assist countries in this regard are Time-bound Programmes. The ILO also adopted the Worst Forms of Child Labour Recommendation No 190 in 1999. This recommendation contains, among others, recommendations on the types of hazards that should be considered for inclusion within a country-based definition of Worst Form Hazards faced by Children at Work.

Predefined Worst forms of Child Labour

Convention 182 includes forms of child labour, which are *predefined* worst forms of child labour. They are also sometimes referred to as *automatic* worst forms of child labour.

The predefined worst forms of child labour are:

1. All forms of slavery or practices similar to slavery, such as
   - The sale of a child;
   - Trafficking of children, meaning the recruitment of children to do work far away from home and

from the care of their families, in circumstances within which they are exploited;

- Debt bondage or any other form of bonded labour or serfdom;
- Forced or compulsory labour, including forced or compulsory recruitment of children for use in armed conflict;

2. Commercial sexual exploitation of children (CSEC), including the use, procuring or offering of a child for:
   - Prostitution, or
   - The production of pornography or for pornographic performances;
3. Use, procuring or offering of a child by others for illegal activities, also known as children used by adults in the commission of crime (CUBAC), including the trafficking or production of drugs.

The last category of worst form of child labour is work which by its nature or the circumstances is likely to harm the health, safety or morals of children, or Worst Form Hazards faced by Children at Work. Here the Convention recommended that the circumstances should be determined in consultation with organisations of employers and workers within a specific country. The Convention recommends that programmes of action should attend specifically to younger children, the girl child, hidden work situation in which girls are at special risk, and other groups of children with special vulnerabilities or needs. Worst Forms of Child Labour Recommendation No 190 contains recommendations on the types of hazards that should be considered to be included within a country-based definition of worst form hazards.

Child Advocacy

Child advocacy refers to a range of individuals,

professionals and advocacy organizations who promote the optimal development of children. An individual or organization engaging in advocacy typically seeks to protect children's rights which may be abridged or abused in a number of areas.

Rights

Rights can be divided into two categories: negative (rights to be free from) and positive (rights to). Children's negative rights are violated when some dangerous or harmful action is taken directly against them. One type of children's advocate typically represents or gives voice to an individual or group whose concerns and interests are not being heard. A child advocate will try to prevent children from being harmed and may try to obtain justice for those who have already been injured in some way.

A child advocate may also seek to ensure that children have access to positive influences or services which will benefit their lives such as education, childcare and proper parenting. Malnutrition is another form of harm-there are many children who go to bed without eating and it is looked over by child welfare or the police. Another form of child advocacy happens at the policy level and aims at changing the policies of governments or even transnational policies. These advocates do lobbying, policy research, file lawsuits and engage in other types of policy change techniques.

Many use Internet based techniques to influence decision makers. Child advocates exist in school, community, and home environments, and work on an individual, group or governmental level(s) to protect and nurture children. In most circumstances, mothers, fathers, family and teachers all advocate on behalf of children, although it is well recognized that we all have the ability and responsibility to advocate on behalf of children. Eight Canadian provinces. including Ontario, have an official Child Advocate whose job it is to protect the interests and welfare of all the children in the province. Within the criminal justice system, child advocates are concerned with the developmental needs of children and young people, and can play an important role in ensuring due process rights for young people in conflict with the law. They can help provide a voice for children and young people, ensure just and humane conditions of custody, and guard the privacy rights surrounding record provisions. They can also work to ensure that the special legal protections assigned to young people are provided with dignity and fairness.

Child Advocacy Centers

Child Advocacy Centers are neutral, safe locations where multidisciplinary teams investigate disclosures of child sexual or severe physical abuse. These multidisciplinary teams are made up of law enforcement officers, child protective service personnel, prosecutors, and advocates. Children who have disclosed abuse are interviewed by a forensic interviewer at such centers. Referrals for medical or mental health treatment are also made for the child and their family members.

The multidisciplinary approach to child abuse investigations is designed with the intention of reducing the secondary trauma associated with the disclosure and subsequent investigation of abuse. Child Advocacy Centers are accredited by the National Children's Alliance. Child Advocacy organizations at the policy level exist at state and national levels and as transnational NGOs. The organizations that they work in vary from smaller organizations at the local level to multinational voluntary organizations concerned about international child rights.

The United Nations

On the international stage, the United Nations has long advocated on behalf of children through UNICEF, whose position on children was formulated and publicly formalized in the Convention on the Rights of the Child. The convention sets out a summary of collective ideals and a covenant of commitments to all children on the planet.

Philosophy

One thing that all child advocates have in common is healthy respect for young children. There is also recognition that in most countries, children are not seen as having the full citizenship status which confers certain rights and responsibilities as adults.

The World's Children's Prize for the Rights of the Child (WCPRC) has, since the start in the year 2000, grown to become the world's largest annual education and empowerment process for the rights of the child, democracy and global friendship for children. As a part of this process, the children award their prizes for outstanding contributions to the rights of the child. 21 million students at 47,000 schools in 94 countries participate in the WCPRC, a number that is growing. 66 million of those children participated 2008 the annual Global Vote to determine who will receive the Global Friends' Award.

An international child jury – consisting of children who are experts on the rights of the child through their own experiences as soldiers, refugees, street children or slaves in brothels or on farms – chooses the recipient of the other major award, the World's Children's Prize. Over 450 organisations all over the world support the WCPRC, which also collaborates with many Departments of Education and youth media projects worldwide. The WCPRC magazine and website are available in ten languages. The magazine is read by over 7 million young people. All schools and child organizations can participate in the WCPRC for free.

Patrons of the WCPRC include Queen Silvia of Sweden, Nelson Mandela, President Xanana Gusmão of East Timor, former Executive Director of UNICEF Carol Bellamy, former UN Under-Secretary-General Olara Otunnu, and

Nobel Prize Winner in Economics Joseph Stiglitz.

The prize money, SEK 1 million (USD 140,000), is to be used in the recipients' work for the rights of the child. It is supported by AstraZeneca, Banco Fonder and pi.se. The WCPRC was founded by the Swedish organisation Children's World, and is a Swedish National Millennium Project. The prize ceremony takes place in April at Gripsholms castle in Mariefred, Sweden.

3

Social Profile of Child Labourers

The 2005 field survey placed the number of child labourers at 1,904. This represents 0.07 per cent of the total child population of the area covered by the survey in the same year. A great majority (64.44%) of the child labourers are the male while 35.56 per cent are female. This implies a ratio of 181 males over 100 females. All provinces followed similar patterns where the proportion of males is higher than the females. This may be attributed to the fact that the type of available jobs are those that does not necessarily need skills but physical agility or strength like construction, and agriculture-related tasks, among others. The data do not provide substantial evidence that females are given preferential attention in families and therefore are sent to schools, instead of males. However, DECS statistics show that as the grade/year level increases, the female elementary/high school participation rates surpass that of their male counterparts.

In general, the proportion of child labourers increases as the age increases. For the four provinces, it is observed that 2 out of 5 child labourers are between 17 and 18; 1 out of 3 is 15 to 16; 1 out of 5 is 13 to 14 and the rest are 12 years old and below. The children start working as early as seven years old. The proportion of child labourers not classified as economically active (below 15) is highest in Rizal with 55.74 per cent and lowest in Cavite with 12.9 per cent. In the case of Laguna, more than half of its child labourers are aged between 17 and 18.

Educational Attainment

Very few (12.97%)of the child labourers have completed high school while almost 3 out of 10 have reached high school but were unable to graduate. More than a quarter (25.74%) have completed elementary education while 21.06 per cent have reached only elementary but did not finish. The high proportions of child labourers unable to finish elementary will have repercussions on the attainment of national goals on functional literacy since researches have shows that children who dropout early from school revert to illiteracy. By province, the child labourers of Cavite and Laguna are better educated with 57.42 per cent and 55.72 per cent, respectively, who have reached high school and up.

This could be attributed to the fact that Cavite and Laguna have more child labourers aged 15-18 than the rest of the provinces and also the type of occupation available. Cavite, for example, has its child labourers in factory work and cottage industries, which require a higher degree of education. It is also interesting to note that in the provinces, there are child labourers who are at the same time studying. Unfortunately, only Laguna and Rizal reported on the number of working students.

However, Batangas also implied the existence of working students as it mentioned "paaral" as one of the benefits received by the child labourers. The total number of working students in Laguna and Rizal is 256 comprising 28.19 per cent of the total child labourers in the two provinces. Furthermore, Laguna noted a total of 317 or 63.65 per cent of the total child labourers who have dropped from school still value education.

Type of Occupation

The child labourers are in diverse occupation, including those looked down by men as the "oldest profession" (i.e. prostitution) and scavenging. Some of occupational categories are extremely hazardous to children like deep sea fishing, construction work, among others. Overall, there are 58 different kinds of occupation in the four provinces. Batangas and Laguna have more diversified types of occupation with 32 and 31, respectively, compared to Cavite and Rizal;. This is attributed to the fact that Batangas and Laguna, specifically the municipalities covered by the survey, have mixed industrial and agricultural activities.

The diversity of occupations where child labourers are engaged in might pose problems to program implementers who would like to reach them. Also, given the fact that child labourers have almost penetrated all occupations that does not necessarily requires skills and higher education, including illegal activities like prostitution, is a cause for concern. The most common type of occupation children are engaged in include construction and related activities with 22.06 per cent; factory work, cottage industry and related occupations, 22.01 per cent; service related, 29.10 per cent; transport services, 1.43 per cent; and others, 1.00 per cent.

Reasons for Working

An overwhelming majority (77.93%) of the child labourers cited family factors as the compelling reason that pushed them to work, even at an early age. In general, the major cause of child labour is often attributed to poverty. The survey supports this as 6 out of 10 children mentioned the need to augment family income as their main reason for working. In addition, the children said they need to work because the head of the family does not have any source of income or is underemployed. The social and cultural aspect of child labour also comes in the picture as more than 10 per cent said that their parents expect them to do work.

It is commonly accepted that the part of socialization process of the Filipino family is to let children work by helping in household chores and other activities like taking care of younger siblings.

However, once the child is forced to work in hazardous jobs, under exploitative conditions, rendering long hours, with no time for studies or recreation, this becomes child labour. Poor family relationship or the disability of the head of the family has been also given as reasons for working. Individual factor, specifically the need to save money to go back to school and community factors like availability of work and peer influence have been cited by 4.33 and 17.74 per cent of the child labourers, respectively.

Working Hours Spent Per Day

Data for the length of hours spent for work per day is not available for Cavite province. But for the three other provinces, almost half (49.17%) of the child labourers work below eight hours. This could be attributed to the fact that these provinces reported the presence of working students. Those who work within the normal working hours of adult is 23.05 per cent while those beyond eight hours is 23.81 per cent. Combining the number of child labourers who work for eight hours and those who work more than eight hours, it appears that 5 out of 10 render adult hours and more, with less time for studies and play. Only 2.54 per cent claim to have variable working hours while 0.89 per cent have no response.

The reports of the provinces do not include whether or not those who work beyond eight hours are given overtime pay. It can be assumed that in informal employment, labour standards are violated and granting that the assumption is true, then this is another form of child abuse.

Wage

The child labourers are paid either cash or kind. Of the total child labourers, most or 82.93 per cent are paid in cash; 4.62 per cent in kind; and 12.45 per cent have no response. Majority (54.97%) of the child labourers receive cash wages below P101 per day; 3 out of 10 receive compensation P151 to P200 per day. The pattern is similar in all provinces with most of Rizal's child labourers or 95.19 per cent receiving daily wage below P101.

Excluding Rizal, the survey reveals that the most common non monetary benefit received is free food with 20.64 per cent, while the least likely to be provided by the employer is free transportation and payment of benefits like PAG-IBIG with 0.06 per cent each. A very minimal or 1.99 per cent enjoyed Social Security System benefits. These child labourers are from Batangas and Cavite who are mostly 15 years old and above and could qualify for formal employment in establishments that adhere to labour standards. Any incidence of hazardous child labour is abominable since it places society's future at stake. It has wide-ranging implications, which are as serious and deep as the right to live.

Based on the foregoing, the primary reasons for child labour is primarily rooted in poverty. Another factor that could influence the level of child labour is migration, which is also related to poverty. Hence, for as long as poverty persists and Batangas, Cavite, Laguna and Rizal remain as destination, child labour continue. While the survey does not provide information on whether or not the child labours are offspring of migrants or not, it has been observed that, to certain extent, migration is one factor that affects the increase of child labour. It is noted, for example, that in Batangas most residents near the seaport working, as baggage carriers, vendors, etc. are migrants belonging to the lower income groups. It is also recognized that there has not been a substantial change on the attitudes of parents regarding children.

To some, children are still investments, thus, are expected to augment family earnings. It should be of utmost concern that in the provinces covered by the survey, child labourers are engaged in hazardous occupations detrimental to their physical, psychological, mental and social development. This indicates the extent to which the welfare of these children has left unnurtured and unprotected. In turn, this should give the impetus for families, communities, nongovernmental organizations (NGOs), national and local leaders, to look into the matter more closely and take meaningful sources of actions to address the problem. In the light of these, the following courses of actions are recommended.

Recommendations:

- Develop and sustain community-based action programs on child labour. As the survey results show, child labour is largely an economic phenomenon but there are underlying social and cultural reasons that contribute to the problem. Unless families and communities are able to understand their situation and are given the means to alleviate their difficulties, children are apt to continue being child labourers. Local officials and community-based support groups should be encouraged to work together to change the conditions in the community which lead to fundamental violations of children's rights.
- Strengthening of local or community structures to monitor and act on child labour cases, abuse and exploitation. Even while there are government agencies mandated to oversee children's welfare and protection, local government units need to establish an efficient and effective structure or mechanism to constantly monitor the situation of child workers and to act for

their protection. Structures in the community such as the Barangay Council for the Protection of Children should be strengthened.

- Mobilization and capability building/advocacy of law enforcement agencies in the fight against child labour The role of law enforcement agencies, particularly in the detection, intelligence and rescue operations for child labourers has to be strengthened.
- Undertake massive and focused advocacy on the rights of children in general and on child labour in particular through the local media (print, radio, TV/cable), posters, and leaflets, among others. Active advocacy and information campaign on child labour targeting local government units, government agencies, legislators, law enforcers, employers, church, NGOs, the private sectors, among others have to be pursued in order to make them and other stockholders aware of the magnitude of the problem and how this can be prevented and acted upon.
- Formulate long-term strategy that will lead to the value shift regarding child work vis-à-vis child labour. The country's goal to eliminate child labour should be supported by an in-depth understanding and complete information of the phenomenon itself accompanied by change in values and attitudes concerning children. Children's rights should be integrated in the school curriculum and taught at all levels of education, including nonformal education projects/activities such as mother's classes, female functional literacy, among others.
- Implement capacity building for child labour implementers and the community to enhance their capability in the prevention, rescue and rehabilitation of child labourers.
- Intensify provision of basic services on health, nutrition, education, income generation to the child labourers and their families, including expansion of scholarship

programs and design of alternative mechanism to enable child labourers pursue higher level of education.

- Continuous updating of local database through regular master listing of child labourers in the community as guide for focused targeting and intervention and to serve as an advocacy tool.
- Engage active participation of socio-civic organizations, NGOs, churches, employers group, labour unions, and the business community, among others as partners in eliminating child labour.

Hazardous child labour is challenging to define and quantify in the context of acute or chronic toxic exposures—either of which may cause significant disease and disability. Epidemiologic occupational studies in adults have documented many harmful outcomes secondary to exposure to toxic substances.

Occupational surveillance efforts often have focused on acute injuries because they are more readily identified. Fassa has been able to compile data concerning injuries to child labourers but notes, "There is great need for studies in developing countries ... on the impact of child labour on illness." Although injuries may be underreported or undocumented among child labourers, acute injury is, at least, potentially recordable. This is in sharp contrast to toxic exposures, where exposure assessment is usually difficult and costly. This is especially true when it is done after an exposure has taken place.

The outcomes of most toxic workplace exposures to children remain unknown. The Agency for Toxic Substances and Disease Registries (ATSDR) notes that in similar environments, children may have greater exposures than adults: "Pound for pound of body weight, children drink more water, eat more food, and breathe more air than adults," and "In some instances, children are less able than adults to detoxify chemicals and are thus more vulnerable."

Children who begin work at an early age have many more years to develop illness than an adult doing the same work. A household survey of child labourers in Ethiopia found that a high proportion (greater than 90%) of children in both urban and rural areas of the country reported non-use of protective equipment. However, it is the experience of present author D.P. that this equipment is rarely if ever adequate, even when made available. For example, protective equipment such as respirators or impermeable gloves are designed for adults, and thus do not properly fit children.

In defining hazardous child labour, the larger context of public health cannot be ignored. The study of child labour needs to take into account the baseline health of exposed individuals. In developing countries, the poorest and most vulnerable children are most often involved in work in order to earn money for survival. These children are also likely to already lack basic necessities of food and medical care, predisposing them to diarrhea, anemia, and micronutrient deficiencies. Underlying nutritional conditions may make children more susceptible to the effects of toxic substances such as lead. In addition, child labourers also may be exposed to lead and other toxic substances from their poor living conditions.

Prenatal exposure to toxic substances can lead to neuro-cognitive and other congenital changes to the fetus. Some children begin life with an elevated lead body burden reflecting the lead body burden of the mother. Thus, the development of children born to exposed mothers can be affected, leading to a cycle of susceptibility. The intergenerational effects of child labour may extend to lead exposure if maternal exposure to lead occurs during pregnancy. While not specifically addressed here, this exposure may take place via several routes: mothers working while pregnant, airborne contamination, and contamination of food and water.

Due to these potential intergenerational effects of lead and other toxic substances, child labourers may begin life with lower intelligence or other neuro-cognitive changes. Thus, when the International Labour Organization's (ILO) Convention 182 injunction against child labour "likely to harm the health ... of children" is considered in a public health context, the definition of hazardous work becomes quite complex. Often, children are working illegally or unofficially as part of their family. Children may be working in remote areas and may be impossible to trace through the years.

Birthdays may be unknown, and families may not have fixed addresses. In addition, the exact nature of the exposure is usually unclear or hidden. The field of industrial hygiene in developing countries is not well-established and hazard reporting and monitoring capabilities are limited. This provides an overview of the extent of hazardous lead exposure in child labourers. Lead was selected because it has been relatively well studied in the general population; however, it is meant to serve as a model for the effects of more numerous, but less studied, substances.

Neuro-toxic Effects of Lead on Children

While there are many health effects attributed to lead exposure, this discussion will focus on the neuro-cognitive changes seen in children, primarily because the link with intelligence quotient (IQ) provides a quantitative basis for discussion. According to the ATSDR, lead is especially toxic to young children and is associated with "decreased intelligence, impaired neurobehavioral development, decreased stature and growth, and impaired hearing." The development of the brain and nervous system begins in the early stages of embryonic life and continues beyond birth into adolescence. Disruptions of this well-organized series of developmental changes will have lasting effects. Schettler notes that the developing brain is extremely vulnerable to toxic effects, though specific neurodevelopmental data in humans are usually unavailable.

Lead exposure in children has been linked to decreased cognitive function and adverse neurobehavioral effects. A meta-analysis of 24 studies of childhood lead exposures related to IQ concludes that lead impairs children's IQ at blood levels less than 10 ìg/dL. Studies have documented lead exposure and decreased cognitive function from age 24 months through age 10 with decreased scores on the Wechsler Intelligence Scale of 5.8 points for each 10 ìg/dL increase in blood lead at age 24 months. An 11-year follow-up of subjects who had been studied as primary school children showed that those with higher blood lead levels than their peers had consistently lower IQ scores in fifth grade and subsequently had lower class standing in high school, increased absenteeism, poorer hand-eye coordination, and longer reaction times, among other neurological findings.

The authors concluded that exposure to lead in childhood is "associated with deficits in central nervous system functioning that persist into young adulthood." Despite continued academic discussion, there is widespread acceptance that lead exposure in childhood causes decreased intelligence and that this effect is present even at low lead levels that are still prevalent in the United States. A generally agreed upon numerical estimate suggests that for each increase in blood lead of 4 ìg/dL, there is a one-point drop in IQ. The effects of lead on delinquent behaviour and antisocial tendencies are equally significant. Of great concern are the recent findings suggesting that even low level lead exposure can have a significant effect on a child's neuropsychological development. Wigg notes that "lead exposed children are at increased risk of adverse effects on both cognition and learning."

As with intelligence, the neurobehavioral impact of early childhood lead exposure can persist into high school and beyond. This is confirmed by data from the ATSDR showing that young adults who had elevated blood lead levels in childhood had poor scores on neurobehavioral tests 15 to 20 years after their initial exposure. In addition, a health assessment of Idaho residents who lived near a mining and smelting facility demonstrated a dose response relationship, with the severity of dysfunction increasing with increasing bone lead concentrations.

As more data have become available on the adverse health effects of lead, the acceptable blood lead level has decreased. In 1990, the U.S. Department of Health and Human Services aimed to eliminate blood lead levels greater than 25 ìg/dL; the new goal in the United States is to eliminate blood lead levels greater than 10 ìg/dL by the year 2010. The threshold level for harmful effects of lead is currently unknown.

Occupational Exposure of Children to Lead

There is almost no information available on toxic occupational exposures in children. Data are lacking on all aspects of this subject: numbers of children exposed, duration of exposure, substances involved, resulting illnesses, and long-term effects. Data were unavailable by country, by region, or globally. We attempted to determine the number of industries around the world that use lead and the total number of people potentially exposed to lead at work, but no accurate data were available.

Our exhaustive search for data on lead exposure in child labourers identified only three manuscripts. Others have encountered the same difficulty: "Official data on child labour are generally fragmentary, underestimate informal sector work and family work, and frequently exclude unpaid work." Children may be exposed to lead in the production of ceramic pottery, battery recycling, stained glass production, automobile radiator repair, construction, and glassworks. Lead exposure also occurs in the smelting and mining industries and through exposure to fuels. In addition, children's industrial exposures to lead are superimposed on higher environmental exposures seen in developing countries where leaded gasoline is in use.

An observational study of the ceramic tile industry in Victoria, Ecuador, describes the local production of roof tiles. Approximately half of the families in this area are involved in producing roof tiles or ceramic objects, usually at small work sites situated next to their homes.

Clay is extracted from the local mountains and then molded into tiles or artifacts. The items are glazed with lead salts made from melted batteries. The ceramics are fired in furnaces for 24 to 48 hours, permeating the local air with dust and fumes from both the ceramics and the fuel. No environmental precautions are in place.

Children as young as 6 years of age were observed working in this trade. Harari et al. enrolled 12 children in a cross-sectional evaluation of lead levels. Ten of these children aged 6 through 15 gave blood samples, and lead levels ranged from 23 to 124 ìg/dL, with a mean of 70. Three of the children had worked for less than three months; their blood lead levels were less than 50 ìg/dL. All of the children who had worked longer than three months had blood lead levels greater than 60 ìg/dL. Corresponding IQ tests were not done, but five of the children had repeated one or more years of school.

Excessive lead levels have been observed in child labourers in occupations where lead exposure is not traditionally suspected. Children who work as scavengers and street vendors also are at risk for hazardous lead exposure. A Philippines study of the child scavengers who worked and lived on Smokey Mountain, a garbage dump that received approximately one-third of Manila's garbage before it closed in the 1990s, found that the 20,000 residents were exposed to waste from chemical, hospital, and slaughterhouse sources.

Children start scavenging when they are as young as 5–7 years old. They begin with a two-year "apprenticeship" and work without any protective equipment. A 1991 survey of 231 scavengers aged 6 through 15 years, recorded mean blood lead levels of 28.4 ìg/dL (standard deviation=11.5). Of the boys, 68.2%, and, of the girls, 58.2% had blood lead levels greater than 20 ìg/dL. The authors compared these data to blood samples from 25 school children in metropolitan Manila who had a mean blood lead level of 11 ìg/dL. Street vendors also are at risk for lead exposure. A 1993 study of 387 school children and 101 child vendors aged 6 through 14 in Manila demonstrated that 10.3% of the school children had blood lead levels in excess of 20 ìg/dL as compared with 32.7% of the street vendors. The mean blood lead level in the street vendors was 17.8 ìg/dL.

Nutrition and Child Labour

Consideration of the effects of toxic exposure in child workers needs to take into account other pertinent public health, economic, and social factors. For example, nutritional status is an important determinant of the impact of lead during early development. Iron deficiency anemia is perhaps the most critical public health issue related to lead exposure and affects more than 3.5 billion people worldwide. Iron deficiency anemia and other indicators of poor nutrition are associated with poverty, and child labourers in developing countries are most often from poverty-stricken families. One would expect significant per centages of child labourers to suffer from malnutrition and micronutrient deficiencies.

The data, however, are limited and conflicting. In the Philippines study of child scavengers, the anemia rate was 10% compared with the rate of 27.7% in metropolitan Manila (Unpublished manuscript, Torres EB, Subida RD, Rabuco LB. Health profile of child scavengers in Smokey Mountain—Balut, Tondo, and Manila. German Agency for

Technical Cooperation and International Labour Organization; 1994). In a study of male child labourers in Jordan, however, 34.1% of the child workers were found to be anemic. Another study of child labourers in Bombay, India, found an anemia rate of 10% in 73 children in the large slum of Dharavi. The authors speculated that the nutritional status of the Dharavi child labourers is better than in "the great numbers of children elsewhere who do not work but who do not eat."

Of particular concern in the study of child labourers exposed to lead is the fact that children appear to be more susceptible to lead toxicity than adults. Children are more vulnerable to absorbed lead than adults because they develop toxicity at lower blood lead levels. In addition, children absorb more lead from the gastrointestinal tract than adults. Adults absorb 10% to 15% of lead ingested with meals; however, children and pregnant women can absorb up to 50%. Epidemiological studies have shown an association between iron deficiency and lead poisoning. Willows et al. found evidence of this association among infants with very low blood lead levels (mean=1.7 ìg/dL).

Wright constructed a model predicting that iron-deficient children are more than four times as likely as their iron-replete peers to have blood lead levels greater than 10 ìg/dL when tested at a second clinic visit. Absorption of lead is even higher in children with low dietary iron, zinc, or calcium intake. Iron deficiency may increase duodenal lead absorption. Low calcium intake activates vitamin D to 1,25-dihydroxyvitamin D, causing increased absorption of calcium and lead in intestinal cells. Low zinc intake could be partly responsible for children's increased susceptibility to lead because lead affects zinc-requiring enzymes in the biosynthesis of heme.

Environmental Exposures

The issues of children's toxic exposure in the workplace

are further compounded by the lack of separation between the job, home, and the external environment. The lack of distinction between these areas is not limited to obvious examples such as:

- Child scavengers who live on the garbage heap where they scavenge garbage for resale and basic sustenance or
- The risks of leaded gasoline that cause more exposure to lead than any other source in the world.

Studies unrelated to child labour have documented the risk of toxic exposures to children from contamination in the homes of exposed workers as well as from environmental sources in industrial areas. An example of occupational disease being transmitted to family contacts in the United States is a National Institute of Occupational Safety and Health (NIOSH) case-control study that examined lead exposure in construction workers and found significantly higher surface lead concentrations in construction workers' homes than in those of controls.

A French study of 125 children with lead-exposed parents found that children's blood levels were significantly higher than the reference group and correlated with their parents' blood lead levels and the lead air concentration at their workplaces. Environmental contamination affecting children was demonstrated in a study of children from a Chinese village with lead smelters located near the residential area. High concentrations of lead dust were found in the air and soil, and on local crops and wheat in the farmers' homes. Mean blood lead levels among children were noted to be extremely high.

The model developed by Landrigan et al., which relies on the calculations by Salkever, was used to assess the costs of childhood lead poisoning in the United States. The methods used by Landrigan were generalized to form a crude estimate of the magnitude of the problem of adverse outcomes (potential per cent decrease in lifetime earnings) associated with lead exposure in child labourers. Salkever determined that the loss of one IQ point corresponds to an overall reduction in lifetime earnings of 2.4%.

Based on the estimate of a 4 ìg/dL increase in blood lead levels causing a 1 point IQ drop, and working on the assumption that there is not a threshold blood lead level for cognitive effects, each 1 ìg/dL of blood lead concentration is associated with a decrease in IQ of 0.25 points. The potential IQ decrease was calculated from the following assumptions: that for each blood lead measurement of 1 ìg/dL, there is a mean loss of 0.25 IQ points per child and that the loss of 1 IQ point subsequently leads to a 2.39% loss of lifetime earnings.

Limitations of this analysis include the fact that Salkever's calculations may not be transferable to developing countries. Moreover, the impact of lead on IQ may vary based on the age of exposure and the acute or chronic nature of the exposure. Another concern is that the lifetime expected earnings calculations from the Philippines and Ecuador studies come from the average annual income in those countries: salaries the average child labourer would not be able to attain for socioeconomic reasons before lead exposure and IQ is taken into account. In addition, simulated earnings models are noted to be difficult to compute reliably and accurately.

This documents the potential magnitude of the problem of lead exposure in child labourers. The definition of hazardous employment will need to be considered for jobs with potentially toxic occupational exposures. Low levels of many toxicants will affect early brain growth and development. Substances such as mercury readily cross the placental barrier or are rapidly absorbed from the intestines of small children. The potential magnitude of the hazard of lead exposure in child labourers is unclear. The remarkable dearth of information adds to the severity of the problem and provides a dramatic example of how toxic occupational exposures in children are overlooked. The definition of hazardous child labour needs to include the consideration of toxic exposures such as lead and other heavy metals.

In addition, the potential for these exposures to interact with pre-existing morbidity such as micronutrient deficiencies should be considered. One example of such an effect is the likely combined impact of lead and iron deficiency on brain growth and development. Both iron deficiency and elevated levels of lead have been shown to impair neurological development in young children. Because these conditions may be present at the same time, studies focusing on the effect of one should control for the effects of the second. Failure to do so allows for the possibility that, for example, the effect of iron deficiency on cognitive abilities is confounded by unmeasured lead poisoning.

Lead was used as an example of a child labour hazard in part because of its prevalence and in part because its link with IQ provides a quantitative element that has not been sufficiently studied for other heavy metal and toxic exposures. Despite the many limitations, several conclusions are quite clear. First, information and research on lead and other toxic occupational exposures in child labourers is in its infancy. Second, the magnitude of the problem is immense. Third, additional data will facilitate the capacity of policy makers to determine the types of work that are most detrimental to growth and development. Finally, the potential impact of toxic exposures may manifest in ways that are not traditionally considered by policy makers.

Suggestions that protective equipment might lessen the impact of hazardous exposures are apocryphal. The cost of such equipment is likely to remain prohibitive to some of the world's poorest children and their families. Even a few cents per day may be greater than the cost that can be absorbed by families that must scavenge garbage for their daily food. Also, it is doubtful that protective equipment that has been designed for adults would serve the needs of children, even if it were available. Lastly, some protective equipment is difficult to use or requires maintenance programs. Training is unlikely to take place, and maintenance programs are expensive.

Efforts to improve nutritional status and micronutrient replacement are crucial. More specifically, a clear policy directive on iron supplementation is necessary because of the relationship between lead absorption and iron deficiency. Unambiguous distinctions between home and work are recommended to prevent adults from bringing contaminants into the home and to ensure that infants and children are not cared for in locations that are contaminated with toxic materials. Global environmental policies such as banning leaded gasoline can also find support from this perspective. Finally, this overview of lead exposure in child labourers provides support for the implementation of ILO Convention 182 in developing countries.

Case studies - Rapid Appraisal of Child Labour in the Tobacco Industry

In Two Ilocos Provinces

The aphorism quoted above captures the essential feeling of millions of parents worldwide. Children are the objects of care and protection, and parents generally feel responsible for them as they move from infancy to childhood and adolescence. The notion that parents exercise care and control over their children defines childhood as a period of dependency. It views children's actions as being under the discipline of their elders, and the scope of their independent behaviour is framed within this social expectation. Filipino families are no different. Ethnographic studies point to the solicitous actions of parents over their children. Every child is valued as a gift from God, deserving of care, nurturance and protection. At the same time, parents are disciplinarians and aim to mold their children into the socially accepted norms of society. Part of this norm, especially in rural areas, is for children to participate early in life in household activities. Hence, it is not unusual to find pre-school children being asked to look after infants and younger siblings. Neither is it exceptional for young children to help in household chores: carrying water, gathering fuel, sweeping, washing dishes and going on simple errands. In families engaged in agricultural production, children are also socialized to become involved in the family's productive activities.

Children's involvement in productive work becomes problematic when it interferes with their physical, emotional and intellectual development. It is in recognition of these risks that the issue of child labour emerges. In 1973, the International Labour Organization adopted Convention No. 138 and Recommendation No. 146 on the Minimum Age for Admission to Employment. This Convention provides a minimum age for admission to employment of not less than the age of completion of compulsory schooling, but in any case, not less than 15 years of age. In 1989, all except two member countries of the United Nations adopted the International Convention on the Rights of the Child. Among others, this covenant provides for "the right of the child to be protected from economic exploitation and from performing any work that is likely to be hazardous or to interfere with the child's education, or to be harmful to the child's health or physical, mental, spiritual, moral or social development." Child labour has been extensively studied in the Philippines since the mid-eighties. However, there have been no researches focusing on child workers in the tobacco industry. For this reason, Philip Morris International and the Philippine Business for Social Progress (PBSP) commissioned PARTNERS, International to undertake a baseline study of child labour in selected tobacco growing areas of the Ilocos Region.

Research Objectives

The general objective of the research is to produce a bird's eye view of child labour in tobacco production within the provinces of Ilocos Sur and La Union. In more specific terms, the study aims to:

- Estimate the incidence of child workers in Ilocos Sur and La Union,
- Describe the situation of child workers in selected areas,
- Document existing programs addressing child labour among governmental and non- governmental agencies in the two provinces, and
- Identify possible areas for program intervention.

Methodology

The research was conducted from mid-November 2001 to February 2002, approximately covering a period of 2½ months. The study sites were selected after consultation with PBSP, the Plans and Projects Office, and other technical staff of the central and branch offices of the National Tobacco Administration (NTA). The criteria for selecting barangays in Ilocos Sur and La Union for the research were the following:

- Tobacco-producing as the main industry of the barangays;
- Having the biggest number of tobacco farmers and farm size among barangays of the provinces;
- Presence of child workers, 7 to 14 years old; and
- Accessibility of the barangays.

Study Sites

The baseline study was conducted in two barangays each from the municipalities of Candon, Ilocos Sur and

Balaoan, La Union. In Candon, Barangays Parioc II and Balingaoan were chosen for the case study. In Parioc II, there are 148 farmers cultivating a total 133.85 hectares of tobacco farms. In Balingaoan, there are 111 tobacco farmers working on 94.20 hectares. In Balaoan, the two contiguous barangays, Calliat and Baracbac Este were selected. These barangays registered a total number of 142 and 178 tobacco farmers, respectively, based on the 2001 barangay profiles. Thirty hectares are devoted to agricultural purposes in Calliat and 50 hectares in Baracbac Este.

Methods of Data Collection

A combination of methods was used for a Rapid Appraisal of Child Labour in tobacco- growing areas of Ilocos Sur and La Union. These methods included a review of documents on child labour, key informant interviews, focus group discussion, drawings and stories by selected child workers from two barangays, and case studies of seven selected households across barangays. Key informant interviews were done with officials, technical staff and extension workers of the NTA. The interviews aimed to elicit the following information: to identify the role of the NTA in the tobacco industry, its strategic programs, projects and services to the tobacco farmers and their families, impacts of these programs on the socio-economic conditions of the farmers and the households, and their knowledge about child labour.

Four selected line agencies of the government in Region I, through their respective heads and key staff, were interviewed to determine what programs, projects and activities were being implemented, and to identify future plans to address the issue of child labour in agriculture, particularly in tobacco farming. These informants belong to the following regional offices: the Department of Labour and Employment, the Department of Social Welfare and Development, Department of Education, Culture and

Sports, and the Department of Health. Ocular visits around the barangays and farm sites were undertaken to get social and resource maps, and to plot the accessibility to roads and transport of the residences, school and production areas.

Since the period of the visits by the Research Team coincided with the planting season of tobacco, they were able to observe some child workers helping their mothers and fathers in watering newly replanted tobacco seedlings. Focus group discussion (FGD) was done in Bgys. Calliat, La Union and Parioc II, Candon, during which time the selected children were asked by the Researcher- Facilitator to draw on papers their participation in the whole process of tobacco production. Work participation refers to the specific work the children do and/or how they help their parents in tobacco farming. After the drawing activity, each child worker was asked to share with the group the story behind his/her drawing.

A Documentor from the Research Team recorded the children's stories and took photos of the drawings. A total of 21 children participated in the FGDs. Case documentation of 7 child workers was conducted to explore the incidence of child labour in the tobacco-growing barangays. Using a data portfolio on child labour devised for the research, the following information was determined;

- Physical features of the barangay,
- Tobacco production profile, including other crops,
- Relations of production,
- Production processes for tobacco growing, and
- Occupational risks and hazards.

These data sets were gathered from interviews with the Barangay Secretaries, Barangay Health Workers, barangay school teachers and barangay extension workers. Child workers and their parents also provided information for the case studies. For the in-depth interview with the child workers and parents, personal information about and the work profile of each of the child workers was obtained. The parents and their children were separately interviewed to validate responses to each question.

Identifying the Child Worker

For the purposes of this study, a child worker is defined as a person below 15 years of age, engaged in any of the phases of tobacco farming, whether on full-time or part-time basis, and receiving remuneration in cash or in kind. The child may be working for his/her parent or relative or for others in the community.

Child Labour in the Philippines

What is Child Labour? The Convention on the Minimum Age for Admission for Employment (ILO Convention No. 138 and Recommendation No. 146) provides a uniform minimum age for admission to all kinds of work or undertakings, without distinction. It stipulates that the age of admission to paid work should not be less than the age of completion of compulsory education, but in any case, not less than 15 years. Exemptions to this rule include the following situations:

- Work done by young persons in schools for general, vocational or technical training.
- Work done by persons at least 14 year of age in undertakings that are an integral part of a course of education or training for which a school or training institution is primarily responsible, or a program of training approved by competent authority.
- Artistic performances given appropriate permits by competent authority.

The Convention, however, allows member-states with an insufficiently developed economy and educational facilities to initially specify a minimum age of 14. Moreover, work for children from 12-14 years is allowed provided these activities are not harmful to their health or development, and will not be prejudicial to their schooling or vocational training (ILS-DOLE 1994). In the context of the Philippine experience, child labour pertains to "the participation of children in a wide variety of work situations, on a more or less regular basis, to earn a livelihood for themselves or for others.

Children's work may be paid or unpaid, and remuneration for their efforts may be made to adults rather than to themselves, or assessed in non-material ways (such as food, education, shelter or clothing). Very rarely are children able to determine the prices of their own labour". Researches have also shown that children's work in the Philippines may be full-time or part-time, regular or seasonal, depending on specific circumstances faced by children. The Labour Code of the Philippines provides that children below 15 years may be allowed to work in non-hazardous activities, provided that such children work under the sole responsibility of a parent or guardian and the activity does not interfere with the children's schooling (Article 139). This is supported by the Child and Youth Welfare Code (R.A. 7610), which allows children to work below the age of 15 under the direct supervision of the parent.

However, R.A. 7658 provides that this situation is permissible only if the child's employment neither endangers his/her life, safety, health and morals, nor impairs normal development. It also requires parents to ensure the enjoyment by the child of either primary or secondary education. R. A. 7610 declares as a state policy the provision of special protection of children from all forms of abuse, neglect, cruelty, exploitation and discrimination, and other conditions prejudicial to their development. It provides sanctions against such acts and allows the state to intervene in behalf of the child when the parent or guardian fails to protect the child. Del Rosario and Bonga (2000) question the assumption that children's work in the home should be allowed because these are likely to be unexploitative.

They particularly point to the situation of child labour in industrial homework for export production where – "Child workers received pittance for the beautiful handiwork from which the foreign importers in developed countries earned much profit. They also worked long hours and were risk in terms of their health. Individually and collectively, these child home workers were being exploited right in their own homes, not necessarily by their parents, but under parental supervision. The home was, therefore, hardly a place free of exploitation, particularly in the context of subcontracting for export production." Not all types of children's work are considered child labour.

Generally, the participation of children in domestic activities, or in efforts that do not produce goods or services, does not constitute child labour. Hence, undertaking household chores is not part of child labour but work in family-owned businesses is. Mendicancy is not child labour because it does not produce a social commodity. But debt-peonage, where children are made to work to pay off their parents' debts, is child labour even if children receive no direct payments for their work. So are children's self-employment activities.

Profile of Child Labour

The National Statistics Office undertook a Survey of Children 5-17 Years Old in 1995. They estimated that 16% of Filipino children were engaged in economic activities during the study period. Boys were more likely to work than girls, and the incidence of children at work increased with age, especially in the 10-14 year age group. About 11% of all rural children work, predominantly in agriculture. A majority of working children attended school in 1995, across all age groups. However, more girls than boys were in secondary school. Consistent with empirical studies, the

NSO survey described few children to be engaged in work alone. More likely, these children were working and studying at the same time. Given this situation, the problems most often cited by the children in relation to their schooling include the high cost of schooling, the distance of their schools from their residences and difficulties in catching up with school work.

These observations are consistent with findings of case studies and other researches on child labour. Statistics on working children in Region I may be summarized as follows:

- 7.1% of all children in the region are engaged in economic activities, with an almost equal number of girls and boys at work.
- A majority of the children are unpaid family workers in household operated farms (80.5%) and only 15.5% work in private establishments.
- Only 14.1% of children are permanent workers.

Close to 39% work as short-term casual workers, while 55% are engaged seasonally and during the summer vacation Boquiren (1987) observed that the child's decision to work is conditioned by a host of factors, including personal characteristics of the child, the household situation, influences of peers and community circumstances. In communities characterized by family-size production units, children are likely to engage in work in the company of one or both parents. In fact, in agricultural communities, most families view their children's work participation as part of the family's routine activities, and find nothing wrong with it. Most parents of working children have their own histories of working early in life, within the same communities where their families are presently situated.

Study results generally show that a majority of working children continue to go to school. However, this pattern is differentiated in relation to the type of work of the children, the production cycle, parents' occupational status, the affordability of intermediate and secondary schools, gender of children and their employment status (whether working full-time or part-time).

The proximity of secondary and intermediate schools is one important factor that discourages children from completely dropping-out of school because of their work activities. The health status of working children is affected by their activities. Child workers tend to be underweight and undernourished.

Children engaged in agricultural work suffer from respiratory ailments, gastro-intestinal complaints, and skin diseases. They are also exposed to a variety of chemical, biological and physical hazards. The paramount chemical risk in farm activities comes from exposure to toxic fumes from insecticides, followed by dust and noxious liquids. In Region I, amoebiasis constitutes the foremost biological hazard, followed by viral, fungal and bacterial infections. Prolonged exposure to the sun, heat, and noise are among the physical hazards in the Region. In the face of these risks to health and physical safety, only about one in five working children use safety gadgets of any kind. The most common safety gadgets used in farming are safety helmets, face shields, and safety boots. Child workers aspire for a better life for themselves.

A majority wants to finish a college education and become professionals. To achieve this, they perceive their work engagement as instrumental. Hence, work is seen as necessary to be able to move out of their present family situations. Despite the efforts of the governments to prohibit child labour since the 1920s through the enactment of laws and policy guidelines, the problem continues to persist. Since child labour is considered as a major economic and societal problem and child labour jeopardizes the children's potential to become productive adults, the government is required to respond more vigorously.

As the perennial problem of child labour is rooted in the economic structure of the country, the objective of the abolition of child labour can be achieved through sustained increases in standards of living. The ILO, in recognition of this fact, adopted a "two-pronged approach" to the child labour problem. The goal is the eventual elimination of child labour by improving the conditions under which children work. There have been government actions to address the child labour problem such as special projects designed to respond to specific needs. One of these projects, a project of the University of the Philippines in collaboration with UNICEF, was the launching of "Breaking Ground for Community Action on Child Labour" in 1988.

It identified and assisted communities in regions with high concentration of child labour through the provision of basic health and education services to children, entrepreneurial skills to children's parents, and advocacy work to convince parents and employers to remove children from heavy or dangerous work. The government formulated the Philippine Plan of Action for Children. It sets specific goals for children in especially difficult circumstances, among which is the banning of children from hazardous occupations/situations by 80% by the year 2000. In 1991, the National Child Labour Program Committee was created to expand the project "Breaking Ground for Community Action on Child Labour." It involved government, non-governmental agencies, and local government units, working together to combat child labour.

In 1994, the Philippine government became a participating country in the ILO-International Programme on the Elimination of Child Labour (ILO-IPEC), after which an agenda of action for attacking child labour in the Philippines was formulated by representatives of various government agencies, NGOs, employers' and workers organizations, local government officials and academics from different regions of the country. The current focus of actions in the country is on the elimination of risk to children than on ending their participation in all form of work. The ILO-IPEC believes that this approach is needed to accommodate the poverty element in child labour and to allow families flexibility in maintaining their essential survival mechanisms while protecting the children involved. The government is focusing on rescue efforts for the most exploited forms of child labour and for high-risk children such as the very young (below age 12 or 13).

For the rest of working children, however, until alternatives for survival are set in place, heightened efforts are recommended be exerted, to assure that they are in jobs that are not harmful to their health and physical and mental development. The present set of findings on child workers was derived from a Rapid Appraisal of Child Labour in four tobacco-growing communities of the Ilocos Region. In this chapter, the principal results of the research will be presented. Brief profiles of the barangays where child workers were identified will be presented first, to enable the reader to place the situation of child labour in the context of community characteristics. Information from informant interviews, ocular surveys, focus-group discussion, and case studies will be combined in the presentation.

The Tobacco-Producing Municipalities and Barangays

The municipality of Balaoan in La Union is made up of 36 Barangays with a total land area of 6,450 hectares. The barangays of Calliat and Baracbac Este in Balaoan comprise 90 and 80.45 hectares, respectively. The topography of Balaoan is generally 60% flat plains suitable for rice, corn and tobacco production, and 40% rolling terrain. The southeast portion going towards the western portion of the municipality is predominantly hilly. Balaoan had a total population of 32,280 for the year 1998. Forty-nine per cent or 3,219 hectares of Balaoan is cropland, with 3,556 total numbers of farmers tilling different farm types and following several cropping patterns where rice is the basic main crop except in upland areas. Barangay Calliat is located at the southern part of Balaoan beside Barangay Baracbac Este.

It is approximately 6 kilometers from the town proper of Balaoan with a road network that stretches from the national highway to its neighboring barangays. It is accessible by passenger jeepneys and tricycles. Social services such as school and health center are visible in the area. Calliat Elementary school is just beside the barangay hall, multi-purpose cooperative and day care center. These resources are also accessible to the residents of Barangay Baracbac Este due to the nearness of the place and its geographical boundaries. It had a total population of 1030 in 2001, and most individuals are engaged in agriculture. Farming and livestock rising are the most dominant and reliable sources of income of the residents.

Ninety per cent of the workers in the area are farmers and their main crops are palay and tobacco. Some of them plant corn and watermelon as alternative cash crops. The remaining 10% of its population are professionals and entrepreneurs. Almost all families are engaged in backyard gardening and livestock rising. Produce is mainly for home consumption although some are sold in the market. The tobacco farmland and facilities for production are just a few kilometers away from farmer's residential area. Most of them who engage in tobacco growing have their own curing barns needed in curing the harvested tobacco leaves. Barangay Baracbac Este is located on the northeastern part of Balaoan, sandwiched by Brgy. Calliat on the east, on the north by Brgy.

Tallipugo, and on the south by the Maluyo River. It is approximately 5 kilometers away from the Balaoan Municipal Hall, with concrete farm to market roads and provincial roads connecting to national highway. The place is accessible through passenger jeepneys and tricycles anytime. Two-thirds of the total land area of the barangay is used for agriculture. Its population numbered 1,284 in 2000. Baracbac Este doesn't have an elementary school in the area. Children normally enroll at Calliat Elementary School, a walking distance from their houses. Most of the residents have electricity supplied by La Union Electric Cooperative while deep wells are the main source of fresh water.

Majority of the residents in Baracbac Este depend on farming as their primary source of income. Rice, corn and sugar are their main products while tobacco is planted during dry season. Farmers who engage in tobacco farming own curing barns that are located near to or beside their houses. Some of them till land in the adjacent areas, particularly in Barangay Calliat. Aside from farming, most of the residents also undertake livestock raising such as swine raising, poultry, cattle, goat and carabao raising. The city of Candon has 42 barangays with a total land area of 10,328.21 hectares. Based on the 2000 census, a total population of 48,456 is projected, with an annual growth of 0.20%. 25,127 of the total population are female and 22,363 are male.

Seventy-four per cent of the total land area of Candon is considered as agricultural land. Majority of the land is used for the production of rice, tobacco, cotton, corn, and vegetables. A small area is devoted to fishing. Commercial establishments located in the city proper make up only 0.03% of its total land area that is used for industrial investments. Barangay Parioc II is 348 north of Metro Manila, and 7.2 kms. from the city proper. It is almost 5 kms. away from the hi-way going north to Vigan, Ilocos Sur, and passing through the road between Brgy, Calaoaan and Brgy and Ayudante. The area is a valley situated between two mountains. Parioc II can be reached by tricycle, the most popular means of transportation going to the highway and vice versa. Twenty per cent of the southwestern part of Brgy. Parioc II is considered as a forest reserve. Its hilly terrain is planted with small trees that are the residents' source of firewood. About 0.1 % of the land is used as fishpond. Parioc II has a population of 1,512, consisting of 831 males and 681 females, occupying 341 residential households scattered in groups across the Barangay. Around 95% of all households have electricity.

Barangay Parioc II is traversed by 18 kms. of concrete roads, with trails in its interior areas commonly used for animal drawn carts. Along the stretch of the road going inside the Barangay proper is a bridge, and almost halfway is the Brgy. Day Care Center (also Multi-Purpose Center) ran by a Barangay Health Worker. The same structure is use by 59 students, who are supervised by a teacher. Since there is no elementary school in the Barangay, elementary grade students walk to Brgy. Parioc I, which has the nearest public school in the area. Approximately 95 % of the household have electricity. A small number of farmers get their water supply from the river, while the major source of water comes from deep wells, run by diesel motors. Majority of the residents are engaged in farming. Approximately 262.5 hectares of land, which is rain dependent, is planted to rice during the rainy season.

After harvest time, other crops that need less water such as corn, tobacco, and vegetables replace the rice in the fields. Barangay Balingaoan is situated 348 kms north of Metro Manila, 4 kms. from the town proper of Candon City. Its total population is 1,393, including 688 males and 705 females, spread across 255 households. There is a 12 km. long barangay road linking the main highway to the interior part of Balangaoan by means of tricycles and other public utility vehicles going to the town proper. It is composed of 6 sitios, linked by 83 % of concrete road, some rough roads (10 %), and trails in the interior. The biggest site is Bariquir where 1/3 of the total number of residential houses is concentrated, spreading along both side of the Barangay road.

The smallest sitio is Kamanggaan where the Barangay Day Care Center is located. The Barangay Hall, church, and the Barangay Elementary School are located alongside the Barangay main road in Sitio Nagbalsaan. Eighty-five per cent of households have electricity and about 35 families have telephones. The source of income of residents in Balangaoan comes from agricultural production in a land area of more or less 287 hectares. The areas are planted with seasonal alternate intercropping of corn, vegetable, and tobacco, but its main product is rice. Balangaoan doesn't have an irrigation system to supply the water needs of the farmers.

Their sources of water come from deep wells constructed beside rice paddies run by conventional diesel motors.

Child Labour on Tobacco Farms

Ten child workers from Calliat, Balaoan and 11 from Parioc II, Candon were separately asked to take part in focus group discussions about their work. In order to stimulate the interest of the children, they were first asked to depict their work in tobacco production through colored drawings. Approximately half of the children who participated in the FGDs were boys and the rest were girls.

The boys from Balaoan had ages ranging from 11 to 14 years, while those from Parioc II were younger: from 9 to 14 years. The female research cooperators were younger than the boys, with one from Parioc II being only 7 year of age. According to community informants and extension workers alike, the participation of children in tobacco production is a common feature in the life of the four barangays in the study. At young ages, sons and daughters are taught to accomplish simple tasks from planting to agtudok ('sticking' tobacco). The drawings shared by the child workers in the FGDs illustrate their involvement in a variety of tasks from seedbed preparation to post-harvest activities. The case studies describe similar work experiences with family members and other persons in the communities.

Types of Work of Child Workers

The types of work engaged in by children, derived from both FGDs and case studies, include:

- In seedbed preparation
- Cultivation of tobacco plants for water percolation (ruc-at)
- Weeding
- Cultivation or plowing (gulis)

Assisting Adults in Chemical Spraying

In planting and transplanting operations:

- Planting
- Transplanting
- Watering
- Fertilizer application
- In harvest and post-curing operations –
- Harvesting (pitas)
- Sticking tobacco leaves on bamboo sticks (agtudok)
- Uprooting the plants
- Preparing the fire for the flue (gatong)
- Sun drying

Work Patterns of Child Workers

There are similarities and slight difference in the patterns of work of children across the two municipalities we studied. To obtain a better picture of the nature of their work in tobacco production, the summary results of the FGDs are reproduced here.

1. *Calliat, Balaoan, La Union:* The children shared their work in the tobacco farms through drawings, which were

shared with the big group. The drawings showed that the children of Calliat were actively involved in six (6) activities of tobacco farming. Panag-sibug (watering) the plants takes place when sowing seeds and becomes a regular activity once transplanting has taken place and until harvest time. Watering is done usually with an older sibling or with a parent.

The children hold the watering hose (2-3 inches in diameter) to avoid trampling on the tobacco plant. Panagturnok (uprooting of tobacco seedlings) for replanting is also participated in by the children. After uprooting the tobacco plant from the sowing plot, the children assist in transplanting (panagmula) to the main plot. Transplanting is a family activity, which is done late in the afternoon, usually from 3-5 p.m. One maintenance work for the tobacco plant is panag-paggot ti ruot (weeding) by the family members. An activity identified as a male role is panag-gulis or plowing along the tobacco plots to loosen the soil for better water percolation during watering.

The last activity in tobacco production where the children are involved is panag-tudok (sticking). It is considered as a favorite among the children not only because it is the easiest but also it is paid. Majority of the children of Calliat do not get paid for their work in their tobacco farm, which they perform before their classes in the morning, and after their classes in the afternoon and usually during weekends. What drives them to work is the desire to help the family. The two that get paid for their work earn from P 20.00 – P 25.00 per hundred sticks. In the above-mentioned activities, the children used their bare hands, which leads to their getting injured or their fingers being pierced during sticking. They however do not consider this as a serious problem.

2. *Parioc II, Candon, Ilocos Sur:* The child workers in Barangay Parioc II are involved in the tobacco production process from planting to the post-curing stage. At the onset of the sowing of tobacco seeds, the plots now have to be watered (panag-sibog) regularly, which is every other day.

This is done very early in the morning before the children attend their classes or late in the afternoon, before sundown. Watering is done using rubber hoses of several meters long and about 2-3 inches in diameter.

An elder sibling or the father is usually the person whom the child helps by holding the hose, making sure that it does not trample on any tobacco plant. After a month the seedlings are ready for transplanting (panag-mula) to the main plot. Transplanting is done early in the morning starting at 7 a.m. – 9 or 10 p.m. then again from 2 p.m - 4 p.m. Since transplanting coincides with the Christmas vacation, the children join their family in this activity. One week after the tobacco plants are transplanted, fertilizer (panag-abono) can then be applied.

The Ammonium Sulfate (2100) or complete fertilizer is placed in a sitaw or small pail and the children using their bare hands apply the granules to the tobacco plant. Spraying or insecticide application is performed by older children, who are 14 years old and above. The adults harvest mature tobacco leaves. Sticking (panag-tudok) is a favorite among the children because it is paid for 30 centavos to 50 centavos per sad-ay which consists of three sticks per sad-ay. On weekdays, the children do sticking from 5-8 p.m., others work from 8 p.m. -11 p.m.; while on weekends, they work from 7 a.m. – 5 p.m. Children who are 9 years old and above help in the fueling of the curing barn (agsungrod) and carrying tobacco in sad-ay (agyawat) to the curing barn. Once the tobacco leaves are cured and removed from the curing barn (panag-yakas), the leaves are removed from the stick (panag-manos).

A complete panag-yakas' is paid P 20.00 with merienda. After removing the leaves from the sticks, the sticks are then bundled and the sad-ay arranged for future use. The children also perform these last two activities. Majority of the children keep all the money they earn for themselves. They save this to buy new clothes (bado) or school supplies. One shares half of her earnings with her mother. The OSY whose farm work is regular earns P 50.00 pesos for a half-day work. Aside from working in their own farms, the children work on the farms of relatives. During weeding and planting time, the children used kumpay (sickle), don sweaters, and wear wide brimmed hats. Two of the participants also sometimes use gloves when sticking tobacco leaves. Aside from this apparel, the children use no other protective clothing so that most experience punctures during their sticking activities. From among the child workers in the FGDs, it was reported that girls as young as 7 years old help in weeding, watering, sticking and uprooting tobacco. The boys, who were older, were occupied with a wider variety of jobs: ruc-at, chemical spraying, weeding gulis, fertilizer application, transplanting, planting and sticking tobacco.

Adult tobacco growers usually accompany the children in the accomplishment of their tasks. Hence, the children report working alongside either parent, with aunts, uncles, cousins, grandmothers, friends, and neighbors. Ocular observation confirms the children's account that these different individuals may work together as pairs or small groups, depending on the phase of tobacco production they are working on. For most of the children, work is part-time and seasonal. They go to the fields before leaving for school, once school is over in the afternoons, on weekends and school breaks. At the time of the study, in December and early January, tobacco growers had just begun to plant. By the time the validation meeting took place in February, some farms had been harvested and most of the children were involved in sticking tobacco, helping fuel the flues, and drying the harvested leaves.

Monetary and Non-Cash Earnings Remuneration for working in tobacco farms varies according to the phase of tobacco production, and is sometimes different across the two municipalities. On the average, for part-time work that may last from 2 to 3 hours on schooldays and 10 hours on weekends, child workers receive P 20 to P 25 daily. The cheapest payment for work is in Calliat, for panag-tudok, or sticking the harvested leaves on bamboo sticks in preparation for curing. Some tasks are unpaid, especially because the children work on small family-owned farms. Some girls reportedly received no payments for doing the same tasks that boys were paid for.

These activities include weeding, transplanting tobacco, fertilizing and weeding. In Parioc II, one child stated that she received money from her parents only after the cured tobacco had been sold to a dealer. Money earned from tobacco production are often used by the children to buy clothes for themselves and other that the need for school. Some buy food for themselves and their siblings or give a portion of the earnings to their mothers. This was shared both by the children in the FGDs and in the case studies. In addition to money, the children perceive certain benefits they receive to be related to their work. These non-cash benefits include merienda (snacks) during the activity, getting uniforms, food and other pieces of clothing from their parents, and their school allowances.

Tools and Equipments used by Child Workers

For certain aspects of tobacco production, some tools and equipment may be required. For fertilizer application, for instance, children use pails (called sitaw), the fertilizer itself (ammonia or complete fertilizer), bottle caps and spoons for measuring the chemical. For panag-tudok, which occupies the children for a great deal of time, bamboo sticks (sad-ay) are fashioned on which the children string the tobacco leaves. Sometimes, gloves are worn to protect them. In many cases, however, the children use their bare hands in undertaking either fertilization or panag-tudok. It may be worth noting at this point, however, that even older persons at work on the farms do not wear protective clothing while applying pesticides or fertilizers. Many of them also go about with bare feet on the fields and use their bare hands for fertilizer application, chemical spraying and panag-tudok.

Profile of the Child Workers: Case Studies

Most of the children included in the case studies are school children, with the exception of Billy, who stopped going to school only this year. Except for Marichu, who is at a lower grade level than her age-cohorts because she had failing grades in the past, the rest have attended school regularly. Work in the fields has not affected the school performance of many of the children. Ricardo is Second Honor in his class while Becky is Seventh Honor. Neither have they been absent on account of work. Rather, illness is the more common explanation of school absences. Visual observation and their own accounts point out that many of the children are underweight and small for their ages. This is especially true among the children from Balaoan.

Despite this poor nutritional profile, the children have not been ill in recent months, suffering only from common respiratory aliments such as coughs or colds. However, Becky states that she gets asthma attack when she is tired. Socialization into Tobacco Production Billy started to work when he was only 4 years of age. Marlon and Marichu learned panag-tudok before they started elementary school, when they were 6 and 7 years old, respectively. Ricardo is the most recent child worker, having been taught only when he was already 10 years old. Hence, the age at which children begin work in tobacco production varies widely. Most probably, the entry of children into tobacco production is linked to the number of adults in a family: the fewer the adults, the more likely a child is involved in work. But panag-tudok is taught even to young children.

All the children report that they learned the needed tasks from relatives, including their own parents, aunts, grandparents, uncles and cousins. These findings are indicative of the fact that tobacco-growing in the two towns are largely family enterprises, and the children are drawn into work as part of their roles as obedient sons and daughters. The 7 children do the same types of simple tasks that the child workers in the FGDs report doing: from planting to post-curing phases of production. Monica and Richard narrate that they work as assistants of older siblings or relatives, from whom they learned the trade. Others reportedly observed older siblings or relatives to learn the tasks. Billy reports that, at the age of 13, he was also taught how to do chemical application. Marichu said she also helps in rice production, as the other children probably also do.

Five of the children work close to their residences, and their family farms can be reached by walking for 5 to 10 minutes only. Billy and Becky, however, need to ride the tricycles or walk for about half-an-hour to their places of work. Certain tasks, according to the children, are done by both younger and older children, while others are for older ones only. Fertilizer application is taught to young children, regardless of sex, who engage in the work along with older children and adults. Weeding, watering and panag-tudok are other activities that young girls and boys can do along with older persons. From these accounts, it can be concluded that most of the work assigned to young children are relatively easy, which they can learn through imitation or after rudimentary instruction from older companions.

Chemical spraying (or pesticide application), firing the flue, and akas (collecting cured leaves from the flue) are tasks reserved for older children and adults. These activities apparently require bigger children (for carrying the sprayers, for instance, or reaching into the flue) and a more developed sense of judgment. However, both boys and girls can do these tasks. Pagpitas, or harvesting mature tobacco leaves is another activity often done by older children. In this case, they have to be tall enough to reach the tobacco leaves (basta't puwede nang maabot ang dahon ng tobacco, they said (so long as the child can reach the tobacco leaves).

Plowing the fields, however, is a task assigned only to older male children. In Parrioc II and Balaoagan, older children help in tobacco curing activities: fueling the curing barn, carrying the sad-ay (tobacco strung on a long pole) to the barn, removing the cured leaves from the sticks afterwards, and arranging the sticks for future use.

The intensity of involvement in tobacco production varies across the children and according to tasks. The youngest, Monica, spends only about a quarter-of-an-hour on weekends for watering the plants or panag-tudok. Five of the other children work no longer than 2 hours at certain tasks. Billy, however, is a fulltime worker, and works an average of 6 hours a day. The most labourious chore is panag-tudok, which can take up to 10 hours, according to Becky, or until midnight, according to Ruben. Some activities have to be done daily (like fertilization, weeding and panag-tudok) but the rest can be done only for certain days of the week (like watering the plants). The nature of activities is also differentiated by the stage of production, such that fertilization and watering are accomplished from December to January, at the start of the production cycle, and panag-tudok from February to March, after the leaves have been harvested.

Physical Risks and Hazards

The children were asked to describe the conditions under which they work. Almost all agree that tobacco cultivation is undertaken under harsh physical conditions. From the months of December to March, the weather can be either hot or cold, although it is generally hot in the open fields. Marichu complains that she gets tired and sleeps late because of her work. Marlon also says his hands get tired from work and his body feels heavy (nangangawit). The children like the simpler tasks like watering and harvesting leaves best because they are easy. They have different opinions about panag-tudok, which is easy for some but risky for the others, who fear having their fingers pricked. Ricardo does not like fertilizer application, either, because he says it is risky (delikado).

The presented complaints and direct observation of their activities in tobacco production lead us to infer that health hazards for children include the following:

- Sleeplessness and fatigue brought on by long work hours, working under hot weather and use of heavy equipment.
- Wounds and injuries, especially from panag-tudok.
- Dermatitis resulting from over-exposure to the sun and fertilizer application.
- Exposure to toxic chemicals resulting from spraying and fertilizer application without protective gear.
- Bites and stings from wasps, bees, mites ants and other insects.
- Asthma and rhinitis resulting from contact with tobacco leaf and dust.

Researches on the health risks associated with tobacco production lists the following possible health effects of work in tobacco farming:

Tobacco croppers and harvesters have been known to experience green tobacco sickness when working with damp tobacco. It is manifested by complaints of headaches, pallor, vomiting and nausea, following contact by the worker with wet tobacco. The skin can also be burned in several ways. Burns can result from dry fertilizer that is hygroscopic and attracts moisture. On the skin, it draws out moisture and causes skin burns. Liquid anhydrous ammonia is used for fertilizing the soil, where it can expand into a gas and combine with moisture. If the liquid or gas gets into contact with the body, especially the eyes, skin and respiratory tract, cell destruction can occur and permanent damage results in the absence of immediate treatment.

The child workers of La Union and Ilocos Sur have reportedly been sick of some of the symptoms described above. They have had coughs, asthma, and strained eyes. A number experienced dizziness, stomachaches, headaches, and vomiting. Others have had skin rashes. Children's Aspirations Education is a value close to the hearts of the children. Billy, who had to stop schooling to enable an older sister to go to college, asserts that he needs to work now to be able to resume schooling. Similarly, Ricardo, Marlon, Becky and Ruben want to continue their work on the farms since it provides money needed to pay off loans, or to purchase household goods. Marichu says she considers the work as part of her routine (nakasanayan na). Thus, none of the children find anything objectionable in their present situation as child workers. They look at work as merely being instrumental for the achievement of a better quality of life. In fact, someday, they would like to see themselves as professionals: as an engineer, a teacher, a nurse or a police officer.

Government Programs in the Ilocos

This describes the programs of key government line agencies in the Ilocos. Originally, we intended to document only programs of agencies dealing with the issue of child labour. However, a description of the work of the National Tobacco Administration is included, inasmuch as it is the most visible agency in the municipalities and barangays we visited.

The National Tobacco Administration

Significance of the Tobacco Industry

The national average annual revenue to the government, as contribution by the tobacco industry during the period 1997-99, was P 21.193 billion. The national average annual volume of tobacco production was 71.635 kilograms, and the average annual value of production reached a P 2.633 B mark. About 1.93 million

Filipinos are dependent on the industry (NTA Brochure, 2001). By geographic coverage of the NTA, Virginia tobacco type covered 23,347 hectares (or 58% of the country's total coverage of 40,297 hectares) in the provinces of Abra, Ilocos Norte, Ilocos Sur (66 %), and La Union.

The native variety ranked second in terms of coverage, where 9,752 hectares (24%) were planted in most provinces, followed by burley tobacco grown in Pangasinan (51%), Tarlac, Nueva Ecija, and Occidental Mindoro. As to demographic coverage of the NTA, the Virginia tobacco is the predominant type cultivated by 32,352 farmers in the provinces of Abra, Ilocos Norte, Ilocos Sur (60%), and La Union. The native variety ranked second (18,729 farmers) while burley was the least variety grown by 11,336 farmers. Tobacco is a dry season crop that is grown during the dry season that is from October or November to April. As a traditional crop, the tobacco farmers are said to have mastered its technology and, in the Ilocos region, tobacco farming is considered as a typical and traditional household activity which members of the family have inherited from their great grandparents.

Hence, all members of a family may be engaged in tobacco production. The production of Virginia tobacco has been on the decline in recent years. The US Department of Agriculture (July 2000) describes the problem in the Philippine tobacco industry thus: "...after a substantial expansion in 1998, the Philippine tobacco in 1999 contracted again as more than 20% of the entire crop was damaged by heavy rains. After gaining some momentum in 1998 to rebuild inventories, this will again lead to substantial declines, primarily as a result of damage to Virginia flue-cured tobacco."

This scenario led to speculation that during the latter half of 1999, due to low prices of the low-grade tobacco leaf resulting from the La Niña phenomenon in 1999-2000, farmers would be discouraged to plant more tobacco. NTA feared that farmers would shift to other crops such as vegetables for 2000 and 2001. This, in fact, is what happened in Ilocos provinces. The decline in the profitability of tobacco production has led to further crop diversification in the Barangays we visited. More areas are now planted to corn, peanuts and vegetables. The NTA has had to extend technical assistance and credit to tobacco farmers, in an effort to help them recoup their losses.

Responsibilities and Functions of the NTA

The National Tobacco Administration (NTA) is the only government agency attending to the development of the local tobacco industry and its major sectors, the tobacco farmers, in particular, and the tobacco buyers and manufacturers, in general. It is mandated by law to (NTA Charter, Executive Order No. 245):

- Administer and regulate the production and trading of tobacco and the manufacture, sale and distribution of tobacco products;
- Improve the living conditions and raise the quality of life of the tobacco farmers, including those who depend upon the industry for their livelihood; and
- Promote the balanced and integrated growth of development of the tobacco industry to help make agriculture a solid basis for industrialization.

Based on the above mandate, the NTA has outlined four strategic programmes for the tobacco industry. These are 1) total market development through responsive research, quality production, fair and equitable trading and efficient delivery of services; 2) total farming, total farmer, total technician development; 3) farmers' organization development; and 4) identification and development of other industrial uses of tobacco.

Among its component services, the NTA is engaged in research such as the production of certified tobacco seeds and technology research/information services. Its extension services are in the form of free distribution of certified tobacco seeds. It extends technical assistance from seed bedding to marketing; provides agricultural inputs and credit assistance for production and/or facility development. It works in collaboration with tobacco companies, congressional leaders, local government units, lending institutions, and other sources.

In the area of marketing services, the NTA provides the following: a) certification of production based on acceptances as required under R. A. Nos. 7171 and 8240; b) trade regulation enforcement; c) establishment of marketing tie-ups; and d) market research and information services. R.A. No. 7171, An Act to Promote the Development of the Farmers in the Virginia Tobacco-Producing Provinces, which was approved on January 9, 1992 serve as the source of financial support to tobacco producers from the national government for beneficiary provinces.

The law stipulates that the funds shall be constituted and collected from the proceeds of fifteen per cent (15%) of the excise taxes on locally manufactured Virginia-type of cigarettes. The funds allotted shall be divided among the beneficiary provinces pro rata according to the volume of Virginia tobacco production.

During the Tripartite Conference constituted by the NTA, representatives of farmer-leaders and traders on December 12, 2001, it was reported in their position paper, "Forging New Directions for the Philippine Tobacco Industry", that the 15% of excise taxes component, amounting to P 1.62 billion, has been given back to the tobacco planters. Part of this money has found its way into Balaoan and Candon. Both the NTA extension workers and farmers report that credit facilities given to farmers have come from excise taxes. In the current year, many farmers have availed of loans from NTA to assist them in a renewed effort at increasing the value of tobacco crops.

From accounts of the tobacco farmers, NTA workers assisted them with interest- free loans after the failure of their crops in 1999. Its extension officers regularly visit their farms to render technical assistance and inspect their curing barns. It has also made available to farmers an innovative design of a curing barn for their possible adoption, with a view to replacing the existing curing barns that have been passed down from generations of tobacco farmers. It helped to establish a cooperative farm among the farmers, which it assists from seedbed preparation to marketing. Residents of the communities visited by the research team generally have positive appraisals of the NTA extension officers.

They are considered to have been a big help to the farmers (malaking tulong), especially because they extend new technologies for tobacco production. They welcome the credit program of the NTA, and farmers wish to avail of bigger loans.

The NTA is not mandated to examine social relations and employment patterns in tobacco production. As such, its programs are not directed to child protection. However, its looming presence in the barangays makes it a significant partner in monitoring and abating problems spawned by child labour. The National Program against Child Labour in Region 1, the Department of Labour and Employment (DOLE) and the Department of Social Welfare and Development (DSWD) are the lead and cooperating agencies in implementing the National Program Against Child Labour.

This Plan is part of the implementation of the National Strategic Framework for Plan Development for Children (2000-2025) or Child 2. The National Strategic Framework aims to ensure that every Filipino child will exercise his or her right to survival, protection, development and participation throughout the life cycle. Related to this, among the strategies that are strategic for child labour are the following (CWC 2000):

- Strengthening of the capability of families to nurture children and provide them with full support for their welfare and development.
- Advocacy towards a paradigm shift to put children first in the use of resources of the family, community and State.
- Transformation of values and practices in the labour market that would protect children from abuse and exploitation.

The goals of the National Program Against Child Labour in Region 1 are the following:

- Establishment of reliable mechanism for identifying and monitoring child labourers, their families and communities through a data base of working children,
- Inspection of tourism establishment for accreditation,
- Visitation of business establishments,
- Compliance with international conventions affecting child labourers through the conduct of symposia,
- Education campaign, linkages and networking with agencies and NGOs,
- Promotion of integrated advocacy and action for child labourers,
- Increased capacity of families employment, livelihood and entrepreneurship, and
- Strengthen the Barangay Council for the Protection of Children and Sagip Batang Manggagawa (Rescue Child Workers) Action Teams.

There is no project that addresses the issue of child labour in agriculture, particularly in the tobacco growing areas. The DOLE Regional Office, for one, believes that children in the Region's tourist establishments are at greater risk of exploitation. Representatives of four agencies interviewed for this project (from DSWD, DOLE, DECS, and DOH) were unanimous in saying that there is no child labour in the tobacco industry in the Region. They perceive children's work in tobacco farms as part of training the children for adult responsibilities. They also state that there is no reported victim of child labour in the Region.

Child Labour in Selected Barangays of the Ilocos

The utilization of the labour of young children below the age of 15 is a common experience in the tobacco farms of La Union and Ilocos Sur. Tobacco production is inherently a family enterprise among tenant farmers and leaseholders in the Barangays we visited, where the average size of the areas under production is half- a-hectare. Thus, it is not unusual to find all hands in a household at work on tobacco farming, including older and younger adults and children of all ages. Both women and men spend time on farming, and this extends to boy and girl children. The norm of working together on tobacco farming is so ingrained that parents may scold or spank children who are recalcitrant, or would rather do something else when there is farm work to be done.

The parents' attitudes keep the children in line and they obediently do whatever they have been assigned to perform. Children are taught at young ages (from 4 years of age) simple tasks related to tobacco production, like watering the plants, weeding and panag-tudok. Eventually, the children help their parents, older siblings and other relatives in all phases of tobacco cultivation – from seedbed preparation to post-curing – engaging in more difficult activities as they grow older.

Observations made during data gathering, findings from the case studies and the FGDs, show that children undertake many of the tasks with older members of the family. For instance, a child may hold the hose for his father or grandfather while the latter waters the plants. An older boy helps carry the chemical sprayer to the fields for his father. Mother and daughter together water the young plants.

Cousins go off to the farms together to weed the tobacco. Panagtudok is essentially the work of women and children sitting around in groups. In many cases, therefore, children's work happens under the supervision of parents and other relatives. The work assigned to children is not always time-consuming and they are able to finish their tasks before they go to school and upon their return in the afternoons. Given the fact that tobacco growing commences in October or November and extends to March or April, school vacations provide time for children to be more intensively engaged in tobacco production.

The average amount of time that children use for working on tobacco farms is 2 - 4 hours. However, on weekends, they may work for as long as 10 hours, especially when the activity involved is panagtudok, sticking tobacco on the sad-ay (bamboo poles). The remuneration derived from children's work is low, given the fact that they are usually given only P 20 for part-time work. This is far below the average nominal wages of adult workers, which was determined to be P 141.00 per day in Region I in March 2001 (BLES-DOLE 2001). Some tasks are unpaid, like watering, weeding and cultivation (gulis). Arrangements for payment and the cost of children's labour vary across family enterprises and barangays. For instance, while a girl child was paid only P 20.00 a day in Balaoan for panagtudok, a boy child in Candon reportedly received P 50.00 daily for the same task. Whatever the arrangements, however, children's work serves to keep down the cost of tobacco production.

Government Concern for Child-Farmers in Tobacco Production

The research determined that, to date, there is no program of government that directly addresses the issue of child labour in the tobacco industry within Region I. Programs and efforts of agencies implementing the National

Plan for Child Labour focus on children in tourism and entertainment rather than on the plight of agricultural child workers. The National Tobacco Administration concerns itself with providing financial and technical assistance to tobacco growers, ignoring completely the risks to children emanating from their labour participation. Consciousness about the need to extend child protection to children at work in tobacco production is not evident among the regional line agencies.

Neither do Barangay officials nor other community workers perceive child labour as an issue. Instead, these community gatekeepers look at children's work participation as part of their childhood responsibilities, which they need to fulfill as obedient children and productive members of their families and communities. Parents are wont to share this view of children at work. A significant area of concern that emerges from the study has to do with the physical and health hazards associated with tobacco production. Children have been observed to work on farms under conditions that can be deleterious to their health. They toil in positions straining their limbs under the scorching heat of the sun. They often wear no protective clothing against sharp or hot objects or chemicals. Children use their bare hands in panag-tudok and fertilizer application.

In the Barangays of Candon, older children continue to be involved in tobacco curing activities, which involves other risks to health. Yet, parents and the children themselves are apparently unaware that there are protective measures that are important to safeguard the health of children.

Recommendations

On the basis of the findings of this Rapid Appraisal of child labour in selected Barangays of La Union and Ilocos Sur, the following recommendations are made:

Information Campaign on Child Labour

It is evident from this study that there is very little awareness on the configuration of child labour in tobacco production. Government officials have not studied the phenomenon, much less designed programs to address the need for child protection in tobacco growing. Community influences, parents and children are also unaware that there are risks to the children's wellbeing that may occur as a result of their work in tobacco farms. The notion that children's work is part of their socialization is a dominant theme.

Yet, the findings of this study describe certain areas that may require attention. For instance, communities have to be made more aware of the rights of children to safety, education and good health. They need to be informed of their responsibility to protect and safeguard their children against the potentially hazardous effects of child labour in tobacco production. In instances where the children are full-time workers, their rights as young workers have to be safeguarded. Work conditions need to be examined, including the conditions and terms of payment. An information campaign should target various groups: regional offices of government and local government units, tobacco producers, parents and their children.

Comprehensive Research on Child Labour in Region I

The rapid appraisal we conducted has merely revealed the 'tip of the iceberg.' Much more needs to be studied concerning the plight of child workers in the tobacco industry. The themes of a comprehensive study may include the following:

- Regional description of the incidence of child labour in tobacco growing Barangays, across provinces, as a way of identifying areas where the children are more disadvantaged.

- Work patterns and work conditions in family enterprises engaged in tobacco production, to identify the range of risks and issues that require child protection measures.
- Analysis of the impacts of children's participation in tobacco production on their health, nutrition, education, values and world views, as a means of identifying useful entry points for program interventions by government agencies, NGOs and the private sector.

Child Protection Measures

Several strategies and directions can be immediately undertaken to alleviate the situation of child workers and to guarantee respect of their rights. Among these are:

- Formulation of municipal ordinances specifically for the protection of working children against exploitation and hazardous forms of employment.
- Formation of a regional or provincial inter-agency committee to address the situation of child workers in the tobacco industry.
- Activation and strengthening of the Barangay Councils for the Protection of Children, with special efforts to educate and capacitate them to address child labour.
- For NTA, to include a monitoring system in its extension efforts in order to assess the extent of child labour in the tobacco industry and to provide child-focused services among its programs in the communities.
- For local governments, to monitor children's work participation in tobacco- growing barangays, as a factor that may negatively affect their health condition.

Community Development

It has been observed that child labour is more likely in families that are economically strapped. The tobacco industry has experienced major setbacks in the past several years and has yet to recover. These conditions will make child labour utilization a more likely phenomenon. Assistance to poor farmers, their families and communities become important in this respect. Given the living conditions of the tobacco farmers, their children and barangays, the following measures are recommended:

- To expand the provision of economic assistance and livelihood projects to tobacco-growing families, especially as a way of preventing their victimization from loan sharks and unscrupulous traders.
- To encourage farmers to apply the integrated farming system approach, which enjoins them to plant a diverse variety of crops at different times in the year, in order to offset the dire effects of losses from mono-cropping.
- To establish elementary schools within the barangays of Parioc II and Baracbac Este, so that the inaccessibility of schools does not become a reason for dropping-out of school among its young population.

The experience of child labour has been proven to exist in the Ilocos provinces. While their work conditions are not alarming, measures still have to be put into place in order to enhance the rights and welfare of children. To paraphrase the UNICEF (2001), it is the right of the child to have the "best possible start in life."

4

Rehabilitation Measures of Child Labour

The Child labour cell is entrusted with the responsibility of formulation and implementation of policy and programmes for tackling problems of child labour. The Cell is respondible for funding and monitoring of the projects taken up under the scheme of National Child Labour Projects. The cell also renders financial assistance to voluntary organizations for taking up action-oriented projects for child labour. In addition, the cell monitors the enforcement of child labour (prohibition and regulation) Act, 1986 and organizes meetings of various committees, workshops, advisory boards, etc.

Child Labour Projects

One of the components of the national child labour policy, 1987, is setting up of the national child labour projects (NCLPs) in areas of high concentration of child labour of their identification, withdrawal and rehabilitation. The package of benefits to child labour for their rehabilitation includes non-formal/formal education, vocational training, nutrition, health care, stipend, etc. The other activities include more strict enforcement of child labour related laws, raising awareness against the evil of child labour and extension of welfare facilities to the child labour.

In keeping with the policy on child labour, the national child labour project scheme was initiated in 12 districts in 1988 with the objective of withdrawing and rehabilitating children working in identified hazardous occupations and processes. The number of projects was increased to 100 during the Ninth plan and has now been expanded to cover 250 districts across 21 states during the tenth plan.

Gants in Aid to Voluntary Agencies

This scheme is for taking up action oriented projects for the rehabilitation of child labour and is implanted through NGOs and voluntary organizations. Financial assistance to the extent of 75 per cent of the project cost is provided to the NGOs for running the projects. The NGOs and voluntary agencies are expected to meet 25 per cent of the projects cost out of their own resources. The scheme allows for flexibility and innovation.

Indo-US-DoL Matching Grant (INDUS Project)

The Ministry of Labour-United States, Department of labour (Ministry of labour-US-DOL) project is being developed as follow up of the joint statement in "Enhanced Indo-US cooperation on Elimination of child labour" signed between the Ministry of Labour and the US Department of Labour in August 2000. The project aims at effecting convergence with the department of education to ensure complete elimination of child labour from identified hazardous industries in identified districts.

The project proposes to cover 21 districts in five states, namely, Uttar Pradesh, Madhya Pradesh, Tamil Nadu, Maharashtra and the NCT of Delhi. The US department of labour would provide US$ 20 million (US$ 13 million for the labour component and US$ 7 million for the education component) to be matched, with equal funding from the Indian government which will be shared between the Ministry of labour (US$ 13 million) and ministry of HRD

(US$ 7 million). The project has been launched on 16.02.2004. Funds have been released to Indo-US-DoL Matching Grant (INDUS) district for setting up for Transitional Education Centre (TECs) and meeting the expense of the project society.

According to the Indian census of 1991, there are 11.28 million working children under the age of fourteen years in India. Over 85% of this child labour is in the country's rural areas, working in agricultural activities such as fanning, livestock rearing, forestry and fisheries.

This labour is outside the formal sector, and outside industry. Moreover, nine out of ten working children work within a family setting. Working in family-based occupations, these children also develop skills in certain traditional crafts, thus augmenting the human capital formation of India's developing economy. India has all along followed a proactive policy in the matter of tackling the problem of child labour. India has always stood for constitutional, statutory and development measures required to eliminate child labour.

The Indian Constitution has consciously incorporated provisions to secure compulsory universal elementary education as well as labour protection for children. Labour Commissions in India have gone into the problems of child labour and have made extensive recommendations.

In India, the post-independence era has seen an unequivocal commitment of the government to the cause of children through constitutional provisions, legislation, policies and programs. The Constitution of India in Article 39 of the Directive Principles of State Policy pledges that "the State shall, in particular, direct its policy towards securing ... that the health and strength of workers, men and women, and the tender age of children are not abused, and that citizens are not forced by economic necessity to enter avocations unsuited to their age or strength, that children are given opportunities and facilities to develop in a healthy manner, and in conditions of freedom and dignity, and that childhood and youth are protected against exploitation, and against moral and material abandonment."

As a follow-up of this commitment, and being a party to the UN Declaration on the Rights of the Child 1959, India adopted the National Policy on Children in 1974. The policy reaffirmed the constitutional provisions and stated that "it shall be the policy of the State to provide adequate services to children, both before and after birth and through the period of growth to ensure their full physical, mental and social development.

The State shall progressively increase the scope of such services so that within a reasonable time all children in the country enjoy optimum conditions for their balanced growth." India has also ratified on December 2, 1992, the Convention on the Rights of the Child which came into force in 1990.

This ratification implies that India will ensure wide awareness about issues relating to children among government agencies, implementing agencies, the media, the judiciary, the public and children themselves. The Government's endeavor is to meet the goals of the Convention and to amend all legislation, policies and schemes to meet the standards set in the Convention.

India is also a signatory to the World Declaration on the Survival, Protection and Development of Children. In pursuance of the commitment made at the World Summit, the Department of Women and Child Development under the Ministry of Human Resource Development has formulated a National Plan of Action for Children. Most of the recommendations of the World Summit Action Plan are reflected in India's National Plan of Action. India's policy on child labour has evolved over the years against this backdrop and its present regime of laws relating to child labour has a pragmatic foundation, consistent with the International Labour Conference resolution of 1979. This ILO resolution calls for a combination of prohibitory measures and measures for humanizing child labour, wherever such labour cannot be eliminated altogether in the short turn.

It should also be mentioned that India is second to none in its commitment to and in the upholding of the core international labour standards such as freedom of association, collective bargaining, non-discrimination, etc. India is signatory to a record 36 ILO labour conventions. The Child Labour (Prohibition & Regulation) Act, 1986 of India prohibits the employment of children below the age of 14 in factories, mines and in other forms of hazardous employment, and regulates the working conditions of children in other employment. India has announced a National Policy of Child Labour as early as 1987, and was probably the first among the developing countries to have such a progressive policy. Through a notification dated May 26, 1993, the working conditions of children have been regulated in all employment not prohibited under the Child Labour (Prohibition and Regulation) Act.

Further, following up on a preliminary notification issued on October 5, 1993, the government has also prohibited employment of children in occupations such as abattoirs/slaughter houses, printing, cashew de-scaling and processing, and soldering.

The announcement by the Prime Minister on India's Independence Day in 1994 that child labour would be abolished in hazardous occupations by the year 2000, reflects a national consensus and commitment. After this declaration, several far-reaching initiatives have been taken by the Government to effectively tackle the problem. With the setting up of the National Authority for the Elimination of Child Labour (NAECL) under the Chairmanship of the

Labour Minister, Government of India, a convergence of services and schemes for eliminating child labour is being achieved.

The NAECL, comprising representatives from the Central Ministries, meets the need for an umbrella organization to coordinate the efforts of the different arms of the Government for the progressive elimination of child labour. The child labour program in India is national in character and involves the Government of India, the governments of the States and the Union Territories of India, as well as such tripartite fora as the Indian Labour Conference and the Standing Labour Committee. A massive national and regional media campaign has been launched to sensitize society against child labour. Funds have been allocated to districts identified as child-labour endemic for surveys to identify child labour, and for awareness generation programs among employers, parents and the working children themselves.

This paper covers the significant aspects of India's constitutional and legislative provisions relating to child labour, the enforcement of these provisions, and programs being undertaken nation-wide to eliminate child labour. India's first act on the subject was the enactment of the Children (Pledging of Labour) Act of February 1933. This was followed by the Employment of Children Act in 1938. Subsequently, twelve additional legislations were passed that progressively extended legal protection to children. Provisions relating to child labour under various enactment such as the Factories Act, the Mines Act, the Plantation Labour Act etc. have concentrated on aspects such as reducing working hours, increasing minimum wage and prohibiting employment of children in occupations and processes detrimental to their health and development. The Child Labour (Prohibition & Regulation) Act 1986 of India was the culmination of efforts and ideas that emerged from the deliberations and recommendations of various committees on child labour. Significant among them are the National Commission on Labour (1966-69), Gurupadaswamy Committee on Child Labour (1979), and the Sanat Mehta Committee (1984).

The Act aims to prohibit the entry of children into hazardous occupations and to regulate the services of children in non-hazardous occupations. The Act, in particular:

- Bans the employment of children, i.e. those who have not completed their 14th year, in specified occupations and processes;
- Lays down a procedure to make additions to the schedule of banned occupations or processes;
- Regulates the working conditions of children in occupations where they are not prohibited from working;
- Lays down penalties for employment of children in violation of the provisions of this Act, and other Acts which forbid the employment of children;
- Brings uniformity in the definition of the "Child" in related laws.

Government of India's Policies and Actions

The National Child Labour Policy

Increasing attention is now being paid to strengthening the enforcement machinery related to child labour. Soon after the enactment of the comprehensive Child Labour (Prohibition & Regulation) Act, 1986, the Government of India adopted a National Child Labour policy in 1987, in accordance with the constitutional provisions and various legislation on child labour. The idea of adopting a separate policy on child labour was not only to place the issue on the nation's agenda, but also to formulate a specific program of action to initiate the process of progressive elimination of child labour. The policy consists of three complementary measures:

- Legal action plan: This policy envisages strict enforcement of the provisions of the Child Labour (Prohibition & Regulation) Act, 1986 and other child-related legislation.
- Focus on general development programs benefiting children wherever possible: The policy envisages the development of an extensive system of non-formal education for working children withdrawn from work and increasing the provision for employment and income generating schemes meant for their parents. A special cell - Child Labour Cell - was constituted to encourage voluntary organizations to take up activities like non-formal education, vocational training, provisions of health care, nutrition and education for working children.
- Area specific projects: To focus on areas known to have high concentration of child labour and to adopt a project approach for identification, withdrawal and rehabilitation of working children.

Central Advisory Board on Child Labour

The Central Advisory Board on Child Labour was constituted on March 4, 1981. The following are the terms of reference of the Board:

- Review the implementation of the existing legislation administered by the Central Government.
- Suggest legislative measures as well as welfare measures for the welfare of working children.
- Review the progress of welfare measures for working children.
- Recommend the industries and areas where there must be a progressive elimination of child labour.

The Board was reconstituted last on November 2, 1994.

The Union Labour Minister is the Chairman of the Board. The other Members of the Board include representatives from the various sister ministries, Members of Parliament, non-governmental organizations, representatives of major trade unions and employers' organizations. The last meeting of the Board was held on December 27, 1995.

Child Labour Technical Advisory Committee

Under Section 5 of the Child Labour (P&R) Act 1986, the Government of India is empowered to constitute a Child Labour Technical Advisory Committee for the purpose of addition of occupation and processes in the Schedule to the Act. The Committee consists of a Chairman and members not exceeding ten. The Committee has been reconstituted on February 5, 1996 under the chairmanship of Director General of Indian Council of Medical Research.

National Child Labour Projects (NCLP)

Under the action plan of the National Policy on Child Labour, there have been National Child Labour Projects (NCLP) set up in different areas to rehabilitate child labour. A major activity undertaken under the NCLP is the establishment of special schools to provide non-formal education, vocational training, supplementary nutrition etc. to children withdrawn from employment.

Under the project based action plan of the policy, 12 NCLPs were started in the States of Andhra Pradesh (Jaggampet and Markapur), Bihar (Garwah), Madhya Pradesh (Mandsaur), Maharashtra (Thane), Orissa (Sambalpur), Rajasthan (Jaipur), Tamil Nadu (Sivakasi) and Uttar Pradesh (Varanasi-Mirzapur-Bhadohi, Moradabad, Aligarh and Ferozabad).

Rehabilitation of Children Working in Hazardous Occupations

A major program was launched on 15th August 1994

for withdrawing child labour working in hazardous occupations and for rehabilitating them through special schools.

Under the program a total of two million children are sought to be brought out of work and put in special schools where they will be provided with education, vocational training, monthly stipends, nutrition and health-checks. As a follow-up, a high powered body, the National Authority for the Elimination of Child Labour (NAECL) was constituted on 26th September, 1994 under the Chairmanship of the Minister for Labour, Government of India. The functions of NAECL are:

- to lay down policies and programs for the elimination of child labour, particularly in hazardous employment;
- to monitor the progress of the implementation of programs, projects and schemes for the elimination of child labour;
- to coordinate the implementation of child labour related projects of the various sister Ministries of the Government of India (to ensure convergence of services for the benefit of the families of child labour).

Secretaries to Government of India in the Ministries of Labour, Information & Broadcasting, Welfare, Rural Development, Textiles and the Departments of Expenditure, Education, Health, Family Welfare and Women & Child Development are members of the National Authority for the Elimination of Child Labour. The NAECL has already met five times on October 1, 1994, November 1, 1994, January 1, 1995, July 10,1995 and December 31, 1996.

Present Coverage Under National Child Labour Project

So far 76 child labour projects have been sanctioned under the National Child Labour Project Scheme for covering 150,000 children. Around 105,000 children are already enrolled in the special schools. The table gives the figures of the state-wise coverage of children under the National Child Labour Project.

Coverage under National Child Labour Project

State	*Districts*	*Sanctioned Schools*	*Coverage Children*	*Actual Schools*	*Coverage Children*
Andhra Pradesh	20	807	43550	610	36249
Bihar	08	174	12200	173	10094
Gujarat	02	040	2000	023	1254
Karnataka	03	100	5000	024	1200
Madhya Pradesh	05	138	9800	087	6524
Maharashta	02	074	3700	024	1200
Orissa	16	430	33000	239	14972
Rajasthan	02	060	3000	054	2700
Tamil Nadu	08	379	19500	307	14684
Uttar Pradesh	04	150	11500	105	7488
West Bengal	04	219	12000	164	8250
Total	76	2571	155250	1810	104615

Assistance to Voluntary Organizations

Under the grant-in-aid scheme, voluntary organizations are being financially assisted to the extent of 75% of the project cost for taking up welfare projects for working children where the children are provided with education, supplementary nutrition, health care and vocational/skill training. The voluntary organizations, which were extended assistance under the scheme during 1996-97 (up to December 1996), are:

1. The Congregation of the Sisters of the Cross of Chavanad, Tiruchirapalli, Tamil Nadu.
2. Indian Council for Child Welfare, New Delhi.

3. Karnataka State Council for Child Welfare, Bangalore, Karnataka.
4. India International Rural Centre, New Delhi.
5. Vivekananda Education Society, Calcutta, West Bengal.
6. Shramik Vikas Sewa Ashram, Allahabad, Uttar Pradesh.
7. Gramin Sansadhan Vikas Parishad, Buxur, Bihar.
8. United Club, Ujini, Orissa.
9. Jibaramjee Club, Orissa.
10. Gram Vikas Seva Samity, Allahabad, Uttar Pradesh.
11. Karimpur Social Welfare Society, District Nadia, West Bengal.
12. Indian Council for Child Welfare, Tamil Nadu.
13. Vijayapuram Praja Seva Samithi, Chittoor, Andhra Pradesh.
14. Bandhuwa Mukti Morcha, New Delhi.
15. Rafi Ahmed Kidwai Shiksha Samiti, Khurda, Bhopal, Madhya Pradesh.
16. Gram Swaraj Abhiyan Sansthan, Baishali, Bihar.
17. Mahatma Gandhi Khadi & Gramodyog Samity, Khurda, Orissa.
18. Gopal Samaj Kalyan Pratishthan, Nalanda, Bihar.
19. Mithila Gram Vikas Parishad, Darbhangha, Bihar.
20. Navachaitanya Academy for Youth Advancement, Vishakapatnam, Andhra Pradesh.
21. All India Santhan Welfare & Cultural Society, New Delhi.
22. Unemployed Young Workers' Society, Burdwan, West Bengal.
23. Village Reconstruction & Development Project, Salem, Tamil Nadu.
24. Daroga Prasad Roy Mahila Prashikshan Avam Audogik Kendra, District Saran, Bihar.
25. Manab Seva Sadan, Dhenkanal, Orissa.

26. Bagmari Youth Progressive Association, Calcutta.
27. Bhagra Diamond Club, Burdwan, West Bengal.
28. Social Environmental and Rural Technology Council, Pallel, Manipur.
29. Manorama Mahila Mandal, Vaishali.

Budgetary Support to Child Labour Programme

A plan provision of Rs. 150 million was made for child labour elimination program in India's Eighth Five-Year Plan (1992-93 and 1996-97). The budgetary allocation was substantially stepped up after the launching of program in August 1994 for the rehabilitation of child labour working in hazardous occupations. The allocation during 1995-96 and 1996-97 was of the order of Rs.344 million and Rs.560 million. As against this, the actual expenditure for these two years was of the order of Rs.343 million and Rs.338 million respectively. The allocation for 1997-98 is Rs.784 million. (In 1995-96 and 1996-97, $1= Rs.35 approximately. In 1997-98, $1 = Rs. 37 approximately).

Status of Free and Compulsory Education

India's National Policy on Education, 1986 gives the highest priority to the program of universal elementary education, and recommends that free and compulsory education of sufficient quality be provided to all children up to the age of 14 years before we enter the 21st century. The present thrust is on three aspects, namely, universal access and enrollment, universal retention of children up to 14 years of age, and substantial improvement in the quality of education to enable all children to achieve essential levels of learning. All these aspects have been incorporated in the various initiatives taken up by the Ministry of Human Resource Development.

All the State Governments have abolished tuition fees in government schools up to the upper primary level Education. In schools run by local bodies and private-aided institutions is almost free. However, unaided institutions (3 to 7%) do charge fees. Compulsory Education Acts have been enacted in 14 states and 4 Union Territories viz. Assam, Andhra Pradesh, Bihar, Delhi, Gujarat, Haryana, Jammu & Kashmir, Karnataka, Madhya Pradesh, Maharashtra, Punjab, Rajasthan, Tamil Nadu, Kerala, West Bengal, Chandigarh, Pondicherry and Andaman and Nicobar Islands.

Supreme Court Directions on Child Labour

The Supreme Court of India, in its judgement dated 10th December, 1996 in Writ Petition (Civil) Number 465/1986, has given certain directions regarding the manner in which children working in the hazardous occupations are to be withdrawn from work and rehabilitated, and the manner in which the working conditions of children working in non-hazardous occupations are to be regulated and improved. The judgement of the Supreme Court envisages:

- Simultaneous action in all districts of the country;
- Survey for identification of working children (to be completed by June 10, 1997);
- Withdrawal of children working in hazardous industries and ensuring their education in appropriate institutions;
- Contribution of Rs.20,000 per child to be paid by the offending employers of children to a welfare fund to be established for this purpose;
- Employment to one adult member of the family of the child so withdrawn from work, and if that is not possible a contribution of Rs.5000 to the welfare fund to be made by the State Government;
- Financial assistance to the families of the children so withdrawn to be paid out of the interest earnings on the corpus of Rs.20,000/25,000.00 deposited in the welfare fund as long as the child is actually sent to the schools;

- Regulating hours of work for children working in non-hazardous occupations so that their working hours do not exceed six hours per day and education for at least two hours is ensured;
- The entire expenditure on education is to be borne by the concerned employer;
- Planning and preparedness on the part of Central and State Governments in terms of strengthening of the existing administrative/regulatory/enforcement framework (covering cost of additional manpower, training, mobility, computerization etc.) implying additional requirement of funds.

Follow up Action on the Directions of the Supreme Court

As a follow up of the directions of the Supreme Court, all the State Governments were sent detailed guidelines on December 26, 1996 indicating the manner in which the directions of the Supreme Court were to be implemented.

A meeting of the NAECL was convened on 31st December 1996 to discuss the directions of the Supreme Court on child labour. It was decided in the meeting that the Ministry of Labour should immediately release funds to the State Governments so as to enable them to conduct surveys of working children before June 10, 1997.

A conference of the Labour Ministers of State/Union Territories was convened on January 22,1997 to finalize an action plan for the implementation of the directions of the Supreme Court on withdrawal and rehabilitation of working children.

In the conference, all the participating States and Union Territories welcomed the judgement and demonstrated their political will to eliminate child labour. However, all the States pleaded for additional and liberal financial assistance from the Central Government for implementing the judgement of the Supreme Court. The following significant recommendations were made in the Conference:

- The survey envisaged in the judgement of the Supreme Court would be in two phases. In the first phase the survey would be conducted in all industries, establishments, shops, work places in urban and semi-urban catchments areas where hazardous processes will be identified. In the event of any child labour being found employed in any such process, simultaneous action would be taken to recover an amount of Rs. 20, 000/from the offending employer. Hazardous establishments in the rural areas would also be fully covered by the survey in the first phase. The door-to-door survey for the purpose of identification and enumeration of working children will be taken up in the second phase.
- While primarily it is the responsibility of the State Governments to provide necessary funds for taking up activities in compliance of the directions of the Supreme Court, funds for conducting the survey will be released by the Central Government to the agencies at the district level immediately.

  If the funds released for the first phase of survey fall short of the actual requirement in any district, the State Governments will provide the additional funds for this purpose. Since this first phase of the survey is concentrated on industrial establishments, the requirement of funds would be worked out by the Central Government and the same would be released immediately.
- Immediate action will be initiated by the State Governments for strengthening the enforcement machinery at various levels and for creation of a separate cell at the State level to monitor and coordinate the activities to be taken up in compliance of the directions of the Supreme Court. They will also send their requirements of funds in this regard, if any, to the Planning Commission at the earliest.

- If the State Governments are not in a position to complete the survey by 10th June, they will apprise the Hon'ble Supreme Court about the reasons for delay and seek extension of time from the Hon'ble Supreme Court well in advance.
- If for some reason, the State Governments find it difficult to give effect to any one or more directions of the Supreme Court, they will seek necessary clarification/directions from the Hon'ble Supreme Court well in time.

As a follow-up of the decision taken in the State Labour Ministers' Conference, the Chief Secretaries of State and Union Territories have been sent detailed guidelines for carrying out the survey as per the directions of the Supreme Court. A copy of the child labour survey form has also been sent to the Governments of State and Union Territories.Funds have been released to all the State and Union Territories governments for the purpose of conducting the surveys. The Chief Secretaries were specifically instructed that if the State Governments could not complete the surveys in time, they should apprise the Supreme Court through an affidavit about the reasons for delay and seek extension of time from the Supreme Court well in advance.

IPEC: ILO'S International Program for the Elimination of Child Labour

The International Program on the Elimination of Child Labour is a global programme launched by the International Labour Organization in December 1991. India was the first country to join it in 1992 when it signed a Memorandum of Understanding with the ILO. The long-term objective of IPEC is to contribute to the effective abolition of child labour. Its immediate objectives are:

- Elimination of the capability of ILO constituents and Non-Government Organizations to design, implement and evaluate programs for Child Labour Elimination;
- To identity interventions at community and national

levels which could serve as models for replication; and

- Creation of awareness and social mobilization for securing elimination of child labour.

At the international level, IPEC has a Program Steering Committee consisting of representatives of the ILO, the donors and participating countries. At the national level in India, there is a National Steering Committee of which the Labour Secretary is the Chairman. This is tripartite in its composition with representation from NGOs as well. There is a National Program Coordinator based at New Delhi who coordinates IPEC work between the Ministry of Labour, the agencies receiving assistance and ILO Headquarters. ILO has made an allocation of $4.15 million between 1992 and 1996 for the IPEC program in India: State-wise projects under IPEC and number of children covered (92-97).

State	*Projects approved*	*No. of Children*
Andhra Pradesh	15	15455
Bihar	3	1340
Delhi	6	4200
Gujarat	5	1350
Haryana	1	300
Karnataka	2	1320
Kerala	2	2000
Madhya Pradesh	6	2050
Manipur	1	500
Maharashtra	7	1750
Orissa	4	1500
Rajasthan	7	5800
Tamil Nadu	17	6710
Uttar Pradesh	11	13939
West Bengal	19	22890
Regional	2	NA
All India Institutions	11	NA
Total	120	81154

As per the Memorandum of Understanding between the Government of India and the ILO, the IPEC program was to continue till December 3 1, 1996. The MOU was extended on January 28, 1997, until December 31, 1997 in the first instance. Thereafter, the MOU continues with mutual agreement.

The problem of child labour continues to pose a challenge before the nation. Government has been taking various pro-active measures to tackle this problem. However, considering the magnitude and extent of the problem and that it is essentially a socio-economic problem inextricably linked to poverty and illiteracy, it requires concerted efforts from all sections of the society to make a dent in the problem. Way back in 1979, Government formed the first committee called Gurupadswamy Committee to study the issue of child labour and to suggest measures to tackle it.

The Committee examined the problem in detail and made some far-reaching recommendations. It observed that as long as poverty continued, it would be difficult to totally eliminate child labour and hence, any attempt to abolish it through legal recourse would not be a practical proposition. The Committee felt that in the circumstances, the only alternative left was to ban child labour in hazardous areas and to regulate and ameliorate the conditions of work in other areas. It recommended that a multiple policy approach was required in dealing with the problems of working children.

Based on the recommendations of Gurupadaswamy Committee, the Child Labour (Prohibition & Regulation) Act was enacted in 1986. The Act prohibits employment of children in certain specified hazardous occupations and processes and regulates the working conditions in others. The list of hazardous occupations and processes is progressively being expanded on the recommendation of Child Labour Technical Advisory Committee constituted under the Act. In consonance with the above approach, a National Policy on Child Labour was formulated in 1987. The Policy seeks to adopt a gradual and sequential approach with a focus on rehabilitation of children working in hazardous occupations and processes in the first instance.

The Action Plan outlined in the Policy for tackling this problem is as follows:

- Legislative Action Plan for strict enforcement of Child Labour Act and other labour laws to ensure that children are not employed in hazardous employments, and that the working conditions of children working in non-hazardous areas are regulated in accordance with the provisions of the Child Labour Act. It also entails further identification of additional occupations and processes, which are detrimental to the health and safety of the children.
- Focusing of General Developmental Programmes for Benefiting Child Labour - As poverty is the root cause of child labour, the action plan emphasizes the need to cover these children and their families also under various poverty alleviation and employment generation schemes of the Government.
- Project Based Plan of Action envisages starting of projects in areas of high concentration of child labour. Pursuant to this, in 1988, the National Child Labour Project (NCLP) Scheme was launched in 9 districts of high child labour endemicity in the country. The Scheme envisages running of special schools for child labour withdrawn from work. In the special schools, these children are provided formal/non-formal education along with vocational training, a stipend of Rs.100 per month, supplementary nutrition and regular health check ups so as to prepare them to join regular mainstream schools. Under the Scheme, funds are given to the District Collectors for running special

schools for child labour. Most of these schools are run by the NGOs in the district.

Government has accordingly been taking proactive steps to tackle this problem through strict enforcement of legislative provisions along with simultaneous rehabilitative measures. State Governments, which are the appropriate implementing authorities, have been conducting regular inspections and raids to detect cases of violations. Since poverty is the root cause of this problem, and enforcement alone cannot help solve it, Government has been laying a lot of emphasis on the rehabilitation of these children and on improving the economic conditions of their families. The coverage of the NCLP Scheme has increased from 12 districts in 1988 to 100 districts in the 9th Plan to 250 districts during the 10th Plan.

Strategy for the Elimination of Child Labour under the 10th Plan

An evaluation of the Scheme was carried out by independent agencies in coordination with V. V. Giri National Labour Institute in 2001. Based on the recommendations of the evaluation and experience of implementing the scheme since 1988, the strategy for implementing the scheme during the 10th Plan was devised. It aimed at greater convergence with the other developmental schemes and bringing qualitative changes in the Scheme. Some of the salient points of the 10th Plan Strategy are as follows:

- Focused and reinforced action to eliminate child labour in the hazardous occupations by the end of the Plan period.
- Expansion of National Child Labour Projects to additional 150 districts.
- Linking the child labour elimination efforts with the Scheme of Sarva Shiksha Abhiyan of Ministry of

Human Resource Development to ensure that children in the age group of 5-8 years get directly admitted to regular schools and that the older working children are mainstreamed to the formal education system through special schools functioning under the NCLP Scheme.

- Convergence with other Schemes of the Departments of Education, Rural Development, Health and Women and Child Development for the ultimate attainment of the objective in a time bound manner.

The Government and the Ministry of Labour and Employment in particular, are rather serious in their efforts to fight and succeed in this direction. The number of districts covered under the NCLP Scheme has been increased from 100 to 250, as mentioned above in this note. In addition, 21 districts have been covered under INDUS, a similar Scheme for rehabilitation of child labour in cooperation with US Department of Labour. Implementation of this Project was recently reviewed during the visit of Mr. Steven Law, Deputy Secretary of State, from the USA. For the Districts not covered under these two Schemes, Government is also providing funds directly to the NGOs under the Ministry's Grants-in-aid Scheme for running Special Schools for rehabilitation of child labour, thereby providing for a greater role and cooperation of the civil society in combating this menace.

Elimination of child labour is the single largest programme in this Ministry's activities. Apart from a major increase in the number of districts covered under the scheme, the priority of the Government in this direction is evident in the quantum jump in budgetary allocation during the 10th Plan. Government has allocated Rs. 602 crores for the Scheme during the 10th Plan, as against an expenditure of Rs. 178 crores in the 9th Plan. The resources set aside for combating this evil in the Ministry is around 50 per cent of its total annual budget. The implementation of NCLP and INDUS Schemes is being closely monitored through periodical reports, frequent visits and meetings with the District and State Government officials.

The Government's commitment to achieve tangible results in this direction in a time bound manner is also evident from the fact that in the recent Regional Level Conferences of District Collectors held in Hyderabad, Pune, Mussoorie and Kolkata district-wise review of the Scheme was conducted at the level of Secretary. These Conferences provided an excellent opportunity to have one-to-one interaction with the Collectors, who play a pivotal role in the implementation of these Schemes in the District. Besides, these Conferences also helped in a big way in early operationalisation of Scheme in the newly selected 150 districts.

The Government is committed to eliminate child labour in all its forms and is moving in this direction in a targeted manner. The multi-pronged strategy being followed by the Government to achieve this objective also found its echo during the recent discussions held in the Parliament on the Private Member's Bill tabled by Shri Iqbal Ahmed Saradgi. It was unanimously recognized therein that the problem of child labour, being inextricably linked with poverty and illiteracy, cannot be solved by legislation alone, and that a holistic, multi-pronged and concerted effort to tackle this problem will bring in the desired results.

The Child Labour (Prohibition And Regulation) Act, 1986 And Rules

Be it enacted by Parliament in the Thirty-seventh Year of the Republic of India as follows:

Comments

Social and beneficial legislation – Social legislation is designed to protect the interest of a class of society who, because of their economic conditions, deserves such protection. With a view to pass the test of reasonable classification there must exist intelligible differentia between persons or thing grouped together from those who have been left out and there must by a reasonable nexus with the object to be achieved by the legislation.

The Court must strive to so interpret the statute as to protect and advance the object and purpose of enactment. Any narrow or technical interpretation of the provisions would defeat the legislative policy. The Court must, therefore, keep the legislative policy in mind in applying the provisions of the Act to the facts of the case.

PART I

Preliminary

1. *Short title, extent and commencement:*

- This Act may be called the Child Labour (Prohibition and Regulation) Act, 1986.
- It extends to the whole of India.
- The provisions of this Act, other then Part III, shall come into force at once, and Part III shall come into force on such date as the Central Government may, by notification in the official Gazette, appoint, and different dates may be appointed for different States and for different classes of establishments.

Comment

May and shall – Where the Legislature uses two words "may" and "shall" in two different parts of the same provision, prima facie it would appear that the Legislature manifested its intension to make one part directory and another mandatory. But that by itself is not decisive. The power of the Court still to ascertain the real intension of the Legislature by carefully examining the scope of statute to find out whether the provision is directory or mandatory remains unimpaired even where both the words are used in the same provision. In interpreting the provisions the exercise undertaken by the Court is to make explicit the intention of the Legislative which enacted the legislation.

It is not for the Court to reframe the legislation for the very good reason that the powers to "legislate" have not been conferred on the Court. In order to sustain the presumption of constitutionality of a legislative measure, the Court can take into consideration matters of common knowledge, matters of common report, the history of the times and also assume every state of facts which can be conceived existing at the time of the legislation.

2. *Definitions:* In this Act, unless the context otherwise requires,

- "Appropriate Government" means, in relation to an establishment under the control of the Central Government or a railway administration or a major port or a mine or oilfield, the Central Government, and in all other cases, the State Government;
- "Child" means a person who has not completed his fourteenth year of age;
- "Day" means a period of twenty-four hours beginning at midnight;
- "Establishment" includes a shop, commercial establishment, work-shop, farm, residential hotel, restaurant, eating-house, theatre or other place of public amusement or entertainment;
- "Family" in relation to an occupier, means the individual, the wife or husband, as the case may be, of such individual, and their children, brother or sister of such individual;
- "Occupier", in relation to an establishment or a workshop, means the person who has the ultimate control over the affairs of the establishment or workshop;

- "Port authority" means any authority administering a port;
- "Prescribed" means prescribed by rules made under Sec.18;
- "Week" means a period of seven days beginning at midnight on Saturday night or such other night as may be approved in writing for a particular area by the Inspector;
- "Workshop" means any premises (including the precincts thereof) wherein any industrial process is carried on, but does not include any premises to which the provisions of Sec. 67 of the Factories Act, 1948 (63 of 1948), for the time being, apply.

Comments

This section defines the various words and expressions occurring in the Act.

Interpretation of section: The Court can merely interpret the section; it cannot re-write, re-cast or re-design the section.

Ambiguous expression: Courts must find out the literal meaning of the expression in the task of construction. In doing so if the expressions are ambiguous then the construction that fulfils the objects of the legislation must provide the key to the meaning. Courts must not make mockery of legislation and should take a constructive approach to fulfill the purpose and for that purpose, if necessary, iron out the creases.

PART II

Prohibition of Employment of Children in Certain Occupations and Processes

3. *Prohibition of employment of children in certain occupations and processes:* No child shall be employed or permitted to work in any of the occupations set forth in

Part A of the Schedule or in any workshop wherein any of the processes set forth in Part B of the Schedule is carried on, provided that nothing in this section shall apply to any workshop wherein any process is carried on by the occupier with the aid of his family or to any school established by or receiving assistance or recognition from, Government.

Comment

This section imposes prohibition on employment of children in the occupation and processes specified in the Schedule.

Proviso: A proviso is intended to limit the enacted provision so as to except something which would have otherwise been within it or in some measure to modify the enacting clause. Sometimes proviso may be embedded in the main provision and becomes an integral part of it so as to amount to a substantive provision itself.

4. *Power to amend the Schedule:* The Central Government, after giving by notification in the official Gazette, not less than three months' notice of its intention so to do, may, by like notification, add any occupation or process to the Schedule and thereupon the Schedule shall be deemed to have been amended accordingly.

Comment

This section empowers the Central Government to amend the Schedule so as to include therein any occupation or process considered necessary.

Construction of a section – It is en elementary rule that construction of a section is to be made of all parts together. It is not permissible to omit any part of it. For, the principle that the statute must be read as a whole is equally applicable to different part of the same section.

5. *Child Labour Technical Advisory Committee:*

• The Central Government may, by notification is in

official Gazette, constitute an advisory committee to be called the Child Labour Technical Advisory Committee (hereinafter in this section referred to as the Committee) to advise the Central Government for the purpose of addition of occupations and processes to the Schedule.

- The Committee shall consist of a Chairman and such other members not exceeding ten, as may be appointed by the Central Government.
- The Committee shall meet as often as it may consider necessary and shall have power to regulate its own procedure.
- The Committee may, if it deems it necessary so to do, constitute one or more sub-committees and may appoint to any such sub-committee, whether generally or for the consideration of any particular matter, any person who is not a member of the Committee.
- The term of office of, the manner of filling causal vacancies in the office of, and the allowances, if any, payable to, the Chairman and other members of the Committee, and the conditions and restrictions subject to which the Committee may appoint any person who is not a member of the Committee as a member of any of its sub-committees shall be such as may be prescribed.

Comment

This section empowers the Central Government to constitute the Child Labour Technical Advisory Committee for giving advice in the matter of inclusion of any occupation and process in the Schedule.

PART III

Regulation of Conditions of Work of Children

6. *Application of Part:* The provisions of this Part shall apply to an establishment or a class of establishments in

which none of the occupations or processes referred to in Sec. 3 is carried on.

Comment

This section lays down that provisions of this Part shall apply to an establishment in which none of the prohibited occupations or processes is carried on.

7. *Hours and period of work:*

- No child shall be required or permitted to work in any establishment in excess of such number of hours as may be prescribed for such establishment or class of establishments.
- The period of work on each day shall be so fixed that no period shall exceed three hours and that no child shall work for more than three hours before he has had an interval for rest for at least one hour.
- The period of work of a child shall be so arranged that inclusive of his interval for rest, under sub-section(2), it shall not be spread over more than six hours, including the time spent in waiting for work on any day.
- No child shall be permitted or required to work between 7 p.m. and 8 a.m.
- No child shall be permitted or required to work overtime.
- No child shall be permitted or required to work in any establishment on any day on which he has already been working in another establishment.

Comment

This section prescribes working hours for a child labour.

8. *Provision if mandatory or directory:* The surest test for determination as to whether the provisions is mandatory or directory is to see as to whether the sanction is provided therein.

Weekly holidays: Every child employed in an establishment shall be allowed in each week, a holiday or one whole day, which day shall be specified by the occupier in a notice permanently exhibited in a conspicuous place in the establishment and the day so specified shall not be altered by the occupier more than once in three months.

Comment

This section lays down that a weekly holiday should be allowed to every child labour.

9. *Notice to Inspector:*

- Every occupier in relation to an establishment in which a child was employed or permitted to work immediately before the date of commencement of this Act in relation to such establishment shall, within a period of thirty days from such commencement, send to the Inspector within whose local limits the establishment is situated, a written notice containing the following particulars, namely:
  - (a) The name and situation of the establishment;
  - (b) The name of the person in actual management of The establishment;
  - (c) The address to which communications relating to the establishment should be sent; and,
  - (d) The nature of the occupation or process carried on in the establishment.
- Every occupier, in relation to an establishment, who employs, or permits to work, any child after the date of commencement of this Act in relation to such establishment, shall, within a period of thirty days from the date of such employment, send to the Inspector within whose local limits the establishment is situated, a written notice containing the following particulars as are mentioned in sub-section (1).

Explanation: For the purposes of sub-sections (1) and (2), "date of commencement of this Act, in relation to an establishment" means the date of brining into force of this Act in relation to such establishment. (3) Nothing in Secs. 7, 8 and 9 shall apply to any establishment wherein any process is carried on by the occupier with the aid of his family or to any schools established by, or receiving assistance or recognition fróm, Government.

Comment

This section makes provision for furnishing of information regarding employment of a child labour to Inspector.

Explanation: It is now well settled that an explanation added to a statutory provision is not a substantive provision in any sense of the term but as the plain meaning of the word itself shows it is merely meant to explain or clarify certain ambiguities which may have crept in the statutory provision.

10. *Disputes as to age:* If any question arises between an Inspector and an occupier as to the age of any child who is employed or is permitted to work by him in an establishment, the question shall, in the absence of a certificate as to the age of such child granted by the prescribed authority, be referred by the Inspector for decision to the prescribed medical authority.

Comment

This section makes provision for settlement of disputes as to age of any child labour.

11. *Maintenance of register:* There shall be maintained by every occupier in respect of children employed or permitted to work in any establishment, a register to be available for inspection by an Inspector at all times during working hours or when work is being carried on in any such establishment showing:

- The name and date of birth of every child so employed or permitted to work;
- Hours and periods of work of any such child and the intervals of rest to which he is entitled;
- The nature of work of any such child; and
- Such other particulars as may be prescribed

Comment

This section makes provision for maintenance of register in respect of child labour.

12. *Display of notice containing abstract of Secs. 3 and 14:* Every railway administration, every port authority and every occupier shall cause to be displayed in a conspicuous and accessible place at every station on its railway or within the limits of a port or at the place of work, as the case may be, a notice in the local language and in the English language containing an abstract of Secs. 3 and 14.

Comment

This section makes provision for display of notice in a conspicuous place at every railway station or port or place of work regarding prohibition of employment of child labour, penalties, etc., in the local languages and in the English language.

13. *Health and safety:*

- The appropriate Government may, by notification in the official Gazette, make rules for the health and safety of the children employed or permitted to work in any establishment or class of establishments.
- Without prejudice to the generality of the foregoing provisions, the said rules may provide for all or any of the following matters, namely:
  - (a) Cleanliness in the place of work and its freedom for nuisance;

(b) Disposal of wastes and effluents;
(c) Ventilation and temperature;
(d) Dust and fume;
(e) Artificial humidification;
(f) Lighting;
(g) Drinking water;
(h) Latrine and urinals;
(i) Spittoons;
(j) Fencing of machinery;
(k) Work at or near machinery in motion;
(l) Employment of children on dangerous machines;
(m) Instructions, training and supervision in relation to employment of children on dangerous machines;
(n) Device for cutting off power;
(o) Self-acting machinery;
(p) Easing of new machinery;
(q) Floor, stairs and means of access;
(r) Pits, sumps, openings in floors, etc.;
(s) Excessive weight;
(t) Protection of eyes;
(u) Explosive or inflammable dust, gas, etc.;
(v) Precautions in case of fire;
(w) Maintenance of buildings; and
(x) Safety of buildings and machinery.

Comments

This section lays down that the Government is required to make rules for the health and safety of the child labour.

PART IV

Miscellaneous

Penalties :

- Whoever employs any child or permits any child to work in contravention of the provisions of Sec. 3 shall be punishable with imprisonment for a term which shall not be less than three months but which may extend to one year or with fine which shall not be less than ten thousand rupees but which may extend to twenty thousand rupees or with both.
- Whoever, having been convicted of an offence under Sec. 3, commits a like offence afterwards, he shall be punishable with imprisonment for a term which shall not be less than six months but which may extend to two years.

Whoever :

- Fails to give notice as required by Sec. 9, or
- Fails to maintain a register as required by Sec. 11 or makes any false entry in any such register; or
- Fails to display a notice containing an abstract of Sec. 3 and this section as required by Sec. 12; or
- Fails to comply with or contravenes any other provisions of this Act or the rules made there under, shall be punishable with simple imprisonment which may extend to one month or with fine which may extend to ten thousand rupees or with both.

Comments

This section makes provision for penalty for contravention of the provisions of the Act.

Penalty – Mens rea – Essential – Penalty proceedings are quasi criminal proceedings.

Before penalty can be imposed it has to be ensured that mens rea has been established.

Penal provision – Object of – The law in its wisdom seeks to punish the guilty who commits the sin, and not his son, who is innocent.

Modified application of certain laws in relation to penalties:

1. Where any person is found guilty and convicted of contravention of any of the provisions mentioned in sub-section(2), he shall be liable to penalties as provided in sub-sections (1) and (2) of Sec. 14 of this Act and not under the Acts in which those provisions are contained.
2. The provisions referred to in sub-section (1) are the provisions mentioned below:
   (a) Section 67 of the Factories Act, 1948 (63 of 1948);
   (b) Section 40 of the Mines Act, 1952 (35 of 1952);
   (c) Section 109 of the Merchant Shipping Act, 1958 (44 of 1958); and
   (d) Section 21 of the Motor Transport Workers Act, 1961 (27 of 1961).

Comment

This section makes provision of penalties under the Act even when any person is found guilty and convicted of contravention of any of the provisions of Sec. 67 of the Factories Act, 1948, Sec. 40 of the Mines Act, 1952, Section 109 of the Merchant Shipping Act, 1958 and Sec. 21 of the Motor Transport Workers Act, 1961.

Procedure relating to offences:

1. Any person, police officer or Inspector may file a complaint of the commission of an offence under this Act in any Court of competent jurisdiction.
2. Every certificate as to the age of a child which has been granted by a prescribed medical authority shall, for the purposes of this Act, be conclusive evidence as to the age of the child to whom it relates.

3. No court inferior to that of a Metropolitan Magistrate or a Magistrate of the first class shall try any offence under this Act.

Comment

This section lays down that any person, police officer or Inspector can make a complaint regarding commission of offences. It also lays down the procedure for disposal of such a complaint.

Court Duty – The Court should meticulously consider all facts and circumstances of the case. The Court is not bound to grant specific performance merely because it is lawful to do so. The motive behind the litigation should also enter into the judicial verdict. The Court should take care to see that it is used as an instrument of oppression to have an unfair advantage to plaintiff.

Appointment of Inspectors: The appropriate Government may appoint inspectors for the purposes of securing compliance with the provisions of this Act and any inspector so appointed shall be deemed to be a public servant within the meaning of the Indian Penal Code (45 of 1860).

Comment

This section empowers the appropriate Government to appoint inspectors for securing compliance of the provisions of the Act. Such Inspector is deemed to be a public servant within the meaning of the Indian Penal Code (45 of 1860).

Public servant – Every public officer is a trustee and in respect of the office he holds and the salary and other benefits which he draws, he is obliged to render appropriate service to the State. If an officer does not behave as required of him under the law he is certainly liable to be punished in accordance with law.

Power to make rules:

1. The appropriate Government may, by notification in the official Gazette and subject to the condition of previous publication, make rules for carrying into effect the provisions of this Act.
2. In particular and without prejudice to the generality of the foregoing power, such rules may provide for all or any of the following matters, namely:
   (a) The term of the office of, the manner of filling casual vacancies of, and the allowances payable to, the Chairman and members of the Child Labour Technical Advisory Committee and the conditions and restrictions subject to which a non-member may be appointed to a sub-committee under sub-section (5) of Sec.5;
   (b) Number of hours for which a child may be required or permitted to work under sub-section (1) of Sec. 7;
   (c) Grant to certificates of age in respect of young persons in employment or seeking employment, the medical authorities which may issue such certificate, the form of such certificate, the charges which may be made there under and the manner in which such certificate may be issued; Provided that no charge shall be made for the issue of any such certificate of the application is accompanied by evidence of age deemed satisfactory by the authority concerned;
   (d) The other particulars which a register maintained under Sec. 11 should contain.

Comment

This section empowers the appropriate Government to make rule for carrying out the provisions of the Act.

Rules for effectuating the purpose of the Act – The general power of farming rules for effectuating the purposes of the Act, would plainly authorize and sanctify the framing of such a rule.

Rules and notifications to be laid before Parliament or State legislature:

1. Every rules made under this Act by the Central Government and every notification issued under Sec. 4, shall be laid, as soon as may be after it is made or issued, before each House of Parliament, while it is in session for a total period of thirty days which may be comprised in one session or in two or more successive sessions, and if, before the expiry of the session immediately following the session or the successive session aforesaid, both Houses agree in making any modification in the rule or notification or both Houses agree that the rule or notification should not be made or issued, the rule or notification shall thereafter have effect only in such modified form or be of no effect, as the case may be; so, however, that any such modification or annulment shall be without prejudice to the validity of anything previously done under that rule or notification.
2. Every rule made by a State Government under this Act shall be laid as soon as may be after it is made, before the Legislature of that State.

Comment

Under this section the rules and notifications are to be laid before Parliament of State Legislature for approval.

Certain other provisions of law not barred: Subject to the provisions contained in Sec. 15, the provisions of this Act and the rules made there under shall be in addition to, and not in derogation of, the provisions of the Factories Act, 1948 (63 of 1948), the Plantations Labour Act, 1951 (69 of 1951) and the Mines Act, 1952 (35 of 1952).

Comment

This section lays down that the provision of this Act shall be in addition to and not in derogation of, the provisions of the Factories Act, 1948, the Plantations Labour Act, 1951 and the Mines Act, 1952.

Power to remove difficulties:

1. If any difficulty arises in giving effect of the provisions of this Act, the Central Government may, by order published in the official Gazette, make such provisions not inconsistent with the provisions of this Act as appear to it to be necessary or expedient for removal of the difficulty: Provided that no such order shall be made after the expiry of a period of three years from the date on which this Act receives the assent of the President.
2. Every order made under this section shall, as soon as may be after it is made, before the Houses of Parliament.

Comment

Under the provisions of this section the Central Government is empowered to remove difficulties which arise in giving effect to the provisions of this Act.

Repeal and savings:

1. The Employment of Children Act, 1938 (26 of 1938) is hereby repealed.
2. Notwithstanding such repeal, anything done or any action taken or purported to have been done or taken under the Act so repealed shall, in so far as it is not inconsistent with the provisions of this Act, be deemed to have been done or taken under the corresponding provisions of this Act.

Comment

The Employment of Children Act, 1938 (26 of 1938) has been repealed by this section.

Implied repeal – It is well settled that when a competent authority makes a new law which is totally inconsistent with the earlier law and that the two cannot stand together any longer it must be construed that the earlier law had been repealed by necessary implication by the latter law.

Amendment of Act 11 of 1948: In Sec. 2 of the Minimum Wages Act, 1948:

i. For Cl. (a), the following clauses shall be substituted, namely:
   (a) 'Adolescent' means a persons who has completed his fourteenth year of age but has not completed his eighteenth year.
   (b) 'Adult' means a person who has completed his eighteenth year of age.

ii. After Cl.(b), the following clause shall be inserted, namely:
   (c) `Child' means a person who had not completed his fourteenth year of age.

Comment

Under this section Sec. 2 of the Minimum Wages Act, 1948 has been amended so as to define the terms "adolescent", "adult" and "child".

Amendment of Act 69 of 1951: In the Plantations Labour Act, 1951:

(a) In Sec.2 in Cls.(a) and (c), for the word "fifteenth", the word "fourteenth" shall be substituted;
(b) Sec. 24 shall be omitted;
(c) In Sec. 26, in the opening portion, the words "who has completed his twelfth year" shall be omitted.

Comment

Under this section, sec. 2 of the Plantations Labour Act, 1951, has been amended so far as it relates to the employment of child labour.

Amendment of Act 44 of 1958: In the Merchant Shipping Act, 1958, in Sec. 109, for the word "fifteen", the word "fourteen" shall be substituted.

Comment

Under this section Sec. 109 of the Merchant Shipping Act, 1958, has been amended so far as it relates to the employment of child labour.

Amendment of Act 27 of 1961: In the Motor Transport Workers Act, 1961 in Sec.2, in Cls.(a), and (c), for the word "fifteenth", the word "fourteenth" shall be substituted.

Comment

Under this section, Sec.2 of the Motor Transport Workers Act, 1961, has been amended so far as it relates to the employment of child labour.

The Child Labour (Prohibition And Regulation) Rules, 1988

G.S.R. 847(E), dated 10th August, 1988 – In exercise of the powers conferred by sub-section (1) of Sec. 18 of the said Act, the Central Government, hereby makes the following rules, namely:

Rule-making power: The general power of framing rules for effectuating the purposes of the Act, would plainly authorize and sanctify the framing of such a rule.

Short title and commencement:

1. These rules may be called the Child Labour (Prohibition and Regulation) Rules, 1988.
2. They shall come into force on the date of their publication in the official Gazette.

Comment

These rules have been framed by the Central Government in the exercise of the powers conferred by Sec.

18 (1) of the Child Labour (Prohibition and Regulation) Rules, 1986.

Rules – Whether validly framed – The question whether rules are validly framed to carry out the purposes of the Act can be determined on the analysis of the provisions of the Act.

Definitions: In these rules, unless the context otherwise requires:

1. "Act" means the Child Labour (Prohibition and Regulation) Rules, 1986 (61 of 1986);
2. "Committee" means the Child Labour Technical Advisory Committee constituted under sub-section (1) of Sec. 5 of the Act;
3. "Chairman" means the Chairman of the Committee appointed under sub-section (2) of Sec. 5 of the Act;
4. "Form" means a Form appended to these rules;
5. "Register" means the register required to be maintained under Sec. 11 of the Act;
6. "Schedule" means the schedule appended to the Act;
7. "Section" means a section of the Act.

Comment

This rule defines the various expressions occurring in the Rules.

Interpretation by a court – The Court can merely interpret the section; it cannot re-write, re-cast or re-design the section.

Otherwise – What amounts to – The words "otherwise" is not to be construed *ejusdem generic* with the word "circulars, advertisement".

Term of office of the members of the Committee:

1. The term of office of the members of the Committee shall be one year from the date on which their

appointment is notified in the official Gazette; Provided that the Central Government may extend the term of office of the member of the Committee for a maximum period of two years;

Provided further that the member shall, notwithstanding the expiration of his term, continue to hold office until his successor enters upon his office.

2. The members appointed under sub-rule (1) shall be eligible for re-appointment.

Comment

"Shall" cannot be interpreted as "may"

Proviso – *In Abdul Jabar Butt v. State of Jammu and Kashmir*, it was held that a proviso must be considered with relation to the principal matter to which it stands as a proviso.

Secretary to the Committee: The Central Government may appoint an officer not below the rank of an Under-Secretary to the Government of India as Secretary of the Committee.

Comment

This rule empowers the Central Government to appoint an officer not below the rank of an Under-Secretary to the Government of India as the Secretary to the Child Labour Technical Advisory Committee.

Allowances to non-official members: The non-official members and Chairman of the Committee shall be paid such fees and allowances as may be admissible to the officers of the Central Government drawing a pay of rupees four thousand and five hundred or above.

Resignation:

1. A member may resign his office by writing under his hand addressed to the Chairman.

2. The Chairman may resign his office by writing under his hand addressed to the Central Government.
3. The resignation referred to in sub-rule (1) and sub-rule (2) shall take effect from the date of its acceptance or on the expiry of thirty days from the date of receipt of such resignation, whichever is earlier, by the Chairman or the Central Government, as the case may be.

Removal of Chairman or member of the Committee: The Central Government may remove the Chairman or any member of the Committee at any time before the expiry of the term of office after giving him a reasonable opportunity of showing cause against the proposed removal.

Comment

This rule lays down procedure for removal of Chairman or member of the Committee by the Central Government.

Cessation of membership – if a member:

1. Is absent without leave of the Chairman for three or more consecutive meetings of the Committee; or
2. Is declared to be of unsound mind by a competent court; or
3. Is or has been convicted of any offence which, in the opinion of the Central Government, involves moral turpitude; or
4. Is, or at any time, has been adjudicated insolvent or has suspended his debts or has compounded with his creditors, shall cease to be a member of the Committee.

Comment

This rule deals with the matter relating to cessation of membership.

Filling up of casual vacancies: In case a member resigns his office under rule 6 or ceases to be a member under rule 8, the casual vacancy thus caused shall be filled up by the Central Government and the member so appointed shall hold office for the unexpired portion of the term of his predecessor.

Comment

This rule empower the Central Government to fill up casual vacancies and it lays down that the member so appointed shall hold office for the unexpired portion of the term of his predecessor.

Time and place of meetings: The Committee shall meet at such times and places as the Chairman may fix in this behalf.

Notice of meetings: The Secretary to the Committee shall give at least seven days notice to every member of the Committee of the time and place fixed for each meeting along with the list of business to be transacted at the said meeting.

Presiding at meetings: The Chairman shall preside at every meeting of the Committee at which he is present; if, however, the Chairman is unable to attend a meeting, any member elected by the members present among themselves shall preside at the meeting.

Comment

"Shall" – It is well-known principle that in the interpretation of statutes that where the situation and the context warrants it, the word "shall" used in a section or rule of a statute has to be construed as "may".

Quorum: No business shall be transacted at a meeting of the Committee unless atleast three members of the Committee other than the Chairman and the Secretary are present.

Provided that at any meeting in which less than three of the total members are present, the Chairman may adjourn the meeting to a date as he deems fit and inform the members present and notify other members that the business of the scheduled meeting shall be disposed of at the adjourned meeting irrespective of the quorum and it shall be lawful to dispose of the business at such adjourned meeting irrespective of the member of members attending the meeting.

Comment

Scope of proviso – The scope of a proviso is well settled. In *Ram Narain Sons Ltd. V. Asstt. Commissioner of Sales Tax,* it was held:

"It is a cardinal rule of interpretation that a proviso to a particular provision of statute only embraces the field which is covered by the main provision. It carves out an exception to the main provision to which it has been enacted as a proviso and to no other."

Decision by majority: All questions considered at a meeting of the Committee shall be decided by a majority of votes of the members present and voting and in the event of equality of votes, the Chairman, or in the absence of Chairman, the member presiding at the meeting, as the case may be, shall have a second or casting vote.

Comment

This rule lays down that the matters considered by the Committee in its meeting should be decided by a majority votes of the members present. The rule further lays down that the Chairman or in his absence the member presiding at the meeting shall have a casting vote.

Sub-Committees: The Committee may constitute one or more Sub-Committees, whether consisting only of members of the Committee or partly of members of the Committee and partly of other persons as it thinks fit, for such purposes, as it may decide and any Sub-Committee so constituted shall discharge such functions as may be delegated to it by the Committee.

Register to be maintained under Sec. 11 of the Act:

1. Every occupier of an establishment shall maintain a register in respect of children employed or permitted to work, in Form A.
2. The register shall be maintained on a yearly basis but shall be retained by the employer for a period of three years after the date of the last entry made therein.

Comment

Under this rule every occupier of an establishment is required to maintain an yearly register showing the children employed or permitted to work and to retain such registers for a period of three years.

Certificate of age:

1. All young persons in employment in any of the occupations set-forth in Part A of the Schedule or in any workshop wherein any of the processes set forth in Part B of the Schedule is carried on, shall produce a certificate of age from the appropriate medical authority, whenever required to do so by an Inspector.
2. The certificate of age referred to in sub-rule (1) shall be issued in Form 'B'.
3. The charges payable to the medical authority for the issue of such certificate shall be the same as prescribed by the State Government or the Central Government, as the case may be for their respective Medical Boards.
4. The charges payable to the medical authority shall be borne by the employer of the young person whose age is under question.

Explanation: For the purposes of sub-rule (1), the appropriate "Medical authority" shall be Government medical doctor not below the rank of an Assistant Surgeon of a District or a regular doctor or equivalent rank employed in Employees' State Insurance dispensaries of hospitals.

Comment

Explanation: It is not well settled that an explanation added to a statutory provision is not a substantive provision in any sense of the term but as the plain meaning of the word itself shows it is merely meant to explain and clarify certain ambiguities which may have crept in the statutory provision.

Policy: The National Policy on Child Labour, August 1987 contains the action plan for tackling the problem of child labour. It envisages:

- A legislative action plan,
- Focussing and convergence of general development programmes for benefiting children wherever possible, and
- Project-based action plan of action for launching of projects for the welfare of working children in areas of high concentration of child labour.

In pursuance of National Child Labour Policy, the NCLP Scheme was started in 1988 to rehabilitate child labour. The Scheme seeks to adopt a sequential approach with focus on rehabilitation of children working in hazardous occupations & processes in the first instance. Under the Scheme, after a survey of child labour engaged in hazardous occupations & processes has been conducted, children are to be withdrawn from these occupations & processes and then put into special schools in order to enable them to be mainstreamed into formal schooling system.

Strategy for Elimination of Child Labour in Xth Plan

Keeping in view the policy of the Government as laid down in the National Agenda and Prime Minister's directions in the National Conference on Child Labour, the evaluation studies carried out by the VVGNLI and the approach defined in the working paper for the Tenth Plan, the strategy adopted during this Plan period aims at bringing qualitative changes in the scheme for elimination of child labour. The details are as follows:

1. Policy and programmes for elimination of child labour would be continued in a more focused, integrated and convergent manner.
2. Focused and reinforced action to eliminate child labour in the hazardous occupations by the end of the Plan period.
3. Expansion of the NCLPs to additional 150 districts during the Plan.
4. Ensuring that the NCLPs have a focused time frame of 5 years with clearly defined targets.
5. Linking the child labour elimination efforts with the scheme of Sarva Shiksha Abhiyan of the MHRD an attempt to ensure that small children in the age group of 5-8 years get directly linked to school and the older children are mainstreamed to the formal education system through the rehabilitation centres. Increased efforts to provide vocational training to the older children.
6. Strengthening of the formal school mechanism in the endemic child labour areas in the country both in terms of quality and numbers in such a manner as to provide an attractive schooling system to the child labour force and its parents so that motivational levels of both the parents and such children are high and sending these children to school becomes an attractive proposition.
7. Convergence with the ongoing schemes of the Dept. of Education, Rural Development, Health and Women & Child Development would be critical for the ultimate attainment of the objective of elimination of child labour in a time bound manner.
8. Large-scale involvement of the voluntary organizations at the district level to assist in the running of the NCLP schools. The attempt during this Plan would be to

encourage the running of the rehabilitation schools only through accepted and committed NGOs so that the Government machinery is not burdened with running of such schools.

Certain important and enhanced parameters that have been introduced in the scheme *now* are as under:

Stipind: In the existing arrangement, the stipend of Rs. 100/- per child per month was being disbursed every month. As per the revised scheme, the monthly stipend of Rs. 100/- per month per child will be disbursed only after the child is successfully mainstreamed into formal system of schooling. Till that period, the amount of stipend will be regularly deposited in the Bank Account of the child. The accumulated stipend amount could be handed over to the child at the time of her/his getting mainstreamed.

Nutrition: The amount for provision of nutrition to the children in the special schools has been doubled from Rs. 2.50/- per child per day to Rs. 5/- per child per day.

Health Component: In the existing scheme, there was no separate budgetary provision for any health component to take care of the health-related aspects of the children. In the revised scheme an amount of honorarium (Rs. 5,000/- per month for one doctor for every 20 schools) has been provided to put in place an institutionalised mechanism for regular and periodical effective health care of the children by a doctor. A health card in respect of every child also needs to be maintained with all the necessary entries.

Vocational Training: In the existing scheme, there was no separate budgetary provision for the services of any Master Trainer for imparting training to the children/ teachers. In the revised scheme, budgetary provision (Rs. 5,000/- for one Master Trainer for each NCLP) has been provided to hire the services of a Master for each NCLP.

Training for Educational Teachers: In the existing scheme, there was no separate budgetary provision for providing training to the educational teachers. In the revised scheme, budgetary provision has been provided to impart training to the teachers twice during the 10th Plan period.

Survey: In the revised Scheme, provision (Rs. 2.75 lakh per survey) has been made to conduct surveys of working children two times during the 10th Plan period. By following the strategy enunciated above and combining this with the existing established mechanisms of enforcement, it is expected that a drastic reduction in child labour would result by the end of Plan period. The problem of child labour requires to be dealt through sustained efforts over a period of time. Government is committed to the goal of eradication of child labour in all its forms. Considering the nature and magnitude of the problem a gradual and sequential approach has been adopted to withdraw and rehabilitate child labour beginning with the children working in hazardous occupations.

5

Role of NGO's in Controlling Child Labour

In developing economies, attention to the issue of child labour – whether at the level of policy, research or interventions – is fairly recent. The involvement of non-governmental organisations (NGOs) in this sector is about a decade old but it has been steadily gaining momentum, partly on account of the availability of funding for child labour programmes. However, only a handful of NGOs has achieved recognition in this field at the national level. The number of organisations that have succeeded in demonstrating a sustainable and wide scale reduction in the incidence of child labour is even smaller. Estimates of child labour in the 5-14 age group vary according to the definition of child labour used by the agency compiling the statistics. While recent statistics indicate some reduction in the overall incidence of child labour, the numbers are still alarmingly large. Given the scale of the problem, the question arises: can NGO interventions add up to a strategy for eliminating child labour?

This will review a number of inter-linked dimensions, starting with the macro context that forms the backdrop against which NGOs develop their strategies. Although NGO interventions are generally designed for the micro, local level, their success in this arena is influenced by a variety of background, overarching considerations ranging from the buoyancy of the economy to the availability of resources and the prevailing legal and institutional frameworks. These factors are largely outside the direct control of NGOs but they both circumscribe and constrain their activities. The following section will highlight some key aspects of the macro dimension, followed by an analysis of the specific strategies that NGOs follow in addressing the issue of child labour. Examples will be taken from across the field to illustrate the wide range of approaches that exist at present.

The Institutional Framework

The Constitution of India provides a sound framework for tackling the issue of child labour when it states that 'No child below the age of fourteen years shall be employed to work in any factory or mine or employed in any hazardous employment' (Article 14). It further directs state policy to ensure that '... the health and strength of workers ... and the tender age of children are not abused and that citizens are not forced by economic necessity to enter a vocation unsuited to their age or strength' (Article 39e). However, this positive environment has not been converted into an adequate legal or institutional framework for eliminating child labour. Government legislation on child labour is piecemeal and does not reflect the dimensions of the problem nor a determination to deal with it. The focus is mainly on prohibiting the most hazardous forms of labour and on regulating conditions of work in sectors that are considered less harmful. Family labour is left outside the purview of the law, which remains silent on the status of countless children who replace or supplement family labour on the farm, in domestic chores and in the informal sector. This situation is made worse by the fact that implementation and enforcement of the meagre legislation that exists is extremely limited. A prime example is the continued existence of bonded labour – for adults and children – despite the Bonded Labour System Act of 1976 which frees all bonded labourers, cancels the debts against them and orders their rehabilitation by the state.

Another striking aspect of child labour policy is that it co-exists or runs parallel to education policy with little cross-reference or discussion between the two. In fact the objectives of the two often clash. For example, universal elementary education has remained a goal, howsoever elusive, of government policy and India is a signatory to the Declaration of Education for All by the year 2000. However, discussions on policy measures to implement these goals have largely taken place without reference to child labour. In fact, by condoning child labour in non-hazardous industries and within the family setting, the government may have built in a mechanism to sabotage its own objective of universalising elementary education. A similar example is provided by the Non-Formal Education Programme which is a key element in the government's strategy for reaching literacy targets. Instead of making a sizeable proportion of the child population literate, this programme may in fact have served to legitimise child labour and keep children away from formal schools, thereby perpetuating the problems associated with non-enrolment.

Resource Availability

The reluctance of the Indian government to undertake programmes to eradicate all forms of child labour – hazardous and non-hazardous - and provide universal elementary education is attributed in large part to the shortage of resources at the national level. However, Sudarshan (2000) estimates that less than 1 per cent extra of GDP is required to universalise elementary education. While this is a substantial amount, and would require some reallocation of resources, it is well within the realm of the possible. The failure to make the necessary commitment can only be attributed to a lack of political will rather than to any real shortage of resources. In this scenario, NGOs become the cheap alternative for assisting government in reaching some of its goals for eliminating child labour and universalising education. While this provides NGOs with a steady source of income, it also constrains their work, as financing for this sector is limited and government grants may be tied to the provision of certain kinds of services such as the delivery of non-formal education to working children, or setting up alternative schools in areas that lack such facilities.

The bulk of non-governmental funding for child labour and education projects is provided by international NGOs. These donor agencies have their own mandates, their own strengths and weaknesses and their own constituencies. Funding for child labour and education projects generally follows current trends that are reflected in frequent changes in programme strategies. Also, the programme cycle may span only 3-5 years with the NGO having to take the responsibility of looking for other sources to continue the project activities. The funding strategies of individual donors will inevitably curtail or enhance the ability of local NGOs to deliver sustainable, long term and coherent programmes for child labour and education. Differences in emphasis and philosophy of donor agencies will be mirrored in the work of NGOs and will determine the outcome and impact of their programmes.

Child Labour Debates

The issue of child labour is layered with controversies and debates. Contested areas include the definition of child labour, in particular the distinction between labour and work; the relationship between child labour and poverty; the impact of child labour on the health and development of children; and the question of children's agency. These are not merely topics for theoretical discussion but have practical implications for the functioning of NGOs. They inform the policy stance of governments, international agencies and the donor community and are expressed in the funding patterns and choice of strategies adopted by them. They also find ready reflection in the thinking and practice of NGOs.

Child labour can be defined broadly to include all children out of school or more narrowly to cover only those who are employed in hazardous occupations. A distinction is also made between child labour and child work – the former refers to occupations that are hazardous or injurious and the latter to those that are claimed to do no harm to the child. It is argued that some forms of work could even be beneficial as they are an integral part of the child's socialisation into adult trades and they empower children by allowing them to contribute to the survival of their families. The poor quality of education in the mainstream government system is frequently invoked as a further reason for preferring work over school. The definition of child labour that is used by NGOs (and their donors) has an immediate consequence for the universe of working children to be covered by an intervention programme. A narrow focus on child labour could be advantageous for NGOs in the short run as it makes their target group more manageable. However, in the longer term this could lead to a perpetuation of child labour as they would fail to take account of the category of so-called 'nowhere children' i.e. those who are neither enrolled in school nor registered as child labour.

These children make up approximately 35 per cent of all children in their age group and the representation of girls is high. They may be engaged in a variety of domestic and other chores that release or supplement adult labour. They also form a reserve pool from which employers can pick and choose according to need and replace children who have been released from labour. Frequently missing from the arguments of those who make a case for the empowering potential of work is any reference to the impact of such work on the health and mental well being of children. Graitcer and Lerer (1998) estimate that the annual cost of child labour related mortality in India lies between 101 million and 2.43 billion US Dollars.

This figure does not include a valuation of impaired physical and mental health resulting from exposure to injuries, toxins, chemicals and pollutants, poor physical and ergonomic conditions, malnutrition, sexually transmitted diseases and sexual abuse, to mention just a few of the hazards children may be exposed to. Studies of children working in the carpet and handicraft industries in Kashmir, making locks in the home based sector in Aligarh, peeling fish in Quilon or as restaurant boys in Bombay, all point to negative consequences for children. Even household work – to which many girls are doomed from an early age – is not without its hazards. The World Bank estimates that, globally, between 400-700 million women and children are exposed to severe indoor pollution caused mostly by cooking fires.

A third disputed issue concerns the link between poverty and the existence and persistence of child labour. The mainstream view - among policy makers and society at large - is that poverty is the main determinant of child labour. In this case the only course open to NGOs would be to develop strategies for alleviating poverty. Any other approach would be meaningless as it would not tackle the root cause of the problem and could, instead, cause further hardship to poor parents. This traditional view is now beginning to be challenged. The experience of NGOs has demonstrated that there is a demand for education, even among the poor and that social and cultural factors are equally responsible for the existence of child labour and low school enrolment. The MV Foundation is one organisation that denies the primacy of poverty and focuses instead on changing values and norms that condone the existence of child labour and tolerate non-school going children. The success of the MV Foundation in creating a demand for education and eliminating all forms of child labour, even under conditions of poverty, has challenged some deep-seated myths about this subject.

The link with poverty is being questioned from other quarters as well. A comparative survey of the impact of poverty alleviation schemes on child labour found that land ownership patterns are similar among households with working and non-working children.

This survey was conducted in two districts each in Andhra Pradesh and Uttar Pradesh – both states with a high population of child labour. A survey in Bangalore showed that one third of working children had parents who were salaried, whereas another study in Bombay revealed that over a quarter of children worked because they had nothing else to do and not on account of poverty. A follow up study of urban slum children in Calcutta who had been withdrawn from work and were now attending school, found that 65 per cent of these children had not handed over their income to parents when they were working. Instead, they spent it on films, sweets, clothes and even gambling. Similarly, research from other developing countries shows that the relationship between poverty and child labour is not straightforward and is frequently mediated by other factors.

The Economic Climate

Underlying some of the positions taken in child labour debates is a presumption that economic growth would be associated with a decline in the incidence of child labour, with the causation running through an assumed decline in poverty. The evidence available suggests, instead, that the relationship is complex and multi-causal. Where economic expansion occurs within a neo-liberal market framework that creates and emphasises labour market 'flexibility', the incidence of child labour could rise rather than fall. The experiences of the garment export sector in Asia and the plantation sector in West Africa provide two illustrations of precisely such an effect.

In the home-based sector as well, improvements in local market conditions or in the production capacity of the household, e.g. through micro credit, could well intensify the use of child labour as the demand for family labour rises. In agriculture, certain forms of commercialisation and restructuring of rural labour relations have also been associated with a rise in the involvement of children. In recent years, there has been a tendency in agriculture towards an increased reliance on family contract labour from landless households. Such family contracts provide a vehicle for the increased induction of children into agricultural labour.

The case of hybrid cottonseed production provides another insightful illustration involving the agency of local labour contractors who have agreements with national and multinational seed companies. This commercial crop was introduced in parts of South India in the early 70's and created a new system of employing girl children as bonded labour. Until then, only adult males and boys had been employed as bonded labour in agriculture. At present, girls between the ages of 7-14 make up 90 per cent of the labour force. They are employed on the basis of long-term contracts that are secured through loans and advances given to parents by local seed producers who have created and propagated the notion that only young girls can do the work of cross-pollination. It is estimated that nearly 400,000 girl children are employed in cottonseed fields. This is more than the total number of children employed in carpet weaving, glass bangles, gem polishing and limestone industries. There is evidence that children have been withdrawn from school to work in the cottonseed fields.

Using inter-state data, Mahendra Dev (2000) has argued that there is no clear linear relationship between higher levels of income and lower incidence of child labour across Indian states. Clearly, other factors must intervene strongly to explain this divergence. Since the relationship between growth and poverty reduction is itself contested, this can only further undermine the general validity of the proposition that growth will lead to a reduction of child labour through its impact on poverty. In the very long run, or viewed across the chasm of the very rich and very poor countries, such a proposition might well hold, but this has little strategic value in the current policy context of developing countries.

NGO Strategies

The majority of NGOs use a combination of strategies in their efforts to eliminate child labour or ameliorate its effects. However, many have a distinct philosophy, and consequently, a clear entry point and areas of emphasis. To take a few examples: Sankalp - an NGO working with tribals in the mining belt of Shankargarh - aims to secure the income and employment of parents as a prior condition to eliminating child labour. The MV Foundation, on the other hand, denies the importance of poverty as the prime motivating factor, and focuses on changing deep-seated mindsets and attitudes about child labour and education in the entire community in villages of Andhra Pradesh. Rugmark - a labelling scheme for carpets made without the use of child labour - approaches this issue from the standpoint of international consumers, whereas CREDA, also located in the carpet belt of Mirzapur and Bhadohi, uses education as the entry point for weaning children away from the looms. CINI-Asha, working in the urban slums of Calcutta, takes a similar stance by providing bridge courses and after school tuition classes to enable working children to join the formal school system and stay there. A radically different standpoint and philosophy is to be found in the work of Concerned for Working Children (CWC), located in Karnataka, who believe that work is part of the reality of some children's lives and is not necessarily harmful for them. Consequently, they aim to give a voice to working children and to organise them so that they can demand better working conditions for themselves.

The following strategies are most frequently used by NGOs:

- Mobilisation and awareness creation
- Provision of education
- Provision of pre-school education
- Facilitating child participation
- Developing income compensatory strategies
- Assuring work and income security for parents
- Facilitating intra-household adjustments
- Social labelling
- Advocacy for legal and institutional reform

Mobilisation and Awareness Creation

Most NGOs subscribe to the view that wide scale changes are possible only through the mass mobilisation and empowerment of the intended beneficiaries. Consequently, campaigns to mobilise children, parents and communities and create awareness about child labour and education are on the agenda of most organisations. A variety of means such as village meetings, theatre, rallies and door-to-door campaigns are used to achieve this objective. However, the intensity with which these activities are undertaken and the capacity to go beyond the rhetoric and follow-up and deliver on the expectations that are raised vary considerably from one agency to the next. It is widely recognised that such campaigns are successful only if the momentum generated by them can be sustained beyond the initial event. The Total Literacy Campaign (TLC) -

perhaps the largest exercise in mass mobilisation around the issue of education - has been an important learning ground in this respect. Its mixed, and eventually disappointing, results can be attributed largely to the failure of the TLC to capitalise on the demand that it created and its inability in following this up with sustained action.

The MV Foundation provides an illustration of how NGOs can ensure that the euphoria created by campaigns is not dissipated. Every mobilisation effort that is undertaken by the organisation results in the creation of a permanent institutional capacity for ensuring follow up at the local level. This is considered vital for sustaining community involvement on the issues of child labour and education long after the campaign is over. Efforts are made to involve already existing structures such as Village Education Committees, women's groups, youth groups and village panchayats by revitalising them and giving them the responsibility for protecting children's rights. These groups can then keep the issue of child labour alive and respond to fresh challenges as and when they arise.

Provision of Education

Compulsory education has been a prime policy instrument in the struggle to eradicate child labour in 19th century Europe, the United States and Japan and more recently in parts of the developing world, including Kerala. While the Indian government has been slow to use this approach, many NGOs have taken up the provision of education as an important plank in their strategy for combating child labour. However, there are major ideological and practical differences between organisations on at least three counts. The first relates to whether they see education as a fundamental right or not. The second variation is in the form in which they deliver education i.e. formal, non-formal, bridge course or vocational. The third refers to the role they see for themselves in delivering this service. The mandate and philosophy of each individual NGO, as well as of their donors, will no doubt determine the stand that they take. This will in turn influence the nature of their lobbying and advocacy work as well as their field practice.

At first glance it may appear unnecessary to question whether education is a fundamental right or not, but a review of the literature and ongoing debates reveals considerable controversy on this subject. The position that is taken in relation to this question will have direct implications for the strategies that NGOs devise and the role that they carve out for themselves. Nor surprisingly, NGOs that take the view that education is a fundamental right are also involved in the call for making elementary education compulsory. But this view is not shared by all. Some argue that making education compulsory would be tantamount to punishing poor families who are dependent on the labour of their children. The quality of education in mainstream government schools and the lack of resources to provide universal coverage are mentioned as further justifications for not making education compulsory. A more extreme corollary to this position maintains that children also have the right to work and to organise. The proponents of this viewpoint argue that school is not the only arena where children learn; they can acquire life skills at the workplace as well. CWC is one of the leading exponents of this position in India as well as in the international arena. At present, this remains a minority position among Indian NGOs, but it may gain ground on account of getting linked to international movements of working children and because of pressure from certain quarters of the donor community.

A variety of educational services are offered by NGOs in their attempt to provide an alternative to child labour. Some NGOs (CINI-Asha, CREDA and Sankalp, among others) provide full day schools that mirror the mainstream formal system in many respects. But these schools are regarded as non-formal on the grounds that they offer the primary school curriculum in a compressed time frame and their teachers are less qualified and are paid lower salaries than government school teachers. The funding for these schools may come from international sources (such as the ILO-IPEC programme) or from various government schemes (such as the Shikhalaya Prakalpa programme of the Government of West Bengal). The rationale for setting them up is to use NGOs to improve school access and accelerate enrolment in areas that are currently lacking in educational facilities. More conventional non-formal programmes such as evening classes and on-the-job literacy classes for working children continue to be offered, despite increasing field evidence to attest to their dismal record.

A radically different approach has been developed by the MV Foundation. It runs residential bridge courses to prepare dropouts, out of school children and erstwhile working children for entry into the formal school system in the class appropriate to their age.

This has proved to be a very successful strategy in easing the transition of working children into the educational system and has been adopted by the Andhra Pradesh government as well as by NGOs such as Pratham, CINI-Asha and Lok Jumbish. A few NGOs provide vocational training for older children who are either unable to make the transition to formal school or who wish to learn a marketable skill. The courses range from carpentry, cycle and motor cycle repair and maintenance to artisanal skills and are usually accompanied by some form of literacy training. However, the number of children who benefit from this kind of hands on training remains limited, largely on account of the costs associating with staffing and running such courses. CWC and MAYA (operating in Bangalore) are two NGOs that offer vocational training to a small number of children.

Given the dependence on external funding, most NGOs find it difficult to take a strong stand on the role that they should play vis-à-vis government and other players in the delivery of educational provision. They may actually be running primary schools even while simultaneously professing that this should be the responsibility of government. However, there are a few organisations that take the clear position that NGOs should not replace government but should restrict themselves to playing a supportive and facilitative role.

This view is espoused most forcefully by MV Foundation and Pratham – both work to strengthen the formal education system and assist it in coping with the influx of students resulting from their mobilisation activities and bridge courses. They also address the issue of quality of education, but in a way that benefits the entire mainstream system, and not just a lucky few who are part of a labouratory experiment on pedagogical improvements. Both NGOs have the mandate to universalise primary education in their respective target areas and have achieved a measure of success in doing this.

Provision of Early Childhood Care and Education

It is well known that early childhood care and education (ECCE) programmes – ranging from child care for the 0-2 age group and pre-school for 2-6 year olds - facilitate the entry of children into primary school and are associated with higher literacy levels, among other longer-term benefits.

In addition, they make an important contribution to releasing siblings from childcare responsibilities and allowing them to attend school. Where suitable provision is not available, infants may be left in the care of older siblings, generally girls, who are frequently little more than children themselves. Despite the obvious need for ECCE facilities – to ease the transition to primary school and release siblings to enter school - this has been an area of low priority so far, in terms of both policy formulation and resource allocation. With a few exceptions, even NGOs working on child labour have been slow to use the provision of ECCE services as a strategy for the elimination of child labour.

Pratham - an NGO working in Mumbai - has developed a network of balwadis in city slums where such services were previously lacking. This has proved to be an invaluable step in its objective of achieving universal primary education in Mumbai. In fact the success of this initiative has encouraged Pratham to extended its mandate to include universal pre school cover for all children as well. The balwadis serve a multiple function. In addition to meeting a much felt community need, they also carry the message of education to the slums, they prepare children for entry into the formal school system, prevent future dropouts, and provide a forum from where the health and nutritional status of children can be monitored and corrected. In 2000, Pratham was running 2,900 balwadis catering to approximately 53,000 of 3-5 year olds. An evaluation of the longer-term impact of this intervention on school attendance, both of children who have attended the balwadis and those that have been released from sibling care, is awaited.

Facilitating Child Participation

Proponents of the view that child work can be empowering and beneficial to children (as opposed to child labour that is harmful) readily align themselves with the move for increased participation of children in deciding their own futures and destinies. In this context, participation can be extended to mean that children have the right to decide whether they want to work or go to school. Children are seen as active agents, indeed as 'partners', and not just as passive recipients, and are considered to be capable of making decisions concerning their lives. The organisations that support this view generally do not favour calls for making education compulsory nor for imposing an outright ban on child labour as this would amount to punishing the child workers and their poor families.

They contend that the problem of child labour has been hugely exaggerated by fundraising departments of development organisations, journalists and the media to serve their own purposes. According to them, depicting the harmful effects of work on children only serves to victimise and exploit poor children and their families.

CWC believes that child labour can be beneficial to children as it provides them with a means of escaping dire poverty and improving their own situation as well as that of their families. While CWC is committed to the eradication of child labour in the long run, it works to empower children who have no option but to work at present. To this end, it focuses on the 'protagonism' of working children i.e. on the need to involve them actively in designing and developing solutions for themselves. One of CWC's primary activities in this direction has been the formation of a union of working children aged 6-18. This union, which currently has a membership of 13,000 working children in Karnataka, sees itself as an advocate for the rights of the child and a means by which working children can participate in local decision making processes.

The members decide their own agenda, priorities and action plans. One of the activities they have undertaken is to develop their own definition of work and to decide what is good and bad work – i.e. work they can and cannot do. This exercise then forms the basis for deciding the interventions that are needed at the local level for dealing with work that is considered 'harmful' by the children. CWC is a leading player in the international movement of working children and has taken delegations of working children to various international conferences and forums.

Developing Income Compensatory Strategies

Income compensatory strategies are a response to the belief that family poverty is directly responsible for the persistence of child labour and poor educational outcomes. Payments to children and their families are suggested as a means to compensate them for the loss of income incurred on account of withdrawing their children from labour and enrolling them in school. No Indian agency offers an income replacement scheme on the Bolsa-Escola model developed in Brazil, where a cash transfer of one minimum wage is made for one year to families below the poverty line who enrol and keep their children in primary school.

This remains one of the most powerful examples of income compensation, but despite its significant potential to eradicate child labour and alleviate family poverty, its impact remains limited in terms of scale and sustainability. This is largely due to the difficulty in finding the resources to extend this programme to reach the entire population of poor families and for the entire duration that their children are in primary school. These problems would be equally relevant, and perhaps even greater in a country like India.

At present there are a variety of income supplementary schemes that provide incentives in cash or kind to encourage school enrolment and prevent dropout. These range from cash stipends, scholarships, free uniforms, books and teaching materials to mid-day meals and nutritional supplements. Such schemes mainly cover the costs of education rather than compensate for the loss of income incurred on account of withdrawing children from labour. They are offered by charitable foundations, as well as by NGOs implementing government programmes and those funded by international donors.

In the absence of any large-scale evaluations, it is difficult to assess the impact of such schemes on reducing child labour. In a global survey of income compensation schemes conducted by Anker and Melkas (1996), respondents expressed concern about corruption and cheating, particularly where cash transfers are concerned. Although the majority were positive about the impact of such schemes, many felt that they would not be sufficient in themselves to keep children in school and would need to be accompanied by more comprehensive strategies. Concern was expressed about creating dependency and taking away initiative from poor families. The sustainability of the programme was also mentioned as a major problem as it was noted that children tend to return to work when the benefits are withdrawn.

Assuring Work and Income for Parents

This is a variant of the above strategy but with a difference. Instead of compensating families by making a transfer to them in cash or kind, the aim here is to assist them in securing work and income. This is done in a variety of ways, through self-help schemes, group savings, rotating loans and micro credit programmes, assistance in setting up income generating activities and organising adult labour to demand minimum wages and better working conditions. This is a more empowering process than giving hand-outs as it strengthens the ability of poor families to take control over their own lives.

This approach is beginning to gain currency with NGOs who feel that their efforts to eradicate child labour will bear fruit only if they are able to help parents to address one of the root causes of their poverty. At present, there are no systematic evaluations of the effectiveness of this strategy in reducing child labour. It would be safe to assume that efforts to assist parents in securing micro loans to develop viable sources of income would be subject to the same problems and constraints that beset micro credit programmes in general. In addition, where these schemes are not linked consciously to the issue of child labour, they could have the unintended consequence of increasing child labour.

Sankalp has succeeding in bypassing some of these problems by making the economic activity conditional on the withdrawal of children from labour. The organisation works with landless kol tribals who are employed at a pittance - the majority as bonded labour - in the silica mines of Shankargarh. Sankalp is organising mineworkers to unite in their struggle for minimum wages, better working conditions and release from bonded labour. They are encouraged to start self-help groups and save even small amounts of money. More significantly, they are enabled to form co-operatives that can apply for mining leases. In return, the mineworkers have to make a commitment that once they are successful in securing a lease, they will send all their children to school. Sankalp is strengthening this process by opening bachpana kendras that function at present as full-time schools, but offering a compressed primary school curriculum, in villages that don't have access to a school.

Sankalp has had some measure of success in its work. 6 villages have secured mining leases and all children are attending school. This is in stark contrast to the previous situation where hardly any child was in school. A campaign for minimum wages has been launched in 40 villages and 25 now have a bachpana kendra. What is perhaps more significant is that Sankalp has opened bachpana kendras in 5 villages where it has not yet organised the mineworkers and there has been no action to demand minimum wages from the employers. These centres were opened in response to a demand from villagers who had seen how these schools functioned in neighbouring villages and wanted the same for their children. At present, their children are denied access to the government schools and consequently end up working as part of family labour. This recent development is very telling as it turns the poverty argument on its head. It demonstrates that the availability of a functioning school can be sufficient incentive to mobilise poor parents to withdraw their children from labour and enrol them in school, regardless of any linkage with any specific form of income compensation.

Facilitating Intra-Household Adjustments

Efforts involving intra-household labour diversification, consumption and expenditure switching, and savings and assets restructuring have been widely observed in the context of sudden fluctuations in the incomes of poor households whether in the context of structural adjustment, natural disasters or loss of family labour due to illness or death. All these point to the resilience of poor families in their struggle for survival.

This view is supported by Chandrasekhar's (1997) study of child labour in the match industry of Sivakasi-Sattur in Tamil Nadu. He argues that the abolition of child labour in this industry would neither lead to industrial distress nor cause problems for individual families. In fact, it would result in higher earnings for adult workers. Some NGOs are beginning to use this resilience as a resource in their efforts to encourage families to give up child labour in favour of education.

CINI-Asha and MV Foundation have been successful in withdrawing children from labour and mainstreaming them in the formal education system in the urban slums of Calcutta and rural Andhra Pradesh, respectively. This has been done without any compensation in cash or kind to the families of these children. Follow up studies of the families of these children show that poor parents make adjustments to compensate for the loss of income and labour incurred by sending children to school. In some cases the children continued to work but reduced their work hours to the time available during holidays and before and after school.

There is also evidence of work sharing. The tasks previously done by the children were now shared between the family members. Some changes have been noticed in the gender division of labour, with fathers taking on some of the tasks traditionally associated with women. Parents also increase their wage work and diversify their income sources. In some cases, family income had actually gone up as parents had sought better paid jobs in order to support their children through school or because adult wages had gone up due to the unavailability of child labour. Changes have been reported in consumption patterns as well with families spending less on festivals, entertainment, alcohol and luxury food items.

Social Labelling

Labelling has been used as a strategy to combat child labour mainly in the hand-knotted carpet industry in the Mirzapur and Bhadohi districts of UP. Social labelling differs from other approaches in that it targets consumers and aims to sensitise them to the issue of child labour. The label provides the guarantee that the product has been made without the use of child labour. Labelling schemes also aim to have a direct impact on the working and living conditions of children and their families through the setting up of schools and other social projects, though this part of their work is not always well developed. The twin strategies of consumer action feeding back through the supply chain and social projects at the local level are expected to result in a beneficial outcome for working children.

Rugmark is the first and best known labelling initiative for carpets, but it has spawned several others such as Care and Fair from Germany, STEP from Switzerland and KALEEN which has been introduced by the Indian government. Although all these labels have the professed aim of reducing child labour in the carpet industry, they differ in some important respects. Some aim to eliminate child labour totally while others want to ameliorate the working conditions of those already employed and prevent future entrants. There are variations in whether the label is provided to the individual product or to the entire establishment and in the monitoring of this process – by the labelling agency or by the producers themselves.

Social labelling is at best a limited approach to tackling the issue of child labour in carpet production. It would have to be accompanied by a wide range of other initiatives including labour legislation, income compensation, substitution of child by adult labour, provision of education and awareness raising for it to have a measurable impact. So far, efforts in this direction have been small-scale and more by way of tokenism. Inspection also remains a problem and it is alleged that it is virtually impossible to give a foolproof guarantee, given the wide area over which looms are spread. But if such a guarantee were possible, all it would do is confirm that a particular carpet has been made without child labour. Apart from catering to the customer's conscience, the label would have limited impact on the totality of child labour in this industry and say little about all the other carpets woven by children. The label could even act to take away attention from the issue of child labour, which is by no means abating in carpet production as a whole.

Advocacy for Legal and Institutional Reform

The social movements of the day have historically played a major role in advocating for the eradication of child labour. Legal reform to make education compulsory and to restrict the minimum working age accompanied by adequate provision of schools and strict enforcement of laws accelerated the process of change. NGOs, along with other civil society institutions, are in the forefront in creating awareness about child labour and advocating for changes in policy at present as well. At the national level, a large number of NGOs took a joint stand on the discussions leading up to the 93rd Constitutional Amendment Bill to make education a fundamental right.

At present there is no counterpart nation-wide movement for legal reform in the sphere of child labour. However, several NGOs are involved in advocating for the abolition of child labour through their membership of forums such as the Global March Against Child Labour and the South Asia Coalition Against Child Servitude. A few NGOs distance themselves from these groups on grounds that they cannot participate in activities that go against children's work. Instead, they work towards increased participation of working children through their involvement in the International Working Children's Movement.

NGOs are more active in their advocacy work at the local level and undertake a wide range of activities in this regard. At the most basic level this involves creating awareness among local communities about child labour, education and existing labour laws. They also engage with the state government in lobbying for legal and institutional reform and better implementation of existing legislation. Some of these initiatives, such as the enforcement of laws regarding minimum wages, abolition of bonded labour or compensation for work related injury do not apply directly to children but are part of the move to improve the economic and living conditions of poor families so that they can withdraw their children from labour. Others are more directly relevant to children. For example, they may seek the extension of existing legislation, such as the Factories Act, to cover sectors such as mining where child labour is rampant but which do not come under the purview of the law at present. Others take a more confrontational stance, for example by seeking penalties for employers of child labour or instituting legal proceedings against employers who hire children as bonded labour.

NGOs working on child labour display a striking diversity in their mandates, networks and target groups as well as in the range of interventions they deploy to reach their objectives. But do these interventions add up to a strategy for eradicating child labour? A successful strategy should stand up to scrutiny on at least three counts.

The individual components of the programmes would need to be integrated in a holistic manner; the programme would have the potential of going to scale, and would be sustainable beyond the life cycle of the project. With a few notable exceptions, the majority of NGOs would find it difficult to score positively on all three fronts. Their approach is often limited to tackling the problem of child labour at the peripheries, while leaving its core intact. Several factors can be held responsible for this. Some stem from deficiencies, limitations and contradictions in the macro context but others are a direct reflection of shortcomings in the approach followed by the NGOs.

Taking a Piecemeal Approach

What is frequently lacking from the approach of NGOs is an integrated operational strategy that addresses the diverse causes of child labour in a holistic fashion. While they may be effective in mounting mobilisation campaigns, releasing children from bonded labour or running non-formal primary schools, these activities are not accompanied by a vision for eradicating child labour in its totality from a given geographical area.

This is largely because these NGOs take a piecemeal approach to the issue of child labour - in terms of their target group, their field practice or their philosophy. Three examples will be used to illustrate this shortcoming. The first and most extreme illustration is provided by efforts to withdraw children from labour without developing parallel activities for rehabilitating them. Obviously, such a piecemeal approach to the complex issue of child labour has the potential to do more harm than good to children and their families.

The most frequently cited case in this regard is of the Bangladeshi garment workers who were dismissed en masse in the early 90's as a result of international pressure. Subsequent reviews showed that these children did not join school but ended up in jobs that were less regulated, less safe and lower paying. Ironically, this example is most readily quoted in the literature by those who seek regulation of child labour in so-called non-hazardous sectors. Rather than pleading for a more complete approach that includes efforts to rehabilitate the children, create awareness about child labour among parents, employers and the community and tackle the issue of family poverty, this example is often used to justify demands for regulating working conditions for children in the garment (and other) industries so that they can continue to contribute to family income.

Most NGOs take a more coherent approach to dealing with child labour but with their focus on a specific target group, rather than on the entire universe of working children in their given area. This target group could range from a narrow category such as bonded labour or carpet weavers to a somewhat broader group such as children working in hazardous industries. No matter how comprehensive the strategies might be for dealing with this particular group, experience has demonstrated that such an approach is doomed to fail in the long run. Developing programmes for an exclusive category of child labourers leaves open the possibility of replacing these children by others who are waiting in reserve to fill these positions. Equally seriously, such an approach has the unintended consequence of condoning child labour in what are considered less harmful or less hazardous sectors. It would be fair to say that contradictions inherent in child labour and education policy find a ready reflection in the practice of NGOs as well.

Efforts to remove child labour in the carpet belt of Mirzapur-Bhadohi provide a telling illustration of the deficiencies inherent in taking a narrow focus. While it is widely acknowledged that child labour has been significantly reduced in this district on account of the combined actions of the NGOs working there, this is by no means the whole picture.

The reduction in child labour is partly accounted for by the fact that manufacturers have shifted their looms to the neighbouring states of Bihar and Rajasthan where they can continue to employ children without coming under scrutiny. The reduction in child labour is also caused by a general fall in the demand for Indian carpets - adult weavers are also unemployed and underemployed. Moreover, despite the concentration of NGOs committed to eradicating child labour, the living and working conditions of weavers and their families is largely unchanged and carpet weaving remains an exploitative industry.

A carpet exporter from Bhadohi summed up the situation neatly, though somewhat cynically, when he was asked why the situation of carpet weavers had not changed despite the concerted efforts of NGOs. "This is how it works: rog bhi bana rahe, dawa bhi chalti rahe (let the disease as well as the medication continue).

The NGOs keep their livelihoods and everything remains the same." The final example is provided by NGOs that focus on child participation. The efforts of these agencies are concentrated on making working children more visible, giving them a voice in determining their own lives, ameliorating their working conditions and, in some cases, organising and unionising them. While listening to children's views will undoubtedly lead to relevant and child friendly strategies, there are certain assumptions underlying this approach that make it problematic, and even counterproductive as a strategy for eradicating child labour.

The first is that child labour can be eradicated by following a twin track system, i.e. eradicate it in the long run but regulate it in the short run as it is a necessary evil. No indication is provided of how long the short run is expected to be. In the absence of other poverty alleviating measures there is the danger of the short run becoming a relatively permanent state. The second set of problems arises from the claim that work is not harmful but empowering for poor children. Organisations that take this approach are generally silent about the consequences of child labour - even when regulated - for the future economic prospects of the child and for society. There is no empirical evidence to support the position that child work is associated with the skills and experiences that contribute to higher earning capability.

Cross-cultural research on urban children shows that between the ages of 6-12 they acquire a strong sense of self by contributing to family income. But those who have been deprived of schooling opportunities may become resentful as adolescents because of their inability to get better-paid jobs. A more dangerous aspect of this approach that is inevitably cloaked in radical statements about participation and empowerment is the clear message that is sent out that certain kinds of work are acceptable for certain categories of children. Condoning child labour – or child work as they term it – for poor children does not amount to a strategy for eliminating it but for perpetuating it. Finally, this approach puts the onus of responsibility on the working child and not on societal norms that apply to all children.

Issues of Scale, Sustainability and Costs

The development of 'good practice' in micro situations is perhaps what NGOs are best at, but they need to go beyond their narrow constituencies and keep the totality of the situation in mind when developing their strategies.

Scale is a crucial dimension that cannot be ignored if NGOs are to make a recognisable impact on the overall child labour situation. NGOs follow several routes to addressing the issue of going-to-scale. One way is to influence the policies of government, which is the only body that has the capacity to deliver programmes at a state-wide or nation-wide level. The problems associated with replicating a model or prototype that has been successful at the local level through government programmes are well known. There is an inevitable watering down of standards and a loss of flexibility and contextual appropriateness in any programme that is delivered by a top-down bureaucracy. Social franchising is another idea that is becoming increasingly popular with NGOs.

The assumption here is that there is a prototype programme developed by one agency that can be replicated by others. This method has been borrowed from the private sector and displays some predictable problems when used in the social sector. A different approach is associated with social movements, where the boundaries of the programme are extended in a more organic way. The essential difference here is that the demand for replication is spontaneous, needs based and comes from below, making the likelihood of institutional ownership higher, and the prospect of sustainability that much greater. For any NGO initiative to successfully go to scale in a manner that is sustainable it should meet another important criterion viz., that of costs. It is often argued that NGO initiatives are expensive in terms of per unit costs for reaching the targeted beneficiaries.

The issue of costs, however, is complex. Three observations need to be registered in this respect. First, NGOs undertake various activities, such as advocacy, the benefits of which are difficult to value. Second, NGOs are often used by government as a low cost mechanism for delivering programmes that would be too costly for the government bureaucracy. It is necessary, therefore, to bear in mind that low cost is not necessarily a virtue as it could also imply low quality. Third, the issue of costs is also tied to the question of local institutional development and ownership. Local communities take on various tasks that are crucial for the success of the overall programme but these efforts are not costed. In the main NGOs it is arguable that NGOs remain an expensive delivery mechanism in terms of the real benefits transferred.

Catering to Donor Demands

Some of the problems mentioned above have no doubt result from the fact that NGO priorities and strategies are per force donor driven. Even when they take an uncompromising stand in the language that they use to describe themselves, their actual functioning is vulnerable to the demands of donors – whether it be national or state government or international agencies. In principle, NGOs can have a role to play in influencing and challenging donor strategies, as most donors prefer to see themselves as partners and profess to be open to dialogue. In practice, however, the flow of influence and ideas tends to be one-way.

It is a rare organisation that can withstand donor pressure and say no to funding for activities that go contrary to its own philosophy and mandate. Only well-established NGOs with assured and varied sources of funding can embark on such an exercise. The vast majority will be forced to compromise or find as close a match as possible between their objectives and the dictates of donors. The contradictions and inconsistencies inherent in government policy and in the stance of international donor agencies then find a reflection in the work of NGOs as well. Some of these have been referred to in the preceding text.

Competition rather than Collaboration

NGOs frequently operate in a competitive environment that defines their space and options and often overrides free choices with regard to strategies and operations. They have to scramble for scarce resources, with a large number of organisations knocking on a few doors. In such an atmosphere, institutional interests gain a life of their own with the sustainability of the organisation becoming an area of prime concern. Competition overtakes collaboration. While there is some scattered evidence of collaboration and interaction between like-minded organisations, there is no significant move at present to unite NGOs behind one common standpoint. In fact, NGOs hold conflicting and diverse viewpoints on the issue of child labour that often work against each other. Donor agencies are equally diverse in their mandates with the result that they fuel this insularity and do not contribute to a culture of cross-fertilisation of ideas and approaches.

Individual NGOs have made remarkable strides in the field of child labour in the short period under review; however, the sector as a whole has a long way to go. Like any other chronic social problems the problem of child labour in our society today has been an issue of concern for all those who care. But it has baffled many social scientists and activists in the field too, as to how to get rid of this blot from our social fabric. There are very few success stories in this regard and one of them is going to be the story of Hisua block of Nawada district of Bihar. Not very long ago one could see the urchins working in every nook and corner of the block but thanks to the initiative taken by the District Administration headed by Smt. N. Vijayalakshmi and the cooperation and active participation of Panchayati Raj Institutions' representatives and NGOs etc. that the Hisua block is going to be declared child labour free within a record time of 100 days. One natural question comes to mind i.e. how was it made possible? One must try and find out by himself/herself. Though here is a brief interim report of the whole process to help anybody who cares to know and learn.

The Process

Under the dynamic leadership of the District Magistrate of Nawada District Smt. N. Vijaya Lakshmi, a "District Vision Exercise"(DVE) was organized on 7th Sept. 2002. The initiative for organizing this one-day exercise was taken by Ms. Saurabh Suman of Bihar Seva Sansathan, Nawada, in close co-ordination and co-operation of Mr. Augustine Veliath, of UNICEF and Dr. Neel Ratan of A.N. Sinha Institute, Patna. People belonging to District Administration, local NGOs and activists and elected representatives of the recently constituted Panchayati Raj Institutions (PRIs) and media participated in this one day exercise and shared their view points about the prevailing menace of rampant child labour in the district. They also put their minds together to prepare a concrete plan of action for eradication of child labour from the district. By the end of the day, it was decided that all the child labour in the Hisua block of the district would be freed in net 100 days i.e. by 17th of December 2002 . It was decided that a committee consisting of all Govt. Officials of Hisua block, NGOs and representatives of PRIs should be formed for accomplishing this task appropriately named as "HAPPY HISUA" Programme.

Following this exercise the team, under the able guidance and leadership of Smt. N. Vijaya Lakshmi, took on themselves the difficult task of implementing the work plan to get the aspired results of the "HAPPY HISUA" Programme. They organized a meeting with all the representatives of Nagar Panchayats and Gram Panchayats of the Hisua block on 14th Sept. 2002. In this meeting the district survey report on child labour which was prepared in the month of Dec. 2001 was shared with all. After discussions with the participants it was decided that a second round of survey would be conducted in the block to ascertain the actual number of children involved in any kind of work in the block. For this a Survey Performa was developed. Finally the second survey was done and the results of the survey showed a very different picture from the earlier survey that was done only last year in the month of December. The number of child-labour came surprisingly low in the second survey report.

The reasons for this difference was given as the non visibility of the child labour in the Agarbatti making families who were too scared to reveal that their children were also working with them and actually they were enrolled in one or the other school of the block. The other reason of such a great difference was explained that most of the brick kiln in the block was closed during the time of survey and the workers in those brick kiln were mostly migratory in nature. So in the season of brick making (i.e. from late December to early June) the migratory workers from the nearby districts of Bihar and Jharkhand State would come bringing with them a large number of child workers too. The problem of child labour become very complex to deal with when it is attached with the problem of migratory workers and requires an in-depth study for better tackling of the situation. After this meeting on 14th of September 2002, a committee was constituted to strategize and implement the plan to make Hisua child labour free. In this committee the District Administration along with the labour department, education department, agriculture department, PRIs and NGOs were made to work together.

This committee met on 25th September and discussed on the plan of action to be adopted. According to one proposal all the *Mukhiya* of ten *Gram panchayat* and Chairman of the *Nagar Panchayat* was made responsible for getting all the child labour in their area free and getting them enrolled in government schools. The other proposal was that the labour department will give notice to all the brick kiln owners (17 in number) in the block to spare all the child labour from any work in the coming season of brick making. The Labour Enforcement Officer (LEO) of the block was entrusted with the aforementioned task and facilitating the work of others besides his other official duties *vis a vis* child labour. But according to his superiors and colleagues he could not get the work done in the given time because of his lackadaisical attitude.

Following which reminder was given to him but to avail. In the end the District Magistrate was left with no other option but to recommend for his suspension to the labour commissioner. This act of recommendation had a great psychological effect on the rank and file of the officials at the block level as they got to know that the DM was very serious about this issue. On 19th of October 2002, another meeting was called by the DM in the district head-quarter to take stock of the progress made. In this meeting Mr. Vasudev Pandey, Mr. Lal Ram, Syed Sirajul Hasan and Mr. Vijay Kumar Singh, LEOs from other blocks were given the responsibility to spearhead the process in Hisua block. The work done by these Labour Enforcement Officers (LEOs) requires to be appraised as they also worked with a missionary zeal that is seldom seen in the ranks and files of government officials. They also gave all the credit to their superiors i.e. the BDO and the DM for their encouragement and support as well.

Though only one LEO works in a block, the initiative to put four LEOs for accomplishing the task helped tremendously. The LEOs themselves say that any one of them alone could not have got the results as it required a team to handle the troubled situation which always arose while conducting the raids. The team spirit and mutual understanding between the four LEOs worked well in dealing with the difficult situations in the field. In return they were named as "BUTRU PAKARWA"(one who catches children) by the employers of the child labour and subsequently by general public. The raids conducted by them and the DM herself, in the town area as well as in the remote areas of the rural Hisua, sent a message to all and sundry that the district administration was very serious about the issue.

The Role of NGOs/Voluntary Sector

The role of NGOs was also praiseworthy and it also raises many questions which will be discussed later. Though the initiative to organize the DVE was taken by the District Administration and the task of organizing it was done by Bihar Sewa Sansthan under due guidance from Mr. Augustine Veliath of UNICEF and Dr. Neel Ratan of A.N. Sinha Institute, but not many other NGOs participated in the whole campaign that followed to make Hisua free from child labour in the set period of 100 day. Ms. Saurav Suman and her team of activists from Bihar Sewa Sansthan and Mukhtarul Haque in his individual capacity of "Bachpan Bachao Andolan" (BBA) representative in the district and as secretary of the District Total Literacy Campaign were very helpful and provided all the support to the district administration in this campaign.

The role of the "Mukti Karwan" group of BBA is lesser to none as their Nukkar-Natak based on the issue of child labour and performed by the freed child labour themselves from 25th to 28th of October had a great effect on the psyche of the people. The group of children from BBA also organized a Bal Chaupal on 28th October which was attended by a large number of people belonging to different caste, community and strata of the block. This Mukti Karwan and Bal Chaupal had a great effect on the awareness and sensitization work which formed the backbone of the whole campaign.

The Role of PRIs

The other strength of this campaign has been the involvement of all the stakeholders since the very inception of the campaign. The role of the representatives of the PRIs and the NGOs/voluntary sector in the realization of campaign objective has been commendable too. The reason for their such keen interest also lies in the genuine motivational and encouragement work done by Smt. N. Vijayalakhmi. The reason that they were involved from the very first phase of planning and strategizing also made them take the ownership of the task at hand and work hard. The role of the PRIs has also been quite commendable. Their representatives, whether it was the Chairman and Members of Nagar Panchayat or Block Samiti or Mukhiya and Ward Members of the Gram Panchayats, they helped the District Administration at every step to obviate the evil of child labour from their soil. Their outreach and knowledge of the population living in their area was a great asset of this campaign.

Rehabilitation Work

On 5th of December 2002, a meeting was called by the DM to consider the rehabilitation work of the children who have been freed. In this meeting it was decided that all the families of the freed child labour will be helped under different government schemes/programmes to improve their economic condition. In this regard the concerned officers were directed to make special arrangements for getting the form filled and get the funds released to the beneficiaries. Following which 71 forms were filled by the family members of the freed child labour under different schemes, such as Bihar State Other Backward Castes Corporation, Special component plan for Scheduled castes and Scheduled Tribes etc. Besides the concerned officers were also directed to facilitate the identified families in getting benefits from other government schemes such as Annapurna, Antayodaya, Scholarships to the needy students and to handicapped children, widow Pension, Old age pension, Protsahan Bhatta, Mid day meal, etc.

In short all concerned official and PRI representatives were asked to strengthen the existing schemes and programmes of the government and ensure that all the needy gets the benefits. A list of all those children, who had either no parents alive or their parents were living in a state of despondency, was also made so that they could be sent to Mukti Ashram of Bachpan Bachao Andolan. Again the committee responsible for freeing the child labour met on 8th of December 2002 at the block office and it was decided that on 12th Decemeber, every *Mukhiya* will take out a padyatra in his/her Panchayat for awareness and sensitization work. The Chairman of the Nagar Panchayat was given the responsibility to take out a similar padyatra on 15th December.

On 10th of December again the DM held a meeting with the managers of different branches of Banks working in the block and guided them to speed up the process of loan sanction to the families of freed child labour under different schemes. She also informed about the decision to set up a Women and Child Development Centre in the Block which will be inaugurated on 17th December 2002, the historic day when Hisua will be officially declared as child labour free block. It was also reported on the occasion that almost all of Hisua has been made Child labour free except for a few who are not at all visible or traceable. This extraordinary achievement was thought to be worth celebrating and on 17th of December 2002 (exactly 100th day after the DVE) the Hisua block of Nawada district will be officially announced as the first "Child Labour Free Block" of the State of Bihar.

In Hisua block, the total number of 291 children were found to be working in hazardous occupation, 117 were working in non-hazardous occupation and 35 were caught while conducting raids. All of these working were set free and were enrolled in the nearby government schools. Besides some more children were also enrolled during the drive. Total number of enrolled children during the campaign is 754.

This commendable accomplishment and the strategy and process adopted for achieving the objective has many overt and covert messages for everyone concerned. The very first lesson according to me would be that "If the District Magistrate of a district wants to lead a campaign against child labour with all the sincerity and genuineness the result won't be difficult to achieve". The second lesson would be that any such campaign against child labour requires the involvement of all the stake holders in the issue, especially the PRIs.

The PRIs have tremendous resources and tapping such resources requires their genuine motivation and regular follow-up. One must also keep in mind that they must be involved from the very first step of the campaign which will make them take the ownership of the campaign and not do this only because some higher authority asked them to do it. The third lesson is the role of the NGOs in the whole campaign. One must keep in mind that the start of the process i.e. DVE was organized by an NGO. Even the initial motivation and sensitivity of Smt. N. Vijayalakshmi (as told) towards child labour issue was generated when she visited the Mukti Ashrams of child labour (run by Bachpan Bachao Andolan) in Delhi and Jaipur.

The awareness building and sensitizational work done by the Mukti Karwan and Bal Chaupal actually formed the very backbone of the whole campaign. The convergent approach which is being applied in the rehabilitational work of the freed child labour also needs special mention. Though it is very early to say anything about the success of this approach in the case of Hisua, according to the DM if "she has to replicate the same campaign in another block she would start applying the convergent approach and rehabilitation work from the very beginning of the whole process".

It was also said that if only all the existing schemes, programmes and services of the government is provided to the deserving beneficiaries then half the battle against the evil of child labour in any block will be over. Most directly linked are the schools and other service system of the government that provides primary education, care and development to the needy children. The very exercise was done in a focused manner and that within target period of hundred days. This, according to the DM, also made every one work with a sense of urgency which bore result in the end. They first of all must become a little sensitive and motivated to do such a novel work. This kind of campaign also requires courage and challenge to get results working in a focused way within a targeted period which everyone must muster before starting on such a campaign.

Beside the position that every DM holds in a district, he/she should be a natural leader with a lot of sincerity and genuineness about the issue, so that he/she could muster the support of one and all by effectively keeping them motivated. The involvement of all the stake holders like all governmental machinery, PRIs, NGOs etc. from the very inception to the very end is also a prerequisite of getting any place free from child labour. Towards the end I must say that this kind of success story is seldom found in the society today. It also shows that how a District Magistrate's initiative can bear fruits within such a limited span of time. Smt. N. Vijayalakshmi and his team of officials in Hisua and Nawada, all the representatives of the PRIs in Hisua block and all the NGOs and individuals who participated in this novel work must be congratulated and it is worth celebrating and aptly being celebrated on the 17th of December 2002, which will go in the history book of this country.

But the actual work will start from 17th of December 2002, because it has to be seen that how the achievement is kept alive and how can the freed child labour be kept away from work in future too. The question of sustainability can only be seen after some time and for that a new assessment will be required to be done. What will happen when the leader of the campaign is not there? Who will keep the light alive? The other stake holders like PRIs and NGOs has all the potential resources of sustaining the campaign's good results.

There are many questions that remain unanswered like what happens to the child workers who come with their migrating parents who work in the brick kiln; what happens to the children who are left behind by the out-migrating parents; what about the children who helps their parents in agarbatti making and other home based work; what about the girl child of the agriculture labour who is left behind to look after their younger siblings when their parents go to work? Such intriguing questions require more in depth studies and time frame, so that such successes of rare nature can be replicated in other places with better knowledge base and experience.

Bihar has decided to use the police to get working children to schools, West Bengal has decided to conduct a survey of child labour, while Delhi has decided to work with NGOs to track and stop child labour. These are some of the responses from various state governments as the ban on child labour entered its second day today. The ban, along with addition of new clauses to the Child Labor (Protection and Regulation) Act, 1986, came into operation yesterday with no indication that it would mean a better tomorrow for the child workforce in the country. The new clauses banning child labor below 14 years in hotels and homes will affect only 5 per cent of this workforce, majority of whom work in agricultural fields. Besides, the ban has no provision for rehabilitation of these children. In Delhi, Business Standard found that the children continued to serve food in roadside *dhabas* and work in houses as domestic helps. "We know about the law, but the boy is 16 years old," a hotel owner in ITO said pointing at a 12 years old serving tea.

At the end of the day, not a single child was removed from his workplace. Delhi Labor Minister Mangal Ram Singhal said, "We have decided to act only on the complaints of NGOs and not on our own." In West Bengal, State Labor Minister Anadi Sahu said the state government was carrying out a survey on the status of child labor in West Bengal. He felt the Centre should come forward in rehabilitating them in alternative avenues. In Bihar, Chief Minister Nitish Kumar seized the opportunity to send back children to school. He has drawn up a plan to use the police to ensure implementation of the ban on child labor by using them to take children to school.

"A meeting chaired by the CM was held last evening where it was decided to take help of the police in bringing street children to schools," Human Resource Development Secretary M M Jha said today. NGOs, while favouring total ban on child labor, have questioned the new notification, pointing at lack of a rehabilitation programme and also absence of any consultation with civil society groups working with children. "How can the Sarva Siksha Abhiyan rehabilitate children? And who will take them to school? Where will they stay for 10 or 15 days before they go to school?" asked Swami Agnivesh of the Bandhua Mukti Morcha.

Sixty one % in Asia, 32% in Africa, and 7% in Latin America, 1% in US, Canada, Europe and other wealthy nations in Asia, 22% of the workforce is children. In Latin America, 17% of the workforce is children. The proportion of child Labourers varies a lot among countries and even regions inside those countries. "In Africa, one child in three is at work, and in Latin America, one child in five works. In both these continents, only a tiny proportion of child workers are involved in the formal sector and the vast majority of work is for their families, in homes, in the fields or on the streets." — UNICEF's 1997 State of the World's Children Report.

Work ranges from taking care of animals and planting and harvesting food, to many kinds of small manufacturing (e.g. of bricks and cement), auto repair, and making of footwear and textiles. More boys than girls work outside their homes. But more girls work in some jobs for instance, as domestic maids. Being a maid in someone's house can be risky. Maids typically are cut off from friends and family, and can easily be physically or sexually abused by their employers. Note: Less than 5% of child Labourers make products for export to other countries. Sources for this statistic include UNICEF's State of the World's Children Report 1997.

Many children in hazardous and dangerous jobs are in danger of injury, even death. Beyond compassion, consider who today's children will become in the future. Between today and the year 2020, the vast majority of new workers, citizens and new consumers — whose skills and needs will build the world's economy and society — will come from developing countries. Over that 20-year period, some 730 million people will join the world's workforce — more than all the people employed in today's most developed nations in 2000. More than 90 per cent of these new workers will be from developing nations, according to research by Population Action International. How many will have had to work at an early age, destroying their health or hampering their education?

Learn about the issue. Support organizations that are raising awareness, and providing direct help to individual children. Four main changes took place:

1. Economic development that raised family incomes and living standards.
2. Widespread, affordable, required and relevant education.
3. Enforcement of anti-child Labour laws (along with compulsory education laws).

4. Changes in public attitudes toward children that elevated the importance of education.

It is a myth that child Labour is only a problem in developing countries. "But in fact, children routinely work in all industrialized countries, and hazardous forms of child labour can be found in many countries. In the US, for example, children are employed in agriculture, a high proportion of them from immigrant or ethnic-minority families.

A 1990 survey of Mexican-American children working in the farms of New York state showed that almost half had worked in fields still wet with pesticides and over a third had themselves been sprayed." It is a myth that child Labour will only disappear when poverty disappears. Hazardous Labour can, and should be eliminated by even the poorest countries.

It is a myth that most child Labourers work in sweatshops making goods for export. "Soccer balls made by children in Pakistan for use by children in industrialized countries may provide a compelling symbol, but in fact, only a very small proportion of all child workers are employed in export industries - probably less than 5 per cent. Most of the world's child labourers actually are to be found in the informal sector - selling on the street, at work in agriculture or hidden away in houses – far from the reach of official labour inspectors and from media scrutiny." It is a myth that "the only way to make headway against child labour is for consumers and governments to apply pressure through sanctions and boycotts.

While international commitment and pressure are important, boycotts and other sweeping measures can only affect export sectors, which are relatively small exploiters of child labour. Such measures are also blunt instruments with long-term consequences that can actually harm rather than help the children involved."

Poverty is widely considered the top reason why children work at inappropriate jobs for their ages. But there are other reasons as well:

- Family expectations and traditions.
- Abuse of the child.
- Lack of good schools and day care.
- Lack of other services, such as health care.
- Public opinion that downplays the risk of early work for children.
- Uncaring attitudes of employers
- Limited choices for women.

"The parents of child labourers are often unemployed or underemployed, desperate for secure employment and income. Yet it is their children - more powerless and paid less - who are offered the jobs. In other words, says UNICEF, children are employed because they are easier to exploit," according to the "Roots of Child Labour" in UNICEF's 1997 State of the World's Children Report. The report also says that international economic trends also have increased child Labour in poor countries. "During the 1980s, in many developing countries, government indebtedness, unwise internal economic policies and recession resulted in economic crisis. Structural adjustment programmes in many countries accentuated cuts in social spending that have hit the poor disproportionately."

Although structural adjustment programs are being revised to spare education from deep cuts, the report says, some countries make such cuts anyway because of their own, local priorities. In many countries public education has deteriorated so much, the report declared, that education itself has become part of the problem — because children work to avoid going to school. Children do some types of low-status work, the report adds, because children come from minority groups or populations that have long suffered discrimination. " In northern Europe, for example, child labourers are likely to be African or Turkish; in Argentina, many are Bolivian or Paraguayan; in Thailand, many are from Myanmar. An increasingly consumer-oriented culture, spurring the desire and expectation for consumer goods, can also lead children into work and away from school."

- Increased family incomes.
- *Education:* That helps children learn skills that will help them earn a living.
- *Social services:* That help children and families survive crises, such as disease, or loss of home and shelter.
- *Family control of fertility:* So that families are not burdened by children.

The ILO's International Programme for the Elimination of Child Labour (IPEC) has explored many programs to help child Labourers. The 1989 Convention on the Rights of the Child calls for children to participate in important decisions that will affect their lives. Some educators and social scientists believe that one of the most important ways to help child workers is to ask their opinions, and involve them in constructing "solutions" to their own problems.

6

Human Rights and Child Labour

It is indisputable. Child labour is a human rights problem, and increasingly recognized as such the world over as well it ought. Of the approximately 246 million children between ages 5 and 17 estimated by the International Labour Organization (ILO) to be engaged in "child labour," large though we define "child labour" as defined in CHILD LABOUR AND HUMAN RIGHTS: MAKING CHILDREN MATTER [hereinafter "CHILD LABOUR AND HUMAN RIGHTS"], to wit, as work done by children that is harmful to them because it is abusive, exploitative, hazardous, or otherwise contrary to their best interests—a subset of a larger class of children's work, some of which may be compatible with children's best interests (variously expressed as "beneficial," "benign," or "harmless" children's work).

In this, the ILO defines "child labour" to mean all "economically active children" except "children 12 years and older who are working only a few hours each week in permitted light work" and "children 15 years and above whose work is not classified as 'hazardous.'" The ILO's estimate of 246 million children engaged in child labour, however, cannot be called exact. Indeed, because so much child labour takes place in the informal sector, such a verdict probably is impossible. At the same time, as a general proposition, the reported overall dimension of the problem and its regional distribution cannot be summarily dismissed.

Of the 352 million children between 5-14 years of age that the ILO estimates to be engaged in "economic activity" worldwide (a broader concept than "child labour"), the Asian Pacific region is said to have the largest number (127 million); sub-Saharan Africa the second largest concentration (48 million); and Latin America and the Caribbean the third largest (17 million), followed by the Middle East and North Africa (approximately 13 million). The remaining 5 million "economically active" children are reported to be found in both developed and transitional economies. It is not unreasonable to extrapolate "child labour" proportions and distributions of rough equivalence.

They can be found in brick factories, carpet weaving centers, fishing platforms, leather tanning shops, mines, and other hazardous places, often as cogs in the global economy. They can be found—most abundantly—in domestic service, vulnerable to sexual and other indignities that escape public scrutiny and accountability. They can be found on the streets as prostitutes, forced to trade in sex against their will. They can be found as soldiers in life-threatening conflict situations. Working long hours under exploitative conditions, often beaten or otherwise abused, and commonly trafficked from one country to another, they are unable to obtain the education that can liberate and improve their lives; their health is severely threatened from years of exposure to hazardous material; many, if they survive, are deformed and disabled before they can mature physically, mentally, or emotionally. Such are the brute facts. Before the 1989 United Nations Convention on the Rights of the Child (CRC), however, the problem of child labour, even in its worst forms, was seldom addressed as a human rights problem.

The practice of the ILO over the years, though long nobly sensitive and attentive to the needs and wants of immediate importance to most people, is illustrative. Reflecting the ILO's traditional labour market perspective, no ILO convention addressing issues of child labour prior to the 1989 CRC couched its provisions in the language of rights, let alone mentioned "human rights," to define its mission or achieve its goals—not even ILO Convention (No. 29) Concerning Forced or Compulsory Labour (ILO C29), nor ILO Convention (No. 105) Concerning the Abolition of Forced Labour (ILO C105), nor ILO Convention (No. 138) Concerning Minimum Age for Admission to Employment (ILO C138).

The first of these important law-making initiatives, concluded in 1930, may perhaps be excused for having been adopted before human rights law began to be taken seriously in world affairs, beginning with the 1945 Charter of the United Nations and the 1948 Universal Declaration of Human Rights (UDHR). But not so the latter two treaties, concluded in 1957 and 1973, respectively, and joining a long list of ILO conventions that address all sorts of worker issues without engaging human rights discourse. The reason seems clear. Although its roots can be traced to antiquity, the idea of human rights is relatively new on the world stage; and, as everyone knows, social change—especially progressive social change—ordinarily takes place slowly, the more so in a context where, both nationally and internationally, command and enforcement mechanisms familiar to mature legal systems are relatively lacking. Thus, even today a human rights understanding of child labour is not widespread.

Yet there are prices to be paid—often steep prices—for human rights myopia or quiescence. As James Gross has observed regarding worker rights specifically: "This lack of [human rights] attention has contributed to workers being seen as expendable in worldwide economic development and their needs and concerns not being represented at conferences on the world economy dominated by bankers, finance ministers, and multinational corporations." It is important to acknowledge, however, that, since the adoption of the 1989 CRC and particularly the 1999 ILO Convention (No. 182) Concerning the Prohibition and Immediate Elimination of the Worst Forms of Child Labour (ILO C182), a commitment to the abolition of child labour as a human rights imperative has taken hold and begun to spread (albeit still too slowly in our judgment).

Key intergovernmental organizations (IGOs) working in the field now actively affirm the link between child labour and human rights—most prominently, even if sometimes equivocally, the ILO and the United Nations Children's Fund (UNICEF). Also committed to a rights-based approach to child labour is the World Health Organization (WHO) whose Department of Child and Adolescent Health and Development (CAH) recognizes that the basic health needs of children and adolescents are fundamental human rights dependent for their protection and fulfillment on the realization of other rights such as "freedom from all forms of exploitation."

Human rights orientations to child labour are now found also, even more conspicuously, among nongovernmental organizations (NGOs) working in this field—for example, Anti-Slavery International (formerly the Anti-Slavery Society) in respect of an estimated 8 million children suffering in slavery and slave-like circumstances worldwide; the London-based International Save the Children Alliance, established in 1919 but principally focused on child labour in the last decade; and Global March Against Child Labour, begun in 1998 and now headquartered in New Delhi. Also noteworthy: Amnesty International relative to child soldiering; the Children's Rights Division of Human Rights Watch, largely focused on forced and bonded child labour; and Defence for

Children International. Certain regional and local NGOs, too, have become well known for combating child labour from a rights-based perspective—Child Workers in Asia as just one example.

The same is true of some national governments as well. Thus, both alone and in growing combination, variously specialized IGOs and NGOs, increasingly in collaboration with national governments, have in recent years placed child labour, especially its worst forms, high among their concerns and in the process confirmed its human rights standing. Perhaps not coincidentally, these organizations also have begun to achieve some discernible progress. But not nearly enough. The circumstance of abused and exploited children remains huge and grotesque—and sometimes seemingly intractable. Why? A primary explanation resides, of course, in the array of economic and political forces worldwide— mostly though not exclusively nationally or locally based—whose various interests are served not by the elimination or reduction of child labour but by its perpetuation and proliferation. But let us be very clear: child labour exists also because, except for a valiant few, the world's governing elites have yet to discover not just the political and economic will that is needed to surmount the problem but, as well, the comprehensive understanding of it upon which solutions adequate to its abolition depend—a critical deficit because such understanding is essential for the vision that is needed to energize the grand will that so far is lacking.

This essay, like the collection from which it is drawn, is intended to help offset this deficit. To this end, it therefore is premised on the following five interrelated propositions: *first*, that child labour—work done by children that is harmful to them for being abusive, exploitative, hazardous, or otherwise contrary to their best interests—constitutes a major blight on human civility and welfare worldwide; *second*, that it therefore begs to be abolished by all who profess ethical-moral conscience and/or pragmatic self-interest in the well-being of present and future generations; *third,* that it manifests itself in complex and diverse ways and thus requires both coextensive (multidisciplinary, multifaceted, and multisectoral) and singly focused approaches and techniques to achieve its eradication in whole or in part; *fourth,* that these approaches and techniques must be informed by frank recognition that no form or level of social organization can claim "business as usual"—i.e., exemption from meaningful, even fundamental change—if the goal of abolition is genuinely to succeed in situations large or small over time; and *fifth,* that such change and the benefits to human dignity that can flow from it are not likely to be achieved except episodically without a dedicated and ongoing commitment to the contextual application of human rights law and policy, including the right of children to have a say about their own lives.

The time is long overdue when, from the most local to the most global circumstance, the rights of working children—not just their needs—must be taken seriously into account in the making and shaping of agendas pertinent to their lives, and especially, of course, when such agendas affect them directly.

A Multidimensional Human Rights Problem

As asserted at the outset of our Introduction, the problem of child labour is indisputably a human rights problem. We reaffirm this claim. The brute facts substantiate it. So does the law. Consider, for starters, the 1966 International Covenant on Economic, Social and Cultural Rights (ICESCR), Article 10(3) of which provides in part as follows: Children and young persons should be protected from economic and social exploitation. Their employment in work harmful to their morals or health or dangerous to life or likely to hamper their normal development should be punishable by law.

States should also set age limits below which the paid employment of child labour should be prohibited and punishable by law. Consider also the 1989 CRC, so widely adopted (more so than any other human rights compact in history) that it may be said to have entered into customary international law.

Article 32(1) of the Convention is explicit: States Parties recognize the right of the child to be protected from economic exploitation and from performing any work that is likely to be hazardous or to interfere with the child's education, or to be harmful to the child's health or physical, mental, spiritual, moral or social development. Article 32(2), requiring the states parties to take "legislative, administrative, social and educational measures" in respect of the foregoing, gives formal muscle to this human rights injunction. Also to the point, albeit less explicitly, is 1999 ILO C182. In its Preamble, it recalls, *inter alia*, the 1989 CRC, the 1998 ILO Declaration on Fundamental Principles and Rights at Work, and the 1956 United Nations Supplementary Convention on the Abolition of Slavery, the Slave Trade, and Institutions and Practices Similar to Slavery.

Thus it predicates its prohibitions of child labour's "worst forms" on a human rights framework, at least in part. But particularly instructive, especially when accounting for the most egregious forms of child labour, are multiple additional provisions of the 1989 CRC, among them:

- *Article 3*, requiring the states parties, "in all actions concerning children," to ensure "the best interests of the child," including "such protection and care as is necessary for his or her wellbeing";
- *Article 6*, requiring the states parties to ensure "to the maximum extent possible the survival and development of the child";
- *Article 8*, requiring the states parties to respect "the

right of the child to preserve his or her identity, including . . . name and family relations";

- *Article 9*, requiring the states parties to ensure that, unless otherwise provided by law, "a child shall not be separated from his or her parents against their will";
- *Article 11*, requiring the states parties "to combat the illicit transfer and non-return of children abroad";
- *Article 12*, requiring the states parties to assure that "the child who is capable of forming his or her own views the right to express those views freely in all matters affecting the child," including "in any judicial and administrative proceedings affecting the child";
- *Article 13*, safeguarding the right of children to "freedom of expression," including "freedom to seek, receive, and impart information and ideas of all kinds";
- *Article 15*, recognizing the right of children to "freedom of association" and "peaceful assembly";
- *Article 16*, protecting children against "arbitrary or unlawful interference with his or her privacy, family, home or correspondence";
- *Article 18*, requiring parents to assume "common" and "primary" responsibility for "the upbringing and development of the child," guided by "the best interests of the child";
- *Article 19*, requiring the states parties "to protect the child from all forms of physical or mental violence, injury or abuse, neglect or negligent treatment, maltreatment or exploitation, including sexual abuse";
- *Article 24*, recognizing "the right of the child to the enjoyment of the highest attainable standard of health";
- *Article 25*, recognizing "for every child the right to benefit from Social security";
- *Article 27*, recognizing "the right of every child to a standard of living adequate for the child's physical, mental, spiritual, moral and social development";

- *Article 28,* recognizing "the right of the child to education";
- *Article 31,* recognizing "the right of the child to rest and leisure";
- *Article 34,* requiring the states parties "to protect the child from all forms of sexual exploitation and sexual abuse";
- *Article 35,* requiring the states parties "to prevent the abduction of, the sale of or traffic in children for any purpose or in any form";
- *Article 36,* requiring the states parties to protect the child "against all other forms of exploitation prejudicial to any aspect of the child's welfare";
- *Article 37,* protecting children against "cruel, inhuman or degrading treatment"; and
- *Article 38,* requiring state parties "to ensure that persons who have not attained the age of fifteen years do not take direct part in hostilities" and to "refrain from recruiting any person who has not attained the age of fifteen years into their armed forces."

The 1989 CRC thus recognizes the factual truth that the problem of child labour is not only a human rights problem, simply put, but a human rights problem that, defying narrow monolithic definition, is multidisciplinary, multifaceted, and multisectoral—in a word, multidimensional. It recognizes it to involve practices that violate children's rights both directly (e.g., slavery) and—more commonly— indirectly (e.g., compulsory labour that results in denial of the right to education) and, beyond that (i.e., in addition to children's rights *per se*), to implicate the broader panoply of entitlements across the whole spectrum of rights with which, at least in theory, *all* members of the human family (children included) are endowed—i.e., the three "generations" of rights that have evolved since at least the English Bill of Rights of 1689 to the present day:

1. Civil and Political rights;
2. Economic, Social, and Cultural rights; and, most recently,
3. Community (or "Solidarity") group rights.

Each has its own historical roots that track the evolution of modern industrial society, including the development of a labour class. Each is thus linked to the problem of child labour in one or more of its manifestations, including such third generation rights as the right to peace, the right to development, and the right to a clean and healthy environment. The exploitative employment of trafficked children for commercial sexual acts, for example, flouts the right to the security of one's person, ergo first generation civil and political rights.

The exposure of working children to toxic and otherwise hazardous substances infringes directly upon the human right to health, ergo second generation economic, social, and cultural rights. Child soldiering subverts not only the first generation right to security of one's person but, likewise, the group right to peace, ergo third generation community (or solidarity) rights. Indeed, few provisions of the three historic instruments that constitute the "International Bill of Human Rights"—the 1948 UDHR, the 1966 ICESCR, and the 1966 ICCPR —are unaffected by the problem of child labour.

This is particularly apparent when one conceives of human rights in terms of "human capabilities" in the manner of Martha Nussbaum and Amartya Sen; that is, by reference less to abstract wants (policy objectives) than to concrete and measurable needs (life functions) —e.g., life itself; bodily health and bodily integrity; senses, imagination, and thought; emotions; conscience; affiliation *qua* friendship and respect; and political and material control over one's environment. It is impossible to disassociate the problem of child labour, especially its worst forms, from any one of these most central of human capabilities and therefore, as well, from any of their human rights correlatives. A mere glance at the 1948 UDHR proves the comparative point. But it is not only the multidimensionality of the child labour problem that reveals its human rights linkages.

Also highly relevant is its interrelatedness with the human rights of the parents or guardians of working children, a point well understood by, for example, UNICEF, which works to advance the rights of children and of women—qua mothers—in tandem.

The safeguarding of children's rights depends not merely on the promotion and protection of their rights, but on the promotion and protection of the fundamental human rights of their parents or guardians as well, and "without distinction of any kind, such as race, colour, sex, language, religion, political or other opinion, national or social origin, property, birth or other status." Denying parents or guardians their human rights contributes to the propagation or perpetuation of child labour and thereby denials of the rights of children. In sum, the nexus between child labour and human rights is both broad and deep. That a number of states, intergovernmental institutions, and nongovernmental organizations engaged in the struggle against child labour have adopted or begun to adopt rights-based policies to prosecute its abolition is thus not surprising.

Still, as previously and hereinafter noted, a commitment to a rights-based approach to child labour is not yet common in official policy or practice. Skeptics assert that rights-based approaches to social ills such as child labour lack pragmatism because, it is sometimes said, they focus on unrealistic, aspirational norms that have little or no connection to the "real world." Indeed, some suggest that, in respect of child labour at least, human rights approaches tend to be counterproductive and, more generally, that the international human rights movement is part of the problem, not the solution. We demur and contest these claims in Section I.B, *infra*.

While the skeptics certainly have some valid points (the human rights movement is, after all, a human—ergo imperfect—project), there is no denying that a rights-based approach to child labour, especially when conceived and executed from a multidimensional, holistic perspective, has strong pragmatic underpinnings and thus can have substantial beneficial results. One can point to numerous instances in which human rights discourse and strategy have had real impact, including in the area of child labour. Given the continued skepticism, however, it behooves us to explain why, and to explain also why the skeptics are mistaken.

Human Rights Approach to Child Labour

Why is it important to think and act upon the problem of child labour as a human rights problem? What purposes are served by such an approach?

Human Rights as "Trumps"

In his germinal book, *Taking Rights Seriously*, legal philosopher Ronald Dworkin asserts unequivocally—and correctly—that when a claimed value or good is categorized as a "right" it "trumps" most if not all other claimed values or goods. Rights discourse confers a special status of importance on claimed entitlements, juridically more elevated than commonplace "standards" or "laws" which, in contrast to "human rights," are subject to everyday revision and recision for lack of such ordination. A proximate analogy is the distinction between a contractual or statutory claim and a constitutional one. Thus, when child labour is designated as a condition from which children have a *right* to be free, not merely an option for which regulating (but comparatively easily revocable) *standards* must be devised, there results an opportunity for empowerment and mobilization that otherwise is lacking.

A rights-based approach to child labour elevates the "needs" and "interests" of children in this context to societal needs and interests—societal goods—with associated claims of legal and political legitimacy. As UNICEF's 1997 State of the World's Children report characterized the organization's strategic decision to use rights to reduce child labour: "The idea that children have special needs has given way to the conviction that children have rights, the same full spectrum of rights as adults: civil and political, social, cultural and economic." Or as UNICEF put it two years later in its 1999 State of the World's Children report: "What were once seen as the needs of children have been elevated to something far harder to ignore: their rights." In other words, rights are not matters of charity, a question of favor or kindness, to be bestowed or taken away at will.

They are high-level public order values or goods that carry with them a sense of entitlement on the part of the rights-holder and obligatory implementation on the part of the rights protector— inter-governmental institutions, the state, society, the family. They are values or goods deemed fundamental and universal; and, while not absolute, they are nonetheless judged superior to other claimed values or goods. To assert a *right* of a child to be free from abusive, exploitative, and hazardous work is, thus, to strengthen a child's possibility for a life of dignity and well-being. It bespeaks duty, not optional—often capricious—benevolence.

Interdependent Agents of Human Dignity

Central to the concept of human rights is the notion of a "public order of human dignity," a public order (*ordre publique*) "in which values are shaped and shared more by persuasion than by coercion, and which seeks to promote the greatest production and widest possible sharing, without discriminations irrelevant of merit, of all values among all human beings." This notion of public order, encapsulating "the basic policies of an international law of human dignity," is embedded in the 1948 UDHR which, in its Preamble, proclaims the concept of human rights to grow out of "recognition of the inherent dignity . . . of all members of the human family" as "the foundation of freedom, justice and peace in the world." Thus, in the struggle against child labour, a rights-based approach signals more than the alleviation of child abuse and exploitation *per se*.

It signals also that notions of nondiscrimination and justice and dignity must be central in all aspects of a working child's life, including provision for her or his education, health, and spiritual, moral, or social development—precisely as the 1989 CRC envisions. A rights-based approach to the child labour problem is part of a complex web of interdependent rights that extends protection beyond one domain to many others in a child's life. Most if not all human rights (e.g., the right to be free from inhumane labour practices) depend on the satisfaction of other human rights (e.g., the right to education) for their fulfillment. Treating freedom from abusive, exploitative, and hazardous child work as a human right thus raises the stakes against those who would put children in harm's way. It transforms the struggle *against* child labour into a struggle *for* human dignity and thus better captures responsible attention and heightened pressure in the search for enduring solutions.

Mobilizing Challenge to Statist and Elitist Agendas

Because they trump lesser societal values or goods and because they are agents of human dignity, human rights challenge and make demands upon state sovereignty. Scores of human rights conventions entered into force since World War II require states actually to cede bits of sovereignty in the name of human rights. Legal obligations of great solemnity, the 1989 CRC and 1999 ILO C182 are among them. Proof is found, too, in the many occasions in which states, international governmental institutions, NGOs, transnational professional associations, corporations, trade unions, churches, and others have relied successfully on this "*corpus juris* of social justice" to measure and curb state behaviour. The legitimacy of political regimes—hence their capacity to govern non-coercively or at all— is today judged by criteria informed and refined by human rights.

All of this is well known. Keenly aware of their interdependencies, most states, however much they may resist human rights pressures from within and without, are mindful that their national interests and desired self-image depend on their willingness to play by the rules and especially those rules that weigh heavily on the scales of social and political morality. Even the most powerful states are thus vulnerable to what has come to be called "the mobilization of shame" in defense of human rights. The case of apartheid South Africa is perhaps the best known in this regard. There is no reason why states that encourage or tolerate abusive, exploitative, and hazardous child work cannot or should not be similarly targeted and shamed. But not only states.

For the same reasons that human rights challenge and make demands upon state sovereignty, so also do they challenge and make demands upon the particularist agendas of private elites. Why? Because human rights have as their core value the value of respect, by definition possessed equally by all human beings everywhere. They insist upon equality of treatment across the board. Writes Virginia Leary, "[e]quality or non-discrimination . . . is a leitmotif running through all of international human rights law." True, no observant person would dispute the widespread disregard of these principles.

Still, there is no denying the potential power of human rights discourse and strategy to stand up, dare, and defy the special economic and political interests, private as well as public, that, usually for selfish reasons, dismiss the equal treatment of all human beings and thus contribute to social ills such as child labour. In sum, ordinary norms, institutions, and procedures are not defined, typically, by the language of human rights and therefore do not have the same *gravitas* as their human rights counterparts. They therefore do not carry with them the same moral authority upon which, in democratic societies at least, governing elites depend to exercise and retain legitimacy and power. The potential for human rights discourse and strategy to dislodge or seriously burden those private exclusive interests that help to perpetuate child labour is likewise manifest.

Human Rights as Empowerment for Children

As noted, human rights carry with them a sense of entitlement on the part of the rights-holder. Indeed, human rights law embraces not only this sense of entitlement, but also "the right of the individual to know and act upon his [sic] rights," hence a sense of duty and redress on the part of the state and other actors. The essence of rights discourse (or human rights law) is that, in Michael Freeman's pointed alert, "if you have a right to x, and you do not get x, this is not only a wrong, but it is a wrong against *you*." This extends inexorably to children as rights-holders. CRC Article 12 expressly requires that states parties "assure to the child the right to express [her or his] views freely in all matters affecting the child" and that "the views of the child [be] given due weight" At least four specific ways have been identified by which human rights accomplish this empowerment.

Each bear obvious relevance to children and others who seek the abolition of child labour. *First,* human rights provide a level of accountability that transcends that of other legal obligations. Like those obligations, human rights provide victims of rights violations with the authority to hold violators accountable, even to the point of criminal liability. However, because human rights entail fundamental values of "superior" moral order, their violation correspondingly entails greater moral condemnation than other wrongs. This is what distinguishes "rights" from "benefits" or from being the beneficiary of another's obligation, and thus what makes possible, for example, "the mobilization of shame" and the condemnation of the international community, commonly without even having to go to formal court.

The "truth and reconciliation" processes of Argentina, Chile, El Salvador, Ghana, Guatemala, Haiti, Malawi, Nepal, Nigeria, The Phillipines, Serbia and Montenegro, South Africa, South Korea, and elsewhere are proof enough. On occasion, they can be more effective than their more formal legal counterparts in overcoming impunity. *Second,* human rights provide access to international institutions dedicated specifically to their promotion and vindication, including the human rights mechanisms of the United Nations and the regional human rights regimes of Europe, the Americas, and Africa. The effectiveness of these institutions as enforcement mechanisms is not consistent and often cumbersome and time-consuming, particularly at the global level. Nevertheless, they confirm that human suffering is and can be taken seriously, providing formal legal tools to remedy or otherwise mitigate abuses and thereby help to prevent future abuse. Like less formal techniques (e.g., a civil society mobilization of shame), their use can result in both specific and general deterrence, potentially ensuring individual and group rights. *Third,* human rights generate legal grounds for political activity and expression because, as already noted, they entail greater moral force than ordinary legal obligations.

This is abundantly seen in the many global and regional conferences and other gatherings commonly called under the auspices of the United Nations (including the U.N.'s former Commission on Human Rights) and such regional organizations as the Council of Europe, the Organization of American States, and the African Union, each providing a forum in which the voices of human rights victims and advocates can be heard. The history of the anti-apartheid movement is replete with examples. Also illustrative are the annual conferences of the ILO and the high-level meetings of UNICEF and other intergovernmental organizations. All contribute to political empowerment, from the adoption of new resolutions and treaties to the recommendation of new norms and mechanisms to the reinterpretation of existing international and domestic norms and procedures—according to which, in Mary Robinson's pithy characterization of the 1989 CRC, "[t]he more fortunate are called upon to assist the less fortunate as an internationally recognized responsibility."

In turn, the resulting rights vocabulary and action plans help to refine the theoretical and operational foundations for human rights projects of all sorts, reinforced by the authority with which the sponsoring organizations and attending participants are regarded. *Finally,* human rights discourse and strategy, which exist to promote and protect human capabilities of all sorts, encourage the creation of initiatives both within and beyond civil society that are designed to facilitate the meeting of "basic needs." Excepting the 1975 Helsinki Accords, such initiatives were not easy to find before the fall of the Berlin Wall in 1989 when tensions sacrificed these concerns on the altar of Cold War rivalries. But since then they have proliferated, especially in the human rights advocacy and scholarly communities. All of which is of profound importance because the provision of basic needs provides the material basis for people to act on their rights—the very definition of empowerment. Despite the relevance of these (and possibly other) forms of empowerment to children and others who seek child labour's abolition, however, some scholars question whether they can in fact extend to children. Onora O'Neill, for one, is skeptical because "[y]ounger children are completely and unavoidably dependent on those [adults] who have power over their lives."

Beyond perhaps the first six to eight years of childhood, we respectfully disagree, as would also most modern anthropologists, historians, and sociologists of childhood. While usually dependent on adults when very young, children are no longer "completely and unavoidably" dependent on them as they mature in age and experience. In fact, children may exhibit considerable independence and self-initiative well before adolescence. Their growing independence may be collective as well as individual. As Michael Freeman has argued, "there are prototypes or at least germs of children's movements already in existence." Indeed, children's movements have long been noted among working children. In early 20th century American cities, for example, the self-organization of child newspaper vendors to defend what they saw as their interests and rights attracted much public attention, and in some places was even supported by far-sighted and creative city officials who linked it to public child protection mechanisms.

Present-day working children's organizations and movements in Africa, Asia, and Latin America have been amply noted and discussed in recent literature, among them organizations linked in an international children's movement (the World Movement of Working Children and Adolescents) which maintains contact between countries and has had two international "summit" conferences, the first in 1996, the most recent in Berlin in April-May 2004, organized with adult assistance. The "Final Declaration" from the latter summit, in which the assembled working children reaffirmed their commitment to "practice protagonism" and fight for "recognition as social actors so that our voices be heard in the whole world," is noteworthy: "We value our work and view it as an important human right for our personal development. We oppose every kind of exploitation and reject everything that hurts our moral and physical integrity. . . . [W]e reaffirm our will to continue constructing a world movement that not only fights for, defends and promotes the rights of working children, but of children in general." In addition, *non*-working children have organized specifically to combat child labour.

A prominent example is the Free the Children network founded by Canadian youth Craig Kielberger, the work and motto of which ("Often assumed to be the leaders of tomorrow, our generation must be the leaders of today") also challenge skepticism of the sort expressed by O'Neill. Further, the Global March Against Child Labour, while an adult-led initiative to mobilize international opinion against child labour, includes ample opportunity for the participation of both working and non-working children to make their views known. At the Children's World Congress on Child Labour organized by Global March in Florence in mid-May 2004, some 200 young persons from 10 to 17 shared their opinions and perspectives and supported the creation of a "network for worldwide, youth-driven action to press international and national efforts towards integrating world resources and responses on poverty, child labour, and education, [including] the development of strategies to enhance national support for implementation of ILO conventions 138 and 182, as well as the 2015 commitment for education for all children."

To be sure, there is room for debate over the extent to which children can or should be selfempowered, as evidenced by the manner in which the above-noted Berlin and Florence events were organized and conducted—the first primarily by working children, the latter primarily by adults. The fact remains, however, that children—including working children—are today demonstrating increasing resolve to assert their own interests and to do so as a self-conscious expression of their universal civil and political rights to access and participate in the decision-making and policy-implementing processes that affect their lives. Indeed, direct involvement by children in the defense and promotion of their interests and rights often is key to the validity and vitality of their claims.

They are themselves often the best witnesses to the harm that results from violations of their rights and thus are uniquely well-positioned to provide the most compelling evidence of the need for redress. Which is why, of course, the 1989 and human rights values generally mandate the right of children to express their views freely and where it counts? Empowerment of children is not only a result of a rights-based approach to child labour, it is, subject to their evolving capacities, virtually a requirement of it.

Contesting Resistance to Human Rights Strategy

However manifest the premise and virtues of a human rights approach to the problem of child labour, our advocacy of it would be incomplete were we not to confront the conceptual, psycho-social barriers that all too commonly are mounted to resist human rights agendas and thwart their potential often from the start (testimony, of course, to the potential of human rights law and policy in the first place). In the ensuing subsections, therefore, we respond to these conceptual barriers and to the vested interests that cluster behind them.

Also, believing that there is nothing as practical as a good theory except the debunking of bad theory, we urge that human rights vis-à-vis child labour be taken seriously and actualized in everyday planning and programming. This may seem an obvious or even redundant thing to say, but it is important to appreciate completely the artfulness of one's detractors in order to weigh in confidently with a human rights orientation to child labour and thereby reap fully its benefits in the making of daily decision and policy. Much hangs in the balance.

There is no disputing that the state has diminished in relative influence in the last half century. Nevertheless, the classical international law doctrine of territorial sovereignty and its corollary of nonintervention remain the central props of our inherited state-centric system of world order. The values associated with these doctrines, however—a legal license to "do your own thing" and an injunction to "mind your own business"—resist the values associated with human rights, which tell us that "you are your brothers' and sisters' keeper" and therefore invite international scrutiny and outside interference in what otherwise would be internal matters. In other words, "human rights qualify state sovereignty and power," and as a consequence governments are naturally resistant to embracing the language of human rights, let alone rights-based agendas. Even governments that have voluntarily consented to human rights treaties, such as the 1989 CRC and 1999 ILO C182, are inclined to demur when it comes to implementation.

However, it is disingenuous of them to tarry when they have committed officially to these legal promises. More importantly, after more than a half-century of mounting international rejection of the claim that "the king can do no wrong," it is no longer tenable for them to do so—least of all when, as in the case of the CRC and ILO C182, the treaty obligations involved command the support of the vast majority of the world's states. In short, a sovereignty defense against human rights violations, particularly of the worst sort, is now, at least theoretically, a thing of the past. To be sure, the radical foundation upon which the scaffolding of contemporary international human rights law and policy has been erected is yet new and fragile. But as evidenced on at least the formal agendas of most international institutions and foreign offices, to say nothing of the agendas of global civil society, the world no longer deems impunity from human rights wrongs acceptable.

The Claimed Sanctity of Corporate Sovereignty

Also explaining resistance to a rights-based approach to child labour is what may be called "corporate sovereignty." Just as states seek to control the territory and populations of their claimed jurisdictions, so business enterprises, in pursuit of market shares and profits, seek sovereignty over the means of production that principally define their more or less private jurisdictions (including of course their labour forces). Human rights agendas, however, tend to be costly and otherwise inconvenient to this fundamental objective and thus often are downplayed or ignored. Not infrequently, business enterprises actively resist human rights agendas—as when, for example, to curry favor with host governments, they break sanctions against repressive regimes, cooperate with such regimes economically, or lend them internal political support of some kind. In these circumstances especially, human rights discourse itself is avoided lest it encourage outside scrutiny, possibly intervention.

True, many—perhaps most—business enterprises strive to be "good corporate citizens" and thus to accept if not actually promote human rights agendas when called upon to do so. True also, corrupt governmental practices often force business enterprises to comply with discriminatory and otherwise repressive legislation. Still, the impulse of corporate sovereignty remains a powerful deterrent to a rights-based strategy opposed to abusive, exploitative, and hazardous child work, especially when large-scale enterprises with great influence are involved. Corporate sovereignty, however, is an impulse to which public policy need not and should not always defer.

Throughout the world, governments adopt and enforce laws to limit factory emissions, regulate product content and safety, set minimum wages, establish occupational workplace standards, and the like. Indeed, labour conditions may be the most heavily regulated of business matters. Business enterprises should not therefore expect that a grotesque problem such as child labour should be subject to any less scrutiny and control. Nor should they, in their own self-interest, want such an outcome. Most business enterprises care more about respected and stable production and marketing climates than they do about ideology, and the surest way to guarantee that such climates prevail is to safeguard the fundamental rights of the populations on which they depend for economic reward.

Irrelevance of Public International Law to Private Actors

Closely related to notions of state and corporate sovereignty as explanations for resistance to a rights-based approach to child labour—indeed supportive of them—is the orthodox theory that, by definition, public international law applies only to public—not private—actors. Given that the vast majority of the world's working children labour on behalf of private—not public—actors, this theory is of no small consequence to the present discussion. Public international law (which includes international human rights law) simply does not apply, so the argument goes, to private business associations, including ones that employ children. Of course, theories are but intellectual paradigms, prototypes of thought that define not only what we look at but also how we go about looking at what we look at. They do not necessarily mirror reality. So when the facts of life no longer fit the theory, it is time, as Copernicus taught us, to change the theory.

In recent years, feminist scholars have urged this kind of rethinking successfully relative to the theoretical structure of international law, particularly in relation to the status of women internationally. There is no reason why the same cannot be done relative to the status of working children in private business enterprises, making such enterprises directly accountable to international human rights norms relevant to them. In any event, there is UDHR Article 30: "Nothing in this Declaration may be interpreted as implying for any State, *group or person* any right to engage in any activity or to perform any act aimed at the destruction of any of the rights and freedoms set forth herein." Additionally, reflecting an emerging consensus that the large economic and political power of at least multinational corporations must be subjected to heightened international accountability, the U.N. Global Compact launched by Secretary- General Kofi Annan in 1999, the former U.N. Commission on Human Rights, and the U.N. High Commissioner for Human Rights, as well as growing numbers of legal scholars now urge theories of international transparency and responsibility that rewrite the relationship between international law and the private sector, including in relation to human rights.

As key beneficiaries of the new economic world order created by international law (e.g., the WTO, NAFTA, etc.), private business enterprises have no standing, it is appropriately argued, to claim immunity from the corresponding obligations established by international law; and trends in actual decision, both national and international, suggest that human rights responsibilities on the part of private persons are being increasingly recognized and enforced. Expressly or by implication, many of the most fundamental human rights instruments recognize human rights obligations on the part of private actors *per se*, while others and cognate treaties require states parties to ensure and enforce the rights enumerated against violations by private perpetrators. States often adopt laws giving domestic effect to human rights norms and standing to seek redress for their violation by private actors.

And, with increasing frequency, corporations commit themselves at least morally to human rights obligations via voluntary "codes of conduct" while consumers and other members of civil society invoke non-juridical mechanisms to hold private actors accountable by voting with their pocketbooks and otherwise mobilizing shame against private human rights violators. True, legal scholars differ over the extent to which developments such as these confer "international legal personality" upon corporations and other non-state actors. Moreover, old canons die hard. But resistance to a rights-based approach to child labour can no longer be justified on the basis of orthodox theory about the "subjects" and "objects" of international law. The world is now far too interpenetrating a place for that.

The Claimed Indeterminacy of Human Rights

Some scholars criticize the language of human rights as lacking conceptual clarity, noting that there are conflicting schools of thought as to what constitutes a right and how to define human rights. For this reason, they claim the concept to be "indeterminate" and therefore distrust its capacity to address pragmatic, "real world" social ills effectively or at all. They observe that there are many unresolved theoretical questions about rights: "whether the individual is the only bearer of rights" (in contradistinction to such entities as families, groups of common ethnicity, religion, or language, communities, and nations); "whether rights are to be regarded as . . . constraints on goal-seeking action or as parts of a goal that is to be promoted"; "whether rights—thought of as justified entitlements—are correlated with duties"; and, not least, "what rights are understood to be rights to" —a certain level of well-being? a certain access to certain resources in one's life pursuit? a certain quality of opportunity in that pursuit?

The recent debate over "Asian values" and its underlying tension between cultural relativist and Universalist approaches to human rights make clear that all this questioning is no idle intellectual chatter. It is very much present in the political arena as well and thus serves as another possible explanation for resistance to a rights-base approach to child labour. The claimed indeterminacy of "human rights," however, is less problematic than perceived. The core of the human rights concept is as well-defined and clearly articulated as any social or legal norm, a fact proven by the numerous widely accepted—and increasingly enforced—human rights norms already noted.

Moreover, even conceding that unresolved theoretical issues relating to human rights remain, this fact should not be allowed to distract from the broadest and most effective actualization of the fundamental principles and values on which there is virtually universal agreement—for example, the right of children to be free from abusive, exploitative, and hazardous labour. Thus, while the concept or language of rights, like most legal language, sometimes suffers ambiguity, it is not to be discarded in the anti-child labour struggle (or any other) simply for this reason. Rather, as with any human—i.e., incomplete and imperfect—system, one must make use of those elements that are established and effective while working to finalize and perfect those that remain vague or incomplete, just as we do all other legal norms as a matter of course all the time.

Perhaps the most confounding of the alleged unresolved theoretical issues about human rights is the claimed absence of a theory to justify human rights. In the presence of ongoing philosophical and political controversy about the existence, nature, and application of human rights in a multicultured world, a world in which Christian natural law justifications for human rights are now widely deemed obsolete, one must exercise caution when adopting a human rights approach to social policy lest one be accused of cultural imperialism. It is not enough to say, argues Michael Freeman, that human beings possess human rights simply for being human, as does, for example, the 1993 Vienna Declaration and Progamme of Action which proclaims that "Human rights and fundamental freedoms are the birthright of all human beings." Writes Freeman: "It is not clear why one has *any* rights simply because one is a human being." We do not disagree. But neither do we accept that there exists no theory to justify human rights in our secular times, ergo no theory to justify a human rights approach to child labour.

The concept of human rights is or can be firmly established on sound theoretical ground. First, there is the proposition, formally proclaimed in both the 1948 UDHR and the yet more widely adopted and revalidating 1993 Vienna Declaration, that human rights derive from "the inherent dignity . . . of all members of the human family" or, alternatively, from "the dignity and worth inherent in the human person." While this proposition informs us little more than the assertion that human rights extend to human beings simply for being human, it does point the way. Unless one subscribes to nihilism, it is the human being's inherent dignity and worth that justifies human rights. Of course, the obvious question remains: how does one determine the human being's inherent dignity and worth? Noteworthy in this regard is the previously noted work of Nussbaum and Sen on "capabilities and human functioning."

In their search for a theory that answers at least some of the questions raised by rights talk, they have pioneered the language of "human capabilities" as a way to speak about, and act upon, what fundamentally is required to be human—*i.e.*, "life," "bodily health," "bodily integrity," "senses, imagination, and thought," "emotions," "affiliation" ("friendship" and "respect"), "other species," "play," and "control over one's environment" ("political" and "material"). While Nussbaum and Sen do not reject the concept of human rights as such —indeed, they see it working hand in hand with their concept of capabilities, jointly signaling the central goals of public policy —they propose emphasis on human capabilities as the theoretical means by which to restore "the obligation of result" and thereby move the discussion from the abstract to the concrete without having to rely on controversial transempirical metaphysics to cut across human differences. There remains, however, the question of how to distinguish those capabilities that are central to human existence—hence worthy of the title "human rights"—and those that are not.

Control over one's political and/or material environment, for example, can lead to some very nasty results. Thus we dig deeper and find the work of the late John Rawls pointing the way. Rawls proposed a thought experiment, akin to Kant's "categorical imperative," in which a group of thinking men and women of diverse characteristics (race, class, creed, etc.) come together in their private capacity (i.e., not as state representatives) in some "original position" to construct a just society with their personal selfinterests in mind, but without knowing their own position in it (economic, social, racial, etc.). Behind this "veil of ignorance," these "original position" decision-makers, rationally contemplating their own selfinterest, freely choose a society that is fair to all, one in which benefits (rights) and burdens (duties) are distributed equally and in which a core of fundamental liberties (freedom of conscience, speech, movement, religion, etc.) and equality of opportunity are protected.

This social constructionism, however, need not be restricted to Rawls' historically Western core values favoring individual civil and political rights. Accounting for *all* the voices assembled, the "original position" decision-makers, transcending personal self-interest even while accounting for it, could equally well choose a set of basic but diverse values (rights and/or capabilities) that would win the general assent of human beings *everywhere*—a set of universal basic values of human dignity that, grounded in principles of reciprocal tolerance and mutual forbearance, define the human rights society. It is such a society that can most guarantee the fairest distribution of basic wants (rights) and needs (capabilities) among all human beings and thereby ensure that all will benefit as much as possible and, by the same token, suffer the least possible disadvantage.

And therein lies, we believe, the theoretical justification for human rights in our secular age: a kind of share-and-share-alike Golden Rule that, in an "original position" behind a "veil of ignorance" and as rational human beings contemplating our own self-interest, we would choose for ordering a society in which all of us would want to live. However interpreted and applied in real world conflict and contestation, human rights are theoretically justified because they satisfy the fundamental requirements of socioeconomic and political justice. In the words of U.N. High Commissioner for Human Rights Louise Arbour before a working group on economic, social and cultural rights of the Commission on Human Rights in January 2005, "uman rights are not a utopian ideal. They embody an international consensus on the minimum conditions for a life of dignity." When joined to the struggle against abusive, exploitative, and hazardous child work, they can be a uniquely powerful tool.

Abolishing Child Labour

In preceding Section I, we challenged a palpable if diminishing reluctance to use human rights to combat child labour. We did so, first, by calling attention to the multidimensional human rights nature of the problem; next, by detailing the virtues of human rights discourse and strategy to combat it; and finally, by contesting claims that would prevent or curtail resort to such rights talk and maneuver. These latter claims, we submit, are as unconvincing as the virtues of human rights law and policy are convincing. And thus we are driven to conclude that the core questions demanding responsible attention are not why or whether to bring human rights to the prosecution of child labour, but how and how quickly. These core questions, we hasten to add, demand urgent as well as responsible attention. Economic globalization, which can be no more arrested than the transition from agrarian to industrial society, is proceeding apace, and while it has its bright sides, it has also its dark sides, negative aspects that threaten human rights generally and the rights of working children in particular.

A human rights approach to child labour, we believe, one that foresees a true culture of respect for children's rights, can help to offset these darker forces if urgently as well as responsibly embraced and pursued. In this section, therefore, using an established typology of decision-making functions to facilitate coverage and coherence, we recommend a more-or-less comprehensive series of concrete policies and courses of action that, in various combination especially, can be effective in combating child labour from a human rights perspective. Without disparaging smaller, incremental approaches when circumstance and opportunity permit—indeed, we wholeheartedly support them when such instances arise—we nevertheless proceed on the belief that a hugely multidimensional human rights problem such as child labour begs for a coextensively multifaceted human rights strategy for its solution, in whole or in major part.

Once the human rights of working children are recognized and their legal content understood, such a strategy, we believe, can translate them into effective policies, programs, and projects that promote, it bears repeating, a true culture of respect for the rights of children. Of course, space limitations require that much of our "nuts and bolts" discussion be restricted to descriptive outline, leaving it to other occasions to fill in the gaps and flesh out the details. Moreover, such recommendations as we do offer here are tendered more in tentative than definitive spirit. Making human rights work for the abolition of child labour must be understood as a continuing process of reflection and debate, open to reappraisal and redirection as time and experience dictate. It is risky to be categorical. At the same time, it is irresponsible to rest content with expressions of theoretical commitment only. Once human rights are recognized and their legal content understood, their formal expressions must be made operational.

Before engaging our "nuts and bolts" discussion, however, we choose to underscore the two central injunctions we made earlier in Section I: *first*, to accept—self-consciously and proactively—the premise and virtues of human rights law and policy on all topical and tactical fronts; *second*, to reject— again self-consciously and proactively—the psychosocial (conceptual) barriers that all too commonly are mounted to resist human rights initiatives and thus thwart their potential from the start. We choose to do so in the first instance because we believe that self-conscious and proactive *acceptance* of human rights as child labour's moral and legal reference point can effectively counter practices that contradict children's best interests and, at the same time, promote those practices that facilitate their human dignity, including their rights to a reasonable standard of living, to education, even to the right to work in ways that are not abusive, exploitative, hazardous, or otherwise contrary to their best interests.

And we choose to do so in the second instance as well because we believe that self-conscious and proactive *rejection* of the conceptual barriers to human rights thought and action in the child labour context unleashes the contributions that states, inter-governmental organizations, NGOs, and others can and must make toward the solution of this complex and pervasive problem. These injunctions to take children's human rights *seriously* are critical "nuts and bolts" in their own right, necessary first steps in any human rights strategy worthy of child labour's abolition and of the social transformations required to make that happen. As Marta Santos Pais has put it relative to the operationalization of UNICEF's approach to development, "[t]he expression of a solemn commitment to human rights legitimizes our work and constitutes a catalyst for our actions."

Although there exists today an emerging commitment to a rights-based approach to child labour (as in the case of UNICEF, for example), the fact is that, as previously noted, it is not common in official policy or practice, especially on the national plane, nor a conspicuous feature even of official rhetoric on the international plane. In contrast to other approaches, it appears to be marginalized or less favored than, for example, the "labour market perspective," long "the dominant international paradigm of government child labour intervention"; the "human capital perspective," which "views the work of children through the lens of national economic development"; and the "social responsibility perspective," which is centrally concerned "with the 'exclusion' of disadvantaged groups from full participation in the protection, benefits and opportunities of society" and which thus proposes "greater social inclusion of those being excluded" by way of remedy.

The ILO, for key example, has been generally marginal in expressly engaging human rights law and policy over the years—except recently in respect of child trafficking—and for this reason, we believe, limited in its ability to ameliorate labour problems of a human rights nature. Virginia Leary, a long-time authority on ILO policy and practice, agrees. Leary, it is important to acknowledge, reached this conclusion in 1992, and not with reference to child labour specifically. Her assessment, therefore, must be weighed against the ILO's current avowed commitment (along with UNICEF and others) to a rights-based approach to child labour. When this is done, however, ILO practice even in relation to child labour appears more to confirm than to invalidate Leary's judgment of more than a decade ago, emphasizing, as the ILO tends to do, negotiable "standards" more than inalienable "rights." The recent and useful ILO study titled *Action Against Child Labour* underscores the point dramatically.

Responding to no less than "the need for comprehensive and practical information on planning and carrying out action against child labour," it mentions human rights only in circumstantial passing and thus seems to eschew the very idea of mainstreaming a rights-based approach to child labour altogether. Not even the more recent report of the ILO Director-General explicitly following up on the ILO's 1998 Declaration on Fundamental Principles and Rights at Work takes the forthright human rights step. Only the 2002 report of the ILO's International Programme on the Elimination Child Labour (IPEC) on the more limited (though huge) problem of child trafficking, it appears, has taken such a self-conscious stand. Indeed, even activists and scholars sympathetic to a rights-based approach to child labour have eschewed the language of rights when making the very point. "Although its intellectual and organizational influence seems to be growing," William E. Myers has written, "the *'child-centered perspective'* [that is, a rights-based approach to child labour] remains surprisingly marginalised in official national policy and programmes guiding child labour action. . . . One might expect from virtually universal ratification of the [Convention on the Rights of the Child] that *a child-centered view* of child labour would have by now become more present in official child labour policy."

In sum, despite a new-found commitment to combat child labour from a human rights perspective, evident since the adoption of the 1989 CRC and especially since the adoption of 1999 ILO C182, the idea of human rights discourse and strategy as an effective tool in this struggle still meets with palpable hesitancy, even among well-wishers. Doubtless this uncertainty is a function of bureaucratic inertia or even general disinterest at least in part—and surely, as well, of incomplete understanding of the virtues of human rights discourse and strategy in the first place. It probably is a function, too, of strongly held beliefs in the minimum age/labour market approach to children's work represented by 1973 ILO C138. We believe, however, that it is also—perhaps even primarily—a function of the statist, elitist, patriarchal, and paternalistic logics that shape our worldviews and lives.

Through many years of psychosocial acculturation, they have come to define not only what, specifically, we see to be possible but also, more generally, how we go about seeing what is possible.

As long as we continue in this way, however, we never will achieve the social transformations that are needed to abolish the abuse and exploitation of working children, in whole or in part, on an enduring basis. The time is long past due when we must unreservedly champion the rights of children not simply as *children's* rights, so labeled at risk of marginalization, but as *human* rights which, at their core, evince concern for the alleviation of *all* human suffering—and therefore also, in Costas Douzinas' evocative phrase, "concern for the unfinished person of the future for whom justice matters." UNICEF's Innocenti Research Centre comes close in its call for "a new global ethic for children." But not, we sense, close enough.

Needed is a wholesale paradigm shift not only in the way we think about children specifically, but also—guided by an ethos of species (human) identity—in the way we think about social governance generally, and therefore a shift away from the statist, elitist, patriarchal, and paternalistic logics that stand in the way of the genuine alleviation of child and other human suffering.

The need is for an internalized worldview or mindset that, on behalf of working children and in continuously persevering ways, actively embraces the premise and virtues of human rights discourse and strategy, consistently contests the psycho-social (conceptual) barriers that impede their operation, and systematically mainstreams the full human rights agenda (civil, political, economic, social, cultural, and communitarian) in each and every policy that is devised and in each and every measure that is taken—all to ensure that children's best interests are served, not as a matter of charity or privilege that may benefit some, but as a matter of right that can benefit all. In short, the need is for a culture of respect for children's human rights, a culture of human rights as a way of life.

It is, indeed, this kind of rethinking that appears first to have shaped the Declaration and Programme of Action of the 1993 Vienna World Conference on Human Rights; that later, in 1997, guided U.N. Secretary-General Kofi Annan, as part of his program for U.N. reform, to summons all U.N. entities to mainstream human rights into the activities and programs that fell within their mandates; and that, as a result, found expression ultimately in a May 2003 Statement of Common Understanding of a U.N. "Inter-Agency Workshop," outlining a human rights-based approach to the development planning and programming of U.N. agencies. While intended for U.N. development agencies specifically, May 2003 SCU points the way as well for all who would seek to abolish child labour by way of human rights discourse and strategy.

First, it identifies several key "human rights principles" to "guide all programming in all phases of the programming process"—which itself is defined to include "assessment and analysis, programme planning and design (including setting of goals, objectives and strategies); implementation, monitoring and evaluation." Specifically, it articulates and explains the following principles: "universality and inalienability; indivisibility; interdependence and interrelatedness; non-discrimination and equality; participation and inclusion; accountability and the rule of law." Next, but first cautioning that "the application of good programming practices does not by itself constitute a human rights-based approach," the SCU cites four "required additional elements" deemed by the May 2003 U.N. Inter-Agency Workshop to be "necessary, specific, and unique to a human rightsbased approach:"

1. Assessment and analysis [to] identify the human rights claims of rights-holders and the corresponding human rights obligations of duty-bearers, as well as the immediate, underlying, and structural causes when rights are not realized.
2. Programmes [to] assess the capacity of rights-holders to claim their rights, and of dutybearers to fulfill their obligations, [and the development of] strategies to build these capacities.
3. Programmes [to] monitor and evaluate both outcomes and processes guided by human rights standards and principles.
4. Programming [that] is informed by the recommendations of international human rights bodies and mechanisms. Finally, the SCU lists thirteen other elements deemed "essential" for a human rights-based approach to development planning and programming.

We quote them in full, modestly amended to demonstrate their especial relevance to the struggle against child labour:

1. People [*including all working children*] are recognized as key actors in their own development, rather than passive recipients of commodities and services.
2. Participation is both a means and a goal.
3. Strategies are empowering.
4. Both outcomes and processes are monitored and evaluated.
5. Analysis includes all stakeholders.
6. Programmes focus on marginalized, disadvantaged, and excluded groups [*including among working children*].

7. The development process [*relative to working children*] is locally owned.
8. Programmes aim to reduce disparity [*between working and non-working children and others*].
9. Both top-down and bottom-up approaches are used in synergy.
10. Situation analysis is used to identity immediate, underlying, and basic causes of development problems [*including the causes of child labour*].
11. Measurable goals and targets are important in programming.
12. Strategic partnerships are developed and sustained.
13. Programmes support accountability to all stakeholders.

All of the foregoing "required" and "essential" elements of the May 2003 SCU can and should be understood to be part of the human rights discourse and strategy that can and should be directed against child labour. At a minimum, a human rights approach to the abolition of child labour requires:

1. Reliance upon human rights criteria and norms when selecting and establishing anti-child labour program priorities, standards, tactics, and strategies;
2. The identification of child labour claims-holders and whether they have the capacity to articulate and advocate for their rights and participate in the process;
3. The identification of dutybearers and their capacity to meet their anti-child labour obligations as well as constraints on their ability to perform; and
4. The establishment of mechanisms for monitoring, assessing, and redressing child labour situations, with human rights norms all the while in mind, shaping one's outlook and purpose.

Proceeding according to this or like-minded designs, programs and projects directed toward the abolition of child labour, even if not conceived initially in human rights terms, become, *ipso facto*, human rights programs and projects by virtue of their deliberate conceptual reorientation. To the extent that the strategic design is adhered to, and regardless of the substantive measures implemented, it works naturally to protect, promote, and fulfill children's human rights, including the human rights of working children. In sum, an ethos of species identity that takes working children's suffering seriously, unaffected by considerations irrelevant of merit, is what is needed if the abolition of child labour is to succeed—a primary even if evolutionary first step in any human rights strategy worthy of child labour's abolition and of the social transformations that are required to make that happen.

It is children's human *rights* we are defending, not just their human *needs*. And we must do so not only in matters of substance but, as well, in matters of procedure—in the invention, design, implementation, monitoring, and evaluation of policies and programs directed against child labour, giving particular consideration to such core human rights values as transparency, accountability, participation, and non-discrimination. If the abolition of child labour is truly the goal, nothing less will do. Even incremental measures, if they are to succeed enduringly, depend on such human rights outlook and strategy.

Promote and Protect Working Children's Rights

This subsection, to minimize redundancies, focuses on the promotion and protection of the rights of working children largely on the international plane. It is essential to appreciate, however, that all that has been said up to now and that much of what has yet to be said applies as well to national policy and decision making. Indeed, the implementation of human rights doctrines, principles, and rules on behalf of working children is, generally speaking, probably most efficiently and effectively achieved at the national or even sub-national level via the institutions and procedures that obtain within each country's own legal political order system—broadly defined to include *both* the formal and informal mechanisms that avail human rights in this setting.

The authority of a domestic legal-political order that provides effective formal and informal "remedies" for violations of international human rights obligations (as well as their national counterparts) can serve richly the promotion and protection of human rights where there is moral and political will. This is as true for working (and non-working) children's human rights as it is for any other category of human rights. And the examples abound: in the formulation and execution of national strategies and agendas for the implementation in the 1989 CRC and 1999 ILO C182; in efforts at national and sub-national policy and law reform based on these same and cognate human rights instruments; in the development of independent governmental institutions at the national level for promoting and protecting the rights of working (and non-working) children; and so forth.

The majority and probably most effective are "extra-legal" in kind and therefore merit the lion's share of responsible attention. Partly for editorial reasons, however, we here focus first, even primarily overall, on the formal legal mechanisms both the global and regional levels for the promotion and protection of human rights (including the human rights of working children). But there is another, more important reason for so doing. Perhaps for lack of sufficient knowledge about them, or because of a preference for consensual diplomacy over adversarial advocacy, or perhaps for both reasons, a comparative few appear to have been pressed into anti-child labour service so far. It seems therefore useful to explicate, however briefly, the explicit human rights enforcement arrangements that, on the international plane and in appropriate instances, can assist child labour's abolition in fact—and potentially to genuine profit.

Formal Legal Mechanisms and Procedures

While resort to formal legal mechanisms may seem inconsistent with goals of social transformation because they represent established officialdom, they should not be dismissed for this reason. To the contrary, if used wisely and with tolerance for quasi and non-legal devices, they have the potential to assist the anti-child labour struggle nobly, both as change agents in their own right and as catalysts for change.

Indeed, resorting to them even only occasionally among the many elements that comprise a human rights approach to child labour's abolition can send a much needed signal that the antichild labour movement means to be taken seriously, sending ripples of persuasion that cut across all levels of resistance in the world system, from the most global to the most local. They deserve, therefore, thoughtful consideration, particularly among persons not trained in the law who tend often to be skeptical (not altogether without justification) about the capacity of legal process to mete out justice and otherwise serve humane values. Some of these formal mechanisms are found at the global level, others at the regional level. In each case, we make specific recommendations that we believe can enhance their ability to help end child labour.

Human Rights Action within the United Nations System

Within the United Nations, the only forum in which *any* country's human rights violations can be challenged, three arenas available specifically to monitor and enforce human rights present themselves as obviously relevant to the abolition of child labour (apart from UNICEF as the U.N.'s chief system-wide promoter of children's well-being and rights): the Committee on the Rights of the Child; the U.N. Commission on Human Rights and its Sub-Commission on the Promotion and Protection of Human

Rights; and, though largely without resort to the language of rights, the ILO relative to the implementation of 1973 ILO C138 and 1999 ILO C182 (as well as other ILO conventions). Also available within the U.N. system, though presently in a supervisory rather than enforcement mode, is the Committee on Economic, Social and Cultural Rights, established in 1987 by the Economic and Social Council.

The Committee on the Rights of the Child

The Committee on the Rights of the Child, established under the 1989 CRC to oversee its implementation, has no mandate to receive and consider in quasi-judicial manner "communications" (i.e., complaints, applications, or cases) from individuals or groups of individuals who claim to be victims of violations of the CRC. Instead, the Committee recommends children or their representatives to refer to the four U.N. "treaty bodies" that have such competence to date and that are relevant to the claim or claims involved: the Committee on the Elimination of All Forms of Racial Discrimination; the Human Rights Committee; the Committee against Torture and Other Cruel, Inhuman or Degrading Treatment or Punishment; or the Committee on the Elimination of Discrimination against Women.

Also, since 1992 when it adopted an "urgent action procedure" to deal with "serious" CRC violations though in nonaccusatory fashion, the Committee has several times responded diligently to urgent children's appeals always on an ad hoc basis and mostly confidentially with a view to sensitizing the states parties to their treaty obligations so as to prevent a further deterioration of the contested situation and thereby safeguard children's rights as much as possible under the circumstances. Beyond these limited interventions, however, the Committee's competence is reportorial and recommendatory only. It receives reports required to be submitted to it by states and other parties to the CRC on measures taken to give effect to the rights set forth in the Convention; it may request further information from the parties if it so chooses; and, on the basis of these communications, it reports to the U.N. General Assembly every two years on its activities.

Additionally, it is authorized to "invite . . . competent bodies as it may consider appropriate to provide expert advice on the implementation of the Convention . . . [and] United Nations organs to submit reports on the implementation of the Convention . Further, it may recommend that the General Assembly request the Secretary General to study "specific issues relating to the rights of the child" and may "make suggestions and general recommendations based on the information received," which recommendations are to be transmitted to any party concerned and reported to the General Assembly. A recent example, highly pertinent to the issue of child labour, was the Committee's request for an international study on the question of violence against children, honored in February 2003 by the U.N Secretary-General's appointment of an "independent expert" (Paulo Sergio Pinheiro) to lead a global study on the subject, on-going at this writing.

These measures afford the Committee, which is at the hub of child labour activities in the U.N. system, significant opportunity to pressure states that engage in, or fail to take steps to correct, violations of the rights enumerated in the CRC and its two optional protocols on the involvement of children in armed conflict and on the sale of children, child prostitution, and child pornography. This includes, of course, Article 32 which proclaims "the child to be protected from economic exploitation and from performing any work that is likely to be hazardous or to interfere with the child's education, or to be harmful to the child's health or physical, mental, spiritual, moral or social development." To enhance the struggle against child labour, however, we recommend that the Committee significantly increase its surveillance and exposé not only of violations of the CRC's child labour-specific Article 32 but, as well, violations of all those CRC provisions that are implicated by child labour.

To the same end, we urge that the Committee appoint special rapporteurs and/or working groups to study, report on, and recommend solutions to all forms of abusive and exploitative child work, and not only the most scandalous. Particularly helpful, we believe, would be a focus on child labour at the intersection of international human rights law and economic globalization. Finally, we recommend strongly that the CRC be amended to empower the Committee to receive and consider individual and group complaints in quasi-judicial manner and to sanction those countries that are found to be in CRC violation.

Without prejudice to the Committee's "urgent action procedure" noted above, the precedent of the 1999 Optional Protocol to the 1967 Convention on the Elimination of All Forms of Discrimination against Women (CEDAW), belatedly extending quasi-judicial authority to receive and act upon complaints to the Committee on the Elimination of Discrimination against Women, is instructive. This step would measurably enhance the opportunity for children themselves, as well as their representatives, to defend and promote their rights against abusive and exploitative child work. The direct involvement of claims-holders in the defense and promotion of their rights usually is key to the validity and vitality of their claims.

The U.N. Human Rights Council

On 16 June 2006, pursuant to a resolution adopted by it on 15 March 2006, the U.N. General Assembly abolished the U.N. Commission on Human Rights created in 1946 as a subsidiary body of the U.N.'s Economic and Social Council (ECOSOC) and replaced it with a new Human Rights Council established under its aegis. In so doing, however, it retained, at least temporarily, most of the innovative mandates and mechanisms of the former

Commission, among them the special investigatory and complaints procedures established under ECOSOC Resolution 1235 of 6 June 1967, ECOSOC Resolution 1503 of 27 May 1970, and "special procedures" put in place by resolutions first adopted in 1979 to address "country" situations and "thematic" issues involving specific violations of human rights. Pursuant to these innovations, the U.N. Commission on Human Rights and its Sub-Commission on the Promotion and Protection of Human Rights were authorized to perform several different operations on behalf of human rights generally, ergo on behalf of those rights implicated by child labour.

This mandate belongs now to the new Human Rights Council and the Sub-Commission under it (or whatever successor expert-advice mechanism may ultimately replace the Sub-Commission). Under ECOSOC Resolution 1235 and by virtue of General Assembly Resolution 60/251 establishing the Council, the Council and the Sub-Commission are empowered "to examine information relevant to gross violations of human rights and fundamental freedoms." Precisely what it means to "examine information" and precisely what constitute "gross violations" are not explicitly clarified by Resolution 1235, but in Paragraph 3 the Resolution authorized the Commission "[to] make a thorough study of situations which reveal a consistent pattern of violations of human rights, as exemplified by the policy of *apartheid* . . . and racial discrimination . . . and [to] report, with recommendations thereon, to the Economic and Social Council." The widespread abuse and exploitation of working children would seem to fit this mold.

In any event, the operational essence of "the 1235 procedure," as it has come to be called, is a public debate that, though entirely in the hands of U.N. Member States (not private individuals or groups) and thus influenced by political considerations, can lead to the establishment of a mechanism ("working group," "observer delegation," "special rapporteur," "special representative," "special envoy," or "representative of the Secretary-General") for study of a country's human rights situation and to the adoption of a resolution concerning the country situation examined or studied. In addition, the Sub- Commission can debate specific country situations and adopt resolutions expressing concern about them.

These resolutions, while not comparable to judicial orders, are not without consequence. They therefore can assist the anti-child labour struggle. "Even a Sub-Commission resolution that does no more than express concern about a particular country's human rights situation," writes Sir Nigel Rodley, "can serve . . . important functions" especially, he adds, "where the Commission has not yet dealt with it.

Sir Nigel continues: "first, it may give political impetus to further action by the Commission; second, even if the Commission is unwilling to act, a Sub-Commission resolution represents the opinion of a formally constituted U.N. body of human rights experts (which is not without independent influence); and, third, it may build up an official documentary record by requesting a report from the Secretary-General on the situation." ECOSOC Resolution 1503, a direct response to the Sub-Commission's reliance upon information derived from non-governmental organizations (NGOs) under the 1235 procedure, gave the human rights complaint initiative for the first time to individuals and NGOs and initially, in contrast to the 1235 procedure, in strict confidence. Limited to general situations that reveal "a consistent pattern of gross and reliably attested violations of human rights and fundamental freedoms" (a "worst form" of child labour?), it nevertheless was seen by many around the time of its adoption as "an enormously valuable precedent, a breach in the citadel of the mutual protection society, one that could be progressively enlarged."

In practice, however, the 1503 procedure, though not without some notable successes, has fallen short of its promise. While it has sometimes facilitated gradually increased pressure on offending governments (often as a precursor to action under ECOSOC Resolution 1235), it is, in the words of Newman and Weissbrodt as long ago as 1990, "painfully slow, complex, secret, and vulnerable to political influence at many junctures."

The utility of the 1503 procedure relative to, say, a "worst form" of child labour is, therefore, open to serious doubt. Nevertheless, with the Sub-Commission formally authorized to receive and act upon complaints and the Council, in place of the former Commission on Human Rights, now empowered to make "a thorough study" or to initiate "an investigation by an ad hoc committee" subject to "the express consent of the State concerned," the 1503 procedure is available to the struggle against child labour at least in principle.

If a pattern of human rights abuse in a country remains unresolved in the early stages, it can be brought to the world's attention through the United Nations human rights system, the procedures of which are more or less transparent. At a minimum, therefore, the potential of the 1503 procedure in relation to child labour should be explored. Given the almost unanimous endorsement of the 1989 CRC and the rapidly growing popularity of 1999 ILO C182, it is not beyond credulity to imagine that the struggle against child labour could even result in the 1503 procedure's reform and reinvigoration. Unlike the public procedures authorized by ECOSOC Resolution 1235 and the confidential procedures authorized by ECOSOC Resolution 1503, each of which deal with general *situations* of human rights violation, the thematic mechanisms (or mandates) developed since 1979 to investigate specific violations of human rights can deal with individual *cases* of human rights violation, both actual and threatened.

And for the most part they do so, typically via special rapporteurs and working groups and particularly in countries where the violations are widespread. Generally they operate impartially, such that their annual reports to the Commission reveal no bias based on the identity of the country being investigated. They operate also relatively efficiently. In these ways, too, they contrast sharply with the 1235 and 1503 procedures, which, as indicated, often are influenced by political considerations and tend to be cumbersome and slow. They thus are ripe for use in the anti-child labour struggle. To our best knowledge, however, only one of the above three human rights enforcement techniques has been pressed into service on behalf of the worldwide struggle against child labour to date. Several of the thematic mechanisms (mandates that have proliferated markedly in recent years) have dealt with child labour issues or issues related to child labour, e.g., the right to education (2002), children and armed conflict (2002), and the sale of children and child prostitution and pornography (2001).

Probably the fact that the 1235 and 1503 procedures are cumbersome and slow, and perhaps also that the 1503 procedure is secret, has dissuaded child labour abolitionists from invoking them. Additionally, direct participation in the Commission's (now Council's) and Sub-Commission's Geneva-based sessions is expensive. "Engaging rapporteurs or working groups is easier," Sir Nigel Rodley writes, "and such an approach is more likely to lead to success in individual cases." consideration of all the enforcement techniques that are provided by the Council and Sub-Commission, and certainly sensitivity to the fact that there are occasions when child labour issues or issues related to child labour must be addressed vis-à-vis countries that are not party to treaty-based complaint procedures.

In any event, there can be no question that at least some of the worst forms of child labour, as defined by 1999 ILO C182, meet the 1235 and 1503 jurisdictional test of "a consistent pattern of gross violations of human rights." At the least, the Council's country and thematic mandates should be given increased and more diverse responsibility for child labour issues—including, in collaboration with the Committee on the Rights of the Child as suggested above, a focus on child labour at the intersection of international human rights law and economic globalization, an intersection in which dwell, we believe, not a few consistent patterns of gross violations of children's rights.

The International Labour Organization

"The procedures developed by the International Labour Organization," writes Lee Swepston, Chief of the Equality and Employment Branch and Coordinator for Human Rights Questions of the Genevabased International Labour Office, "form part of what may be the most effective and thorough international mechanism for the protection of human rights"—though almost completely, it must be added, without benefit of rights language per se. The procedures, predicated on the adoption of conventions and declarations enunciating principles and standards pertinent mainly to organized and unorganized labour (including 1973 ILO C138 and 1999 ILO C182) are of two distinct but interdependent types:

1. Regular and systematic monitoring by the ILO Committee of Experts on the Application of Conventions and Recommendations and the ILO Conference Committee on the Application of Conventions and Recommendations; and
2. Complaint procedures premised on the ILO Constitution and ILO basic principles.

The first of these procedures is defined more by advocacy, encouragement, and technical cooperation than by adversarial confrontation. It involves mainly five sequential monitoring operations, the first three at the hands of the ILO Committee of Experts:

1. The examination of governmental reports on ILO convention compliance;
2. Essentially quiet diplomacy in the form of "Direct Requests" where compliance is found wanting;
3. Published "Observations" where non-compliance is deemed serious or persistent; and, in the most severe cases of non-compliance, either
4. Mandatory appearance before the ILO Conference Committee (which reflects the ILO's tripartite structure of governmental, workers', and employers' representatives) for a public accounting of the reasons for non-compliance or
5. "Direct contacts" between the International Labour Office and the delinquent government to resolve the problem without public criticism.

The second (complaint) procedure entails any one of three essentially adjudicative operations. They include:

1. "Representations" to the ILO Governing Body by trade unions or employer organizations (not necessarily associated with the subject of the complaint) as authorized by Article 24 of the ILO Constitution whenever a country "has failed to secure in any respect the effective observance within its jurisdiction of any Convention to which it is a party";
2. "Complaints" to the ILO Governing Body (and an assisting Commission of Inquiry usually established by the Governing Body) by governments, International Labour Conference delegates, or the Governing Body itself on its own motion, as authorized by Article 26 of the ILO Constitution, alleging that a country is not "securing the effective observance" of a convention it has ratified; and
3. "Complaints" directly to the ILO Governing Body's Committee on Freedom of Association (CFA) and indirectly via the CFA to an assisting Fact-Finding and

Conciliation Commission on Freedom of Association (FFCC) by governments or by employers' or workers' organizations alleging violations of the ILO's basic principles on freedom of association whether or not the state concerned is a party to any ILO convention on the subject.

The last mechanism mentioned above—the complaint procedure involving the ILO Governing Body's CFA—is reliably reported to be "one of the most widely used international complaint procedures for the protection of human rights," and "[t]he most widely used ILO petition procedure." This comes as no surprise. The principle of freedom of association, including but not limited to the right to form trade unions and to collective bargaining, is fundamental to the protection of worker rights generally. It also is critical to children who are the victims of abusive and exploitative labour practices. Not only do they or their surrogates need its protection to resist particular abuses, they need its protection also to safeguard the right of children under CRC Article 12 "to express [their] views freely in all matters affecting the child," including "in any judicial and administrative proceedings affecting the child." It is essential to the empowerment of child workers and to their direct involvement in the vindication of their rights. A strategy that seeks the abolition of abusive and exploitative child work on a comprehensive basis must therefore embrace the ILO's CFA procedure to the maximum extent needed. Much the same may be said of the ILO's "representations" and "complaints" procedures under articles 24 and 26 of the ILO Constitution.

It appears, however, that these procedures have not been widely used, although for reasons that have more to do with the ILO's successful monitoring and supervision of its many standard-setting conventions than with any ineffectiveness that might be attributed to these procedures. Writes Swepston: If these procedures are used relatively infrequently, it is because they are but one part of a comprehensive and active system of regular supervision. It is rare that governments do not cooperate fully in the ILO's investigations . Even if a government does not implement the ILO's conclusions immediately, in the longer term the government often adopts legislation and practices that closely follow the recommendations made. When it comes to the implementation of ILO C138 and ILO C182, however, credit must be given particularly to the ILO's International Programme on the Elimination of Child Labour (IPEC), established in 1992 and, as of this writing, now active in 60 countries worldwide.

Working toward the elimination of child labour through a phased, multi-sectoral strategy of technical cooperation that includes a Legal Unit for monitoring and evaluation, it reinforces the ILO's supervisory system and, along the way, confirms that technical cooperation and normative action can be complementary. In fact, in part because of its monitoring and evaluation procedures, IPEC has hastened ratifications of both 1973 ILO C138 and 1999 ILO C182. True, in the years preceding IPEC, work to eliminate child labour barely existed at the global level even after the entry into force of ILO C138 in 1976, and when it did it was slow and incoherent. Still, it is wise not to leap hastiiy to the conclusion that the ILO's "representations" and "complaints" procedures need never be pressed into service on behalf of the struggle against child labour.

To the contrary, a comprehensive strategy to abolish child labour, by definition multifaceted, requires that they be placed in active reserve. The ILO's supervisory procedures probably would not be nearly as effective as they are without the threat of its adversarial procedures lying in wait. Finally, as it is not easy for human rights NGOs to gain access to the ILO's enforcement machinery, cooperation with trade unions is strongly recommended, especially with those that are human rights oriented. At the same time, however, we urge greater ILO leniency toward human rights advocacy groups, preferably as part of an ILO policy shift that, like UNICEF in 1997 and 1999, would signal a strategic decision to use rights discourse to abolish or at least reduce child labour.

Committee on Economic, Social and Cultural Rights

Article 10 of the 1966 ICESCR, which provides for the "widest possible protection and assistance . . . to the family," decrees, as noted earlier, that "[s]pecial measures of protection and assistance should be taken on behalf of all children and young persons"; that [c]hildren and young persons should be protected from economic and social exploitation"; that "[t]heir employment in work harmful to their morals or health or dangerous to life or likely to hamper their normal development should be punishable by law"; and that "States should also set age limits below which the paid employment of child labour should be prohibited and punishable by law." Like all the other of the provisions of the ICESCR that bear upon the problem of child labour, the implementation of this provision is monitored by the Committee on Economic, Social and Cultural Rights (CESCR).

Established in 1987 by ECOSOC, the CESCR is not, at this writing, empowered to receive and adjudicate complaints of violations of the ICESCR, as is, for example, the Human Rights Committee under the companion ICCPR. The absence of a direct complaints procedure, the CESCR has noted, "places significant constraints on the ability of the Committee to develop jurisprudence or case-law and, of course, greatly limits the chances of victims of abuses of the ICESCR obtaining international redress." protocol similar to the one provided for in the first Optional Protocol to the ICCPR. Thus far unsuccessfully, however; and as a consequence the CESCR has signaled that, "[p]ending the addition of an optional protocol, beneficiaries of the rights contained in the Covenant may still have recourse to the general procedures of the Committee, and may utilize what has been called an "unofficial petition procedure" based on the modalities of the Committee."

Also, the Committee has drawn up a "Plan of Action to Strengthen the Implementation of the International Covenant on Economic, Social and Cultural Rights" with emphasis on "substantive, analytical, expert, and general support (a) to facilitate the Committee's work with States parties in relation to the reporting process; (b) for the preparation of various substantive background papers to enable the Committee to contribute effectively to the various activities which it is increasingly being called upon to perform; and (c) to enable the Committee to work constructively with States parties and United Nations agencies and others in following up on its recommendations designed to enhance the realization of economic, social and cultural rights." Meanwhile, the CESCR's legal competence is to oversee the ICESCR's state reporting process. Pursuant to ICESCR Articles 16 and 17, the states parties to the ICESCR are obligated to submit periodic reports to the CESCR on the programs and laws they have adopted and on the progress they have made in protecting the rights pronounced in the ICESCR.

With the help of state delegations, specialized U.N. agencies, and relevant NGOs on behalf of civil society, the CESCR reviews the reports, entertains both written and oral testimony, and then concludes its consideration of a state party's report by issuing "Concluding Observations." The "Concluding Observations" constitute the CESCR's decision and variously include both positive and negative assessments of a state party's performance together with suggestions and recommendations for improvement. A possible Committee conclusion is that a state party has failed to comply with an ICESCR obligation and, hence, is in violation of the Covenant. It is important to note, however, that the CESCR's Concluding Observations are not technically binding and that, to date, there is no method to enforce them.

At the same time, the CESCR has stated that "for States parties to ignore or not act on such views would be to show bad faith in implementing their Covenantbased obligations" and that "in a number of instances, changes in policy, practice and law have been registered at least partly in response to the Committee's concluding observations." Finally, it is important to note that, at its third session in 1988, in response to an invitation from ECOSOC, the CESCR began to prepare and issue "general comments" on the rights and provisions contained in the ICESCR for the purpose of assisting states parties to fulfill their ICESCR reporting obligations, and also to provide greater interpretative clarity as to the intent, meaning and content of the Covenant. The CESCR views the adoption of such comments as a way to promote the ICESCR's implementation of the Covenant. It also sees them as a way to generate a consensual jurisprudence relative to the ICESCR's substantive provisions. To date, however, the CESCR has issued no general comment on Article 10's proscription of child labour.

We urge it to do so as an important and potentially persuasive further element in a comprehensive human rights strategy for child labour's abolition. Additionally, and to the same end, we urge the CESCR to move swiftly in winning acceptance of its proposed individual complaints procedure. Even though many economic, social, and cultural rights are perhaps best secured via group action, individual complainants as victims or representatives of victims of abuse can speak with unmatched moral authority. Meanwhile, we urge the CESCR to fulfill its Plan of Action and use its existing supervisory power over the state party reporting process to heighten its scrutiny of dubious labour practices involving child workers and thereby energize states parties, international organizations, and civil society to work yet harder at Article 10's full realization.

While the Committee on the Rights of the Child, the ILO, and UNICEF, along with several rapporteurs and working groups, currently dominate anti-child labour activity within the U.N. system, there is no apparent reason why responsibility for this issue should not extend to other United Nations mechanisms and procedures where appropriate. For example, it is well known that children from lower socioeconomic status, especially when from unfavored ethnic or tribal groups, often suffer severe discrimination and other abuse at the hands of unscrupulous parties and that, as a consequence, they commonly end up working on the street and in other abusive contexts rather than going to school. In such a setting, it seems appropriate that the Committee on the Elimination of Racial Discrimination (CERD), established under the 1965 International Convention on the Elimination of All forms of Racial Discrimination and with authority to adjudicate claims of violation under that convention, could and should have a role to play in the anti-child labour struggle.

Equivalent conclusions might be reached about the similarly constituted Committee against Torture established under the 1984 Convention against Torture and Other Cruel, Inhuman or Degrading Treatment or Punishment. Our point is simple. Given the multidimensionality, interrelateness, and interdependencies of the worldwide child labour problem, the entire U.N. human rights system, especially at the committee level, should be brought to bear in the antichild labour struggle in a comprehensive and coordinated way—and, what is more, in a fashion that invites the active participation of interested governments and civil society. It is this kind and degree of reordering and mobilization that is needed to ensure child labour's abolition, perhaps with the help of a working children's ombudsperson in the form, say, of a new U.N. High Commissioner for Children (analogous to, for example, Norway's Cabinet-appointed Ombudsman for Children). The Committee on the Rights of the Child, the ILO, and UNICEF are indispensable actors, without a doubt. But they cannot alone win the day. Needed is a kind and degree of reordering and mobilization within the U.N. system that can raise the moral and legal stakes dramatically higher on the scales of human aspiration and endeavor.

Regional Human Rights Systems

There exist today three regional human rights systems, each with state-to-state and individual complaints procedures for judicial or quasi-judicial redress of human rights violations: *in Europe,* pursuant to the 1950 European Convention for the Protection of Human Rights and Fundamental Freedoms and the European Social Charter (Revised); *in the Americas,* pursuant to the 1948 Charter of the Organization of American States (OAS) and the 1969 American Convention on Human Rights; and *in Africa,* pursuant to the 1981 African Charter on Human and Peoples Rights and 1990 Charter on the Rights and Welfare of the Child. Space does not allow a detailed analysis of these complaint procedures. A brief summary, however, is helpful, as all are relevant to child labour's abolition.

The European Human Rights System

Of the three regional human rights systems, the most established is the European. After more than four decades of implementing the European Convention via both a commission and a court, Protocol No. 11 to the European Convention established a unified, full-time European Court of Human Rights with jurisdiction extending to both inter-state and private petitions alleging Convention violations.

What matters here, of course, is that this juridical machinery—involving the encouragement of "friendly settlements" and the rendering of final and binding judgments on the merits enforced by the Committee of Ministers to the Council of Europe, even to the point of threat of expulsion from the Council—is available for the adjudication of the rights of working children.

While the European Convention focuses primarily on "first-generation" civil and political rights, it is nonetheless relevant to the consideration of child labour in that, child labour practices impinge potentially on *all* human rights (for example, freedom of speech and expression).

Moreover, specific rights enumerated in the European Convention—*e.g.*, the right to life and the prohibition of slavery and forced labour manifestly are implicated by certain "worst forms" of child labour. In contrast to the European Convention and its focus on civil and political rights, the European Social Charter (Revised) specifically covers "second generation" economic, social and cultural rights, including many that are of particular relevance to working children. Again, therefore, the anti-child labour movement should take notice. Under the Social Charter, the parties commit to the rights set forth in it "by all appropriate means, both national and international in character."

Under an additional protocol that provides for a system of collective complaints, non-governmental organizations of employers, trade unions, and others may file a complaint with a Committee of Independent Experts alleging violations of the Charter by a state party (indeed, the first complaint filed in this context alleged violation of Social Charter Article 7 prohibiting the employment of children below age 15). The P Committee reviews the complaint, may hold a hearing, and reaches a decision on the merits. The decision is forwarded to the Committee of Ministers of the Council of Europe, which may recommend specific measures to redress any violation.

The Inter-American Human Rights System

The American Convention on Human rights also addresses primarily civil and political rights, calling only for the "progressive development" of measures by the states parties to achieve the "full realization" of economic and social rights. However, among the civil and political rights enumerated in the Convention are the right to life, freedom from slavery, freedom of association, and measures of protection specifically for children. Moreover, an optional Additional Protocol in the Area of Economic, Social and Cultural Rights entered into effect in 1999 and boasts 13 ratifications at this writing (July 2006).

The OAS Charter, in addition, commits all OAS member states to "devote their utmost efforts to accomplishing basic goals," including, in pertinent part, fair wages, acceptable working conditions, and expansion of educational opportunities. OAS member states also obligate themselves to "dedicate every effort" to the application of such "principles" as "a right to material wellbeing and spiritual development under circumstances of liberty, dignity, equality of opportunity, and economic security"; work under conditions of "fair wages, that ensure life, health, and a decent standard of living"; and the right of association and collective bargaining. Furthermore, the OAS Charter requires member states to "exert the greatest efforts to ensure the effective exercise of the right to education."

The American Convention provides for two organs to enforce the rights set forth in the Convention and Additional Protocol—the Inter-American Commission on Human Rights and the Inter- American Court of Human Rights. Both are potential tools for implementing the above-mentioned human rights norms in support of working children. The Commission is charged under the Convention with promoting "respect for and defense of human rights."

In addition, as an organ also of the OAS Charter, it is charged to "promote the observance and protection of human rights and to serve as a consultative organ of the OAS in these matters." Thus, while the Commission's authority under the Convention is limited to those states parties to the *Convention*, as an organ of the *Charter* its purview includes the activities of all OAS member states, including those not party to the Convention.

The Inter-American Commission receives individual petitions against any state party and inter-state petitions involving states parties, determines admissibility, conducts fact-finding, and attempts to reach friendly settlement of cases, whereupon it reports to the OAS Secretary-General and the parties regarding the facts and friendly settlement. Such reports are made public. Under the Convention, where friendly settlement is not achieved, the Commission, after preparing a confidential report, may offer proposals and recommendations, and may submit the case to the Inter-American Court of Human Rights. The Inter-American Court interprets and applies the American Convention via contentious and advisory jurisdiction. When exercising its contentious jurisdiction (as in the case of claims of human rights violations), the Court may order compensation and/or issue injunctions, but then only with regard to states parties that have consented to such jurisdiction. The Commission brings claims to the Court, and the Court's judgments are final and binding. Judgments are enforced via the OAS General Assembly, which may adopt whatever sanctions it deems appropriate.

The African Human Rights System

Under the African Charter, not only are civil/political and economic/social/cultural rights recognized, so also are third generation community or solidarity rights. Specifically, the Charter binds the states parties to recognize and give effect to, *inter alia*, the rights to dignity and freedom from exploitation such as slavery, association, work under equitable and satisfactory conditions and equal pay for equal work, the best attainable state of physical and mental health, education, and protection of morals—all relevant, of course, to the safeguarding of the rights of working children. And this task is left to both an African Commission on Human and Peoples' Rights and, since January 2004, a new African Court on Human and Peoples' Rights. In addition to promotional functions (providing information, offering conferences and seminars, assisting national governments in formulating policy), the Commission has both contentious and advisory jurisdiction to consider complaints lodged with it under the African Charter.

In contentious cases, the Commission may resort to "any appropriate method of investigation," receive, investigate, report on, and make recommendations concerning alleged violations of the Charter, pursuant to either inter-state or individual communications involving any state party to the Convention. For its part, pursuant to the protocol that established it, the Court may receive complaints submitted to it by the Commission, by a state party that has lodged a complaint to the Commission, by a state party whose citizen is an alleged victim of a human rights violation, or by one of the African Intergovernmental Organizations. Further, the Court is authorized to "entitle relevant Non Governmental Organizations (NGOs) with observer status before the Commission, and individuals to institute cases directly before it" vis-à-vis states parties that have consented to such jurisdiction.

The Court will hear cases, try to reach amicable settlement, and may order remedies/reparation, deemed final and binding on the parties. It remains, of course, to be seen how the Court develops in practice. But clearly, given the high incidence of child labour in Africa, both the new Court and the Commission should be taken seriously and thoroughly explored in the struggle against African child labour. Likewise relevant to the safeguarding of the rights of working children and therefore to be taken seriously is the African Charter on the Rights and Welfare of the Child which entered into force in November 1999 and which obligates the parties to it to recognize, and take steps to give effect to, the rights enumerated in it. Many of them, not surprisingly, are applicable to the problem of child labour generally, e.g., rights to free association, education, rest and leisure, and the best attainable state of health. But the Charter also addresses child labour specifically, requiring states parties to take legislative and administrative measures to establish minimum ages of employment and regulation of hours and conditions, and prohibiting the recruitment of children for armed conflict, their sexual exploitation, and and their abduction and trafficking.

To serve all these rights-based objectives, the Charter establishes a Committee on the Rights and Welfare of the Child empowered to receive communications "from any person, group or nongovernmental organization recognized by the OAU, by a Member State, or the United Nations." Like the African Commission on Human and Peoples' Rights, the Committee may use "any appropriate method of investigating" matters brought to its attention, and, further, is required to report its activities to the Assembly of Heads of State and Government every two years. Also, according to Charter Article 42(a), the Committee is empowered to (a) "interpret the provisions of [the Charter] at the request of a State Party, an Institution of the [AU] or any other person or institution recognized by the [AU], or any State Party"; (b) "monitor the implementation and ensure protection of the rights enshrined" P in the Charter; and (c) "where necessary give its views and make recommendations to Governments."

All of which constitutes broad power to investigate violations of child-labour-related human rights and both to report on such violations and to make specific recommendations to states parties on redressing them. However, the Committee has only just begun operating in the last few years so that, as in the case of the African Court on Human and Peoples' Rights, only time will tell whether the Committee lives up to its potential. A thoroughgoing commitment to child labour's abolition, however, would make sure that it does.

Notwithstanding the lofty goals espoused by the instruments establishing the regional human rights systems discussed above, each of these systems has been criticized for failing to protect human rights effectively or efficiently. In the case of the European system, for instance, huge backlogs and insufficient resources caused cases to drag out over years—providing the impetus for reforming the system with a single, full-time human rights court. Similar criticism, coupled with charges of ineffectiveness, propelled the member states of the OAU (now AU) to establish the Court of Human and Peoples Rights. Only time will tell whether these courts will become the effective and efficient arbiters of human rights contests that their architects hope. Despite the well-founded criticisms of the three regional systems, however, it is clear that, for reasons of cultural and geographic propinquity, these systems have had a positive effect on human rights promotion and protection in their respective regions. Indeed, it is fair to say that the enforcement of human rights at the regional level has proven generally more effective than at the global level.

On the whole, states have responded cooperatively to the judgments of the regional tribunals, complying with their orders and changing their laws and practices as a result. Moreover, the regional systems collectively encourage further development and improvement of the global human rights system via interaction and collaboration. It thus is clear that the regional human rights systems are another potentially useful tool for addressing abusive, exploitative, or hazardous labour practices affecting children. Their enforcement or implementing potential in the anti-child labour struggle should be actively explored and invoked, in terms of both their direct impact and their catalytic ripple or demonstration effect.

Extra-Legal Means

As international lawyers, we naturally gravitate toward juridical solutions to the problem of child labour. However, though formal legal institutions and procedures created specifically to promote and protect human rights are indispensable components of a comprehensive strategy for the abolition of child labour, by no means are they the only components—indeed, possibly not even the most effective or important components in many instances.

As previously stated, the abolition of child labour requires broad and deep social change, and for this is needed far more than the law and its formal arrangements, even when dedicated specifically to the promotion and protection of human rights. Legal solutions tend frequently to be "top-down" or "elitist" solutions, often suspect because they are inclined to overlook disparities in power—especially at points of conflict—between those who prescribe solutions and those who, typically less powerful, are on the receiving end of them.

Though nonetheless indispensable, they are not likely to make much headway against abusive and exploitative child work without calling into collaborative service a host of more or less informal approaches to the problem. Many of these are "bottom-up" or "grass roots" approaches. Generally they are of an "extra-legal" (quasi- and non-legal) sort that interface closely with education, international trade, and other such societal infrastructures—and commonly, too, with those who daily fight in the trenches on behalf of working and non-working children: intergovernmental organizations such as the ILO and

UNICEF; NGOs such as Anti-Slavery International, Save the Children, Global March; and a host of others from civil society—trade unions, business enterprises, consumer groups, children's service providers, working children's groups/organizations, faith-based groups, women's organizations, academic institutions, and so forth. Increasingly scholars and activists expert in these "extra-legal" realms are bringing their expertise publicly to bear on the problem of child labour.

For this reason and because of space limitations, we limit ourselves here to outlining a *multifaceted problem-solving/policy-implementing typology* whose individual elements, we believe, hold out the potential for child labour's true abolition, especially when they are conceived in human rights terms coherence and coordination as possible likewise in such normative terms. And this is so even if these elements are not perceived by their owners as components of a comprehensive human rights strategy against child labour. If this be the case, it is simply that their owners have not yet fully understood or internalized the power of a human rights outlook on child labour, in which event human rights education becomes the first imperative. Indeed, given the necessity of social transformation in the child labour context, human rights education— particularly that kind of human rights education that, from the nuclear family to the cosmopolitan state, impels all levels of social organization and action to view human rights as *a way of life*—may be the single most important thing that anyone can do at this time.

To each facet of each function recorded or capable of being recorded in our problem-solving/policy-implementing typology must be brought all of the conceptual and tactical elements we noted earlier that define what we mean by a human rights approach to the abolition of child labour. It is, at any rate, from this perspective that we identify in summary fashion the problem solving/

policy-implementing functions and their principal components that, including formal legal institutions and procedures, must be pursued if child labour is ever to be abolished or significantly reduced.

The problem of child labour, we recognize, is a polychromatic problem that insists upon polychromatic solutions. In no way do we presume to have exhausted the options. Nor do we presume that our cataloguing of them reflect an always precise, exclusive fit. What follows is meant to be heuristic, suggestive—*not* definitive. Broadened/ strengthened domestic (national and local) plans and legislation prohibiting child labour and related abusive practices, coupled with the creation of permanent governmental institutions competent to ensure the effective implementation of human rights norms applicable to working children. Expanded ratification and enforcement by states of international law-making instruments directed at the elimination of child labour.

7

Child Labour and International Human Rights

Children constitute part of the labour force in virtually every country. An estimated 246 million people between the ages of 5 and 17 work in the agricultural, industrial, and craft sectors worldwide. Approximately 180 million of these children work under the worst forms of child labour as defined by the International Labour Organization (2002). In spite of conventions and protocols designed to eradicate the worst forms of child labour, international human rights violations concerning children in the workplace persist. This Digest defines child labour and its worst forms within the context of international human rights, describes several key protocols and conventions aimed at eliminating these worst forms, proposes a rationale for teaching about certain issues in child labour, and offers parameters for choosing instructional strategies that teach about the worst forms of child labour.

Not all economic activity performed by children is necessarily a "worst form" of child labour. The International Labour Organization (ILO) distinguishes between acceptable forms of work by children and child labour that should be eradicated. The ILO defines child labour as "all children under 15 years of age who are economically active excluding (i) those who are under five years old and

(ii) those between 12 to 14 years old who spend less than 14 hours a week on their jobs, unless their activities or occupations are hazardous by nature or circumstance".

Of course, any form of labour that endangers a child, denies a child's right to an education, or exposes a child to illicit activities is unacceptable. The unacceptable, worst forms of child labour include work such as bonded labour, prostitution and pornography, illicit activities, armed combat, and physically and mentally hazardous labour. These worst forms manifest themselves in violations of a nation's minimum age laws; threats to a child's physical, mental, or emotional well being; intolerable abuses such as child slavery, forced labour, or hazardous working conditions; illicit activities such as drug and contraband trafficking or debt bondage; and work that prevents a child from going to school.

Protocols and Conventions

In 1973, the ILO adopted Convention 138, commonly known as the Minimum Age Convention, which sought to regulate the minimum acceptable age for different categories of work ranging from light work to work that is hazardous to a child's growth and development. In most cases, 15 is the minimum acceptable age, but in some underdeveloped countries age 14 is allowable (ILO 1973). For years after Convention 138 was adopted, scholars and activists debated its effectiveness to progressively eliminate child labour and began working toward a more effective solution. Eventually, the ILO adopted a new convention. ILO Convention 182 on the Worst Forms of Child Labour, unanimously adopted by ILO member countries in June 1999, was aimed at the immediate elimination of intolerable forms of child labour (ILO 1999).

Convention 182 has focused the attention of the ILO, various national governments, and civil society organizations' resources on working toward eliminating child labour. The United Nations also adopted the Convention on the Rights of the Child (CRC) in 1989. The CRC is the most widely ratified convention in the history of the United Nations. Two specific protocols related to the CRC that deal with the worst forms of child labour were also adopted one dealing with prostitution and pornography and the other addressing the issue of children in armed combat situations (United Nations 1989). These conventions and protocols are only a handful of the international human rights instruments that are relevant to child labour. In addition, Articles 23 and 26 of the United Nations Universal Declaration of Human Rights seek to guarantee "just and favorable conditions of work" and the "right to education," both of which are violated constantly and globally through the exercise of the worst forms of child labour (United Nations 1948).

Issues for Teaching and Learning

Despite the widespread adoption of these international conventions, declarations, and protocols, child labour continues in our global society. Given the nexus between international human rights and the worst forms of child labour, students need to know and understand the international laws and conventions that protect them and other students around the world from unfair, harmful, and cruel child labour practices. As citizens of the twenty first century, students should be prepared to recognize and evaluate the conditions and situations under which approximately 180 million of their peers work and live each day.

The ultimate goal of such learning experiences is for students to become motivated to act on behalf of all the children of the world in abolishing the violations of human rights found in the damaging and harmful practices associated with child labour. Failure to abolish child labour in general, in particular its "worst forms," has led to the suggestion that the issue of child labour is not simply an issue of worker rights or child rights, but an issue of basic human rights which apply to all human beings.

Thus, any curriculum that addresses human rights as a national or international imperative would include child labour as a pertinent topic.

Levels of income, forms of democratic constitutionalism, and cultural regard for education are all determinants in the plight of children in the workforce. Data show that in places where working parents are able to improve working conditions and establish acceptable labour standards (such as adequate salaries), children are much less likely to have to work and, therefore, are much less likely to become victims of harmful labour practices that deny them the essentials of education that underpin a democratic society.

Choosing Instructional Strategies

Felisa Tibbitts developed three models for teaching about human rights that emerged from her research in several countries (2002). By their nature, these models also apply to teaching about child labour as an aspect of human rights. Each of the models-the values and awareness model, the accountability model, and the transformational model-is tailored to a different teaching style and approach.

Regarding the knowledge component of a curriculum that teaches about child labour, the University of Iowa Center for Human Rights (UICHR), through a contract with the United States Department of Labour, is compiling the largest database on child labour laws and statistics in the world. As part of this contract, the UICHR began developing pre-collegiate curricular models that emphasize the following knowledge and skills objectives for learning about child labour that should be included in any course or set of instructional materials that deal with this human rights topic on an international scale.

They recommend that students studying child labour, especially its worst forms, should be able to:

1. Recognize and understand international laws, protocols and conventions enacted to abolish or ameliorate harmful child labour practices around the world, as set forth particularly in ILO Conventions 138 and 182, the United Nations Convention on the Rights of the Child, and the United Nations Universal Declaration of Human Rights;
2. Understand reasons for the failure of many of these laws and conventions;
3. Become knowledgeable about all forms and practices of child labour, particularly those identified as the "worst forms"; understand the context and/or culture in which child labour is often used or practiced; and
4. Develop ideas and commit to action and activities that will significantly aid in the eradication of child labour everywhere.

Essentially, Tibbitts and the UICHR offer criteria for developing and making decisions about instructional materials that offer students and teachers a well-considered approach to learning about child labour, a topic in international human rights that is as delicate as it is important for the advancement of the rights of children everywhere.

The Indian government is failing to protect the rights of hundreds of thousands of children who toil as virtual slaves in the country's silk industry, Human Rights Watch said in a new report. The 85-page report, "Small Change: Bonded Child Labour in India's Silk Industry," calls on the Indian government to implement its national laws to free and rehabilitate these "bonded children." Bound to their employers in exchange for a loan to their families, they are unable to leave while in debt and earn so little they may never be free. A majority of them are Dalits, at the bottom of India's caste system.

"The Indian government claims there are no bonded children in India," said Zama Coursen-Neff, counsel to Human Rights Watch's children's rights division. "In fact, they're everywhere. They are easy to find." Human Rights Watch interviewed children, employers, government officials and members of nongovernmental organizations in three states that form the core of India's sari and silk industries: Karnataka, Uttar Pradesh and Tamilnadu.

At every stage of the silk industry, bonded children as young as five years old work 12 or more hours a day, six and a half or seven days a week. Children making silk thread dip their hands in boiling water that burns and blisters them. They breathe smoke and fumes from machinery, handle dead worms that cause infections, and guide twisting threads that cut their fingers. As they assist weavers, children sit at cramped looms in damp, dim rooms. They do not go to school and are often beaten by their employers. By the time they reach adulthood, they are impoverished, illiterate, and often crippled by the work, the report said.

Human Rights Watch first investigated bonded child labour in India in 1996. Since then, the Supreme Court made rehabilitation of child workers a legal requirement, and India's National Human Rights Commission has successfully pressured some local governments to act. "The government has taken a number of steps in the right direction since our first investigation. The National Human Rights Commission's involvement is especially encouraging," Coursen-Neff said. "However, many of the small improvements are now being rolled back."

High-level government officials interviewed by Human Rights Watch denied that children were bonded or work in factories; they claimed to have therefore shifted their focus to raising public awareness about child labour, instead of freeing children and prosecuting employers. "Most government efforts never reached beyond high-profile industries like carpets and beedi cigarettes," said Coursen-Neff. "Instead of living up to its promises, the Indian government is starting to backtrack, claiming the problem is being solved. Our research shows that it is not."

Human Rights Watch also urged the government to recognize and address the connection between caste and bondage. Coursen-Neff pointed out that caste-based violence and discrimination, not just poverty, keep many *Dalit* families in bondage. "Caste is one of the foundations of the bonded labour system," said Coursen-Neff. "Dalits are denied access to land, forced to work in degrading conditions, and expected to perform free labour. Upper-caste communities inflict violence and economic boycotts on Dalits who challenge their expected social roles, keeping Dalit families in bondage and a perpetual state of poverty."

Human Rights Watch called on international donors to pressure the national and state governments in India to enforce the child labour and bonded labour laws. International donors are increasingly funding some schools for former child workers. "Funding schools is important, but international donors should do more," said Coursen-Neff. "Donors must pressure the Indian government to enforce its own laws to free bonded children. Otherwise, schools won't reach children who can't leave work voluntarily - those who are working under force." Human Rights Watch also called on the national and state governments to greatly expand cooperation with nongovernmental organizations to address the problem of bonded child labour.

Major Silk States:

- Karnataka is India's primary producer of silk thread. There, production still depends on bonded children.

Most are under age 14 and are Dalit or Muslim. In 2001, the state government promulgated an ambitious plan to eliminate all child labour, but it was not in operation at the time of Human Rights Watch's investigation one year later. A nine-year-old boy bonded in Karnataka told Human Rights Watch: "At work the supervisor used to beat me with a belt. He tied me up and beat me with a belt on my back. He did this two or three times. He tied a chain that was attached to the wall to my leg. [The owner beat me] if I didn't do my work properly."

- In Uttar Pradesh, most attention has been paid to child labour in the carpet industry, not silk. While bonded child labour in carpets has not been eliminated, vigilance from the National Human Rights Commission and pressure from domestic and international activists has provoked the government to better enforce the law and to provide schools and other social services. Much less attention has been paid to silk weaving, where child labour that was in factories has been pushed into individual homes. A 14 year-old boy who worked as a weaver's assistant in Varanasi, Uttar Pradesh, told Human Rights Watch that he could not leave his loom owner because he was paying off a loan, which in two years he had only reduced from Rs. 2,500 (U.S. $52) to Rs. 475 (U.S. $9.90). "The owner pays [a small salary] but deducts for the advance [loan]," he said. "He deducts but won't write off the whole advance. We only make enough to eat."
- In Tamilnadu, which has successfully identified more bonded labourers than any other state, most state initiatives have focused on children working in match and fireworks manufacture. However, the state government has simply abandoned Supreme Court-mandated rehabilitation of child workers for those children found after 1997, in clear violation of the court's

order. In Kanchipuram district, a major silk sari weaving area in Tamilnadu, child bondage flourishes openly. A 13 year-old girl working in a silk weaving factory in Kanchipuram told Human Rights Watch: "Always [the weavers and owners] are beating me - I don't like to work. They always scold and shout. They beat me on the back and head. They are always knocking their fists on my head or hitting me with a comb [wood piece in the loom]. We don't play at all."

Child Labour and Human Rights Abuses

Nearly 50,000 children are estimated to work in the mines of Katanga in the Democratic Republic of Congo (DRC). Much of the cobalt they mine ends up in batteries for portable electronics that young people in Europe love to buy, such as mobile phones, laptops and MP3 players. In South Africa, local communities have been forced to leave their farmland without proper compensation to make way for platinum mines supplying the computer industry. make IT fair, a new network of organizations from across Europe, is calling on companies such as Sony, Nokia, Hewlett-Packard and Philips to start addressing the ethical and environmental risks related to purchasing of metals.

Metal prices are booming, but many of the mine workers in African countries have not noticed this, as revealed in a recent survey conducted by the make IT fair network. Wages commonly do not cover basic needs, especially among the industry's growing numbers of subcontracted workers. Emissions and discharges are destroying the environment for generations to come. Death and injury rates are notoriously high. A new report1 from one of make IT fair's Swedish partners, SwedWatch, shows that about a quarter of the world's cobalt goes into products such as mobile phones, laptops, camcorders, digital cameras, MP3 players and electronic games. More than half of the world's cobalt comes from Zambia and the DRC, where local communities complain about severe pollution causing health problems and loss of livelihoods. Eighty people suffered fatal accidents in the mines of Zambia in 2005 alone.

In the DRC about one third of all people working in the mining industry are estimated to be children and adolescents. Some of them are as young as seven years old. Sara Nordbrand at SwedWatch says: "They live a very risky and unhealthy life, working without protective gear, inhaling mineral dust that might damage their lungs and irritate their eyes." Anglo Platinum, the world's largest platinum company, mines its platinum and palladium for computer hard drives, mobile phones and flatscreen TVs in South Africa. In order to make way for platinum mining operations, this company is forcing 17,000 local inhabitants to leave their ancestral lands, without proper compensation, reveals the Dutch organisation SOMO in its report.

Esther de Haan from the Dutch organisation SOMO says: "Forty per cent of the miners we met during our research are contracted labourers who have few rights and earn substantially less than other workers. They often perform the most dangerous tasks with very little safety training." Currently, none of the market leading electronics companies are dealing with these risks, even though metals play an essential role in their electronic gadgets. Make IT fair is calling on consumer electronics companies to play their part by taking responsibility for human rights and labour abuses in their supply chain. "Even though the consumer electronics industry is a significant consumer of many metals, and many of these metals are extracted in high-risk countries such as China, Russia and various African states, the industry does not address the problems. So far they have not tried to investigate where their metals come from. We urge them to do this and to start to make IT fair for people everywhere," says Esther de Haan from SOMO.

Human Rights and the Capability Approach

The issue of child labour is sometimes debated on the basis of a cultural framework. More precisely, child activities are perceived either as a socializing way for children or an apprenticeship way of life. In a certain meaning these arguments deny the value of human rights. If Sen does not focus particularly on child labour, he rejects clearly the cultural point of view. Moreover, in its discussion about human rights Sen (2005) establishes a distinction between substantive opportunities and freedom of processes. He focuses essentially on substantive opportunities as the capability approach seems more in phase with this way of thinking. Human rights become entitlements to capability. This analyses the application of the capability approach to the issue of child labour.

Firstly, we discuss the cultural argument of child labour. We argue, on the one hand, that this point of view is not sustainable and cannot be opposite to human rights approach; and on the other hand, that the distinction between child work and child labour may be in accordance with the cultural framework, but does not constitute a rejection of human rights. Secondly, starting from the distinction made by Sen between substantive opportunities and freedom of processes, we show that substantive opportunities renews the issue of child labour by bringing critical aspects in debate. However, this aspect leads us to consider only a part of the child labour question. Freedom of processes also plays its role. Focusing on a single approach of substantive opportunities enlightens the importance of the process of decision dealt with the intra-family issue related to children.

Thirdly, we go beyond this first limit to the capability approach using Nussbaum (2000) capabilities list. We argue about capabilities articulation as processes. In this vein we defend capabilities processes of freedom. We underline that opportunity to education needs to be completed with other capabilities like emotional capability. The capability approach is then seen as processes. This point of view implies nonetheless an opportunity to be educated but moreover non violent processes of education is required. Cultural framework versus child's rights - Interpretation of the cultural framework, the attempts to assert human rights or child's rights are often confronted with the accusation of violation and non respect of countries cultural specificities.

This inquisition is too excessive and most of the time does not rest on any foundation. To us, three arguments clearly reject a "caricatured" conception of defence of cultural specificities. Firstly, as Sen (1999) underlines, if we have to consider these specificities, then they indeed do not concern countries but even more restrained geographical areas and sometimes do concern only with some individuals. It is in fact impossible in most cases to consider that the individuals of the same country have homogenous cultural traits. Significative differences between regions or States, as well as within the same region or country really exist. And these differences do not limit themselves to large countries like India or the USA, but also affect countries of small size like France or Togo. The defenders of cultural specificities should agree that cultural specificities have to be maintained at the finest level that could lead to accept specificities applying to restricted individual groups. But under no circumstances, they can be considered valid for a given country.

Secondly, specificities saying "cultural" constitute a serious attack for human life. Let us imagine that a cultural specificity in a given geographical area consists in mutilating children severely at birth, for instance by cutting them a hand. On what foundation this specificity could be defended? It is clear that the defenders of cultural specificities are badly comfortable to defend cases affecting seriously human life. But they do not provide any appropriate criteria for distinguishing the specificities that can be rejected from those that can be accepted. Unless they accept that some individuals may attack human life, whereas others do not. Many countries experience dramatic practices. Let us choose two examples: the infibulation and the cramming (force- feeding) are both practices having destructive impacts on children.

The former, a deeper and serious form of excision consists of the ablation of clitoris with the suture of sex. The latter practiced essentially in West Africa consists in forcing young girls to eat a huge amount of food (more often, it is puree) in order that they gain weight substantially and become enough fat to respect the standards of beauty and perform a "good and nice" marriage. This practice leads in most cases to serious problems of obesity and health and invalidates severely the young girls, who indeed are subjected to their husband. Moreover, various practices, saying cultural traits, are indeed not as ancient as it appears and are the results of socioeconomic evolution. They have no only "cultural" foundations since they result from economic strategies in a context of survival or wealth rising. The dowry issue in India illustrates perfectly this specificity. Marriage and the practice of dowry are strongly embedded in a rigid social context of norms and caste rules. At the same time, new economic and development opportunities have a considerable impact on social organisation in Indian society. The social status of a person is determined by his caste. Within a context of economic development, particularly in urban areas, the social status takes into account of several elements: caste, education, nature of the occupation and income.

Within such context, the identity, and therefore the social status, of an individual is not determined by rigid, hereditary factors such as community and caste affiliation, but by economic factors (income, education, occupation).

In well-developed urban areas, this leads to a bigger socio-economic heterogeneity within a given caste. So, a striking social change is operated across India and implies new strategies notably within the family. The changes in social status play indeed a major role in the marriage institution, which is regarded as a mean to strike up family relations and to enhance social mobility. In particular, the fact that some families pay higher dowries is for them a way of entering into a prestigious alliance and of distinguishing themselves within their own community. This matrimonial strategy through dowry payments is associated with a strategy of differentiation and distinction, which enables the families to improve their social status and shape new identities for themselves.

Thus the contemporary practice of dowry is seen for families as a strategy of investment in social status. It leads to a process of identity distinction involving spatial and social expansion of dowry and its inflation. The argument of cultural specificities is often a wrong argument in the hands of the conservatives finding a special interest to maintain situation in the state. This argument is not relevant taken in a broad sense which would include all practices. In this sense, it is not an opposable argument to human rights and child's rights. It does not mean that it is necessary to deny any contextual specificity. But on one hand these contextual specificities are not necessarily cultural and can be led to change with context; on the other hand they have to be confronted to human rights and to child's rights to establish if they do not constitute a fundamental violation of these rights. The convention of the child's rights and its implications.

The United Nation has implemented the convention on the rights of the child in 1989 to endow children with the same rights as adult and comfort the idea that children as human being having a fragile status must need rights which protect them. The convention comprises 54 articles and two protocols. The convention is based on five fundamental principles stipulating that all children throughout the world regardless to its race, colour, religion, ethnic, caste, opinion, gender, wealth must beneficiate of the right to survival, to develop to the fullest, to be protected from harmful influences, abuse and exploitation, to participate fully in family, cultural and social life. The convention has been ratified by 187 countries except the United States of America and Somalia. If only it was sufficient to illustrate by an example that the non ratification of the convention of the child's right does not stem from the defence of the cultural specificities, the fact that two different countries like the USA and Somalia do not sign this convention would be significant.

Even if the convention is largely ratified and accepted by governments, it remains nonetheless problematical concerning its application in developing countries particularly when it challenges the issue of child labour. Developing countries have lately recognised the existence of child labour. Therefore, all the countries having ratified the convention take the engagement to include it in their constitutions and they accept to implement all the means to protect children. The refusal to sign this convention on behalf of the United States is rather linked to their will not to compromise the practices of multinationals in terms of exploitation operating in South. The signature of this convention can indeed be meant systematically so that the governments act against the practices of these companies. Nonetheless, the fundamental principles of the convention raise some main issues of discussion.

The survival of children is the main problematical issue. In the literature on child labour the survival of a child depends on that of the household living standard. The poverty approach stipulates that a child for the survival purpose has to work as long as the family income is unable to ensure his living. Hence, child labour becomes a mean for the household survival. The policy implication of such a principle consists in improving the household income particularly those of the parents and denies the problem of children of the street who have to work for their survival on the street. If this aim is easily attainable in developed countries and in wealthier household, it is not the case in developing countries.

Thus the fundamental constraint for applying this convention is not cultural but economic. A number of studies deal with this issue, for instance the papers of Ray examine cases of several single countries but also comparative analyses studies. The empirical studies reveal the fact that child labour is directly and indirectly related to poverty depending on the structures of the economies. The second problem faced by the convention is its objective of "to develop to the fullest". This objective is the main core of the millennium goal led by the United Nations. For the harmonious development of children, the States members of the UN must educate their children, give health services, as well as social services. In most of the low income countries the rate of enrolment is under 50% and the gap between boys and girls enrolment is quite high and particularly in rural areas.

UNESCO has implemented in 1992 the programme "education for all (EFA)" in order to attain the millennium goal. The objective of such a programme is to have 100% of enrolment for both boys and girls. Two difficulties have to be considered to reach this goal. The first one is of economic nature. The reason for non enrolling children at school is explained by income poverty, lack of parents' education, worst school infrastructures, and lack of school in rural areas. In such an environment it is very difficult to fulfil the objective of EFA.

The second dimension is cultural. Some countries count in the rate of access to education the children who are registered in schools always not offering basic programmes allowing a "normal" schooling. For instance, some coranic schools only supply coranic teaching without any consideration of other subjects or disciplines. It is a wrongly cultural feature since these schools, in addition to the coranic teaching, can also offer basic teachings required for a normal schooling. Moreover, a number of them and probably the best make it.

The third problem addressed by the UN convention is those of exploitation and child abuse. The convention forbids the recruitment of children for the industry of sex, pornography, and prostitution and also for armed conflicts. Lately in 1999, the ILO has adopted the convention on the worst forms of child labour.

The convention C182 challenges the issue of child rights and the ILO makes its priority to eradicate the worst form of child labour as it is detriment to the child development for the fullest. Hence, the ILO distinguishes between child labour and child work. If the former is seen as dangerous for the physical and mental development of the child, the latter is considered as beneficial to children as it can be a way of socialization.

Acknowledging the possibility for children to exercise a socializing activity (for instance to milk cows in rural area) does not however justify to put them in work during long hours, even if this activity does not present any danger in itself. It is necessary to distinguish what is of the resort of socializing activity from what dealt with economic constraint affecting the household. The economic conditions such as the lack of family resources, time constraint for women, etc. often imply children occupations for completing these resources or for freeing women's time. And if some activities, more or less traditional, can be linked to apprenticeship, it is also necessary to distinguish them from the economic constraints. From this point of view, the number of the performed hours, the conditions in which they are executed are significative elements.

It is then obvious, under these conditions of boundary that traditions do not enter in contradiction with the child's rights but can favor their promotion. In the sense, the argument of cultural specificities cannot be opposed to human rights and child's rights. If it is necessary to take it into account, it is because cultural specificities reinforce the implementation of these rights.

Child Labour and the Concept of Childhood

In society, a child is a passive person without having any possibility to express his desires. The convention gives children the possibility to voice their wishes and to participate actively in the family decision particularly when they are directly concerned with. A child becomes an active person inside the family. Nevertheless, the perception of childhood is quite different in most developing countries. The convention on the child rights gives a universal concept of childhood. Every child in every part of the world must have the same childhood which consists in going to school for basic education, playing game for the physical and mental development. The UN defines a child as a person being under the age of 18. This definition of a child does not allow a child to work as long as it is detrimental to her/ his development. The ILO convention 138 fixes the minimum age of work at 15 years old and encourages the States ratifying the convention to take actions to fight against child labour and to raise gradually the minimum age of work.

Moreover the convention 138 stipulates that the national legislations must not be in conflict with the compulsory education. Considering the real economic state of a lot of low income countries, the ILO accepts that the age of work can be decreased to the age of 13 and 12 in non detrimental activities and the age of work in dangerous activities is maintained at 18 years old. However, derogation can be given of working in dangerous activities to children of 16 years old belonging to the poorest household. Meanwhile, the ILO has engaged a lot of means to fight against child labour and in 1999 a special convention has been ratified aiming to fight against the worst forms of child labour. The convention on the worst forms of child labour has been widely ratified contrarily of the convention 138 which is more in debate; especially because it is more difficult to find a consensus about the minimum age of work among States.

The concept of childhood is not universally accepted and concepts of childhood and adulthood depend on societies. According to Aries (1969) the concept of childhood is a recent creation; it is a transitional step common to every child which is characterised by basic physical changes. Therefore according to James and James (2001) if childhood is common to all children, it is not the same for all, it varies due to cultural factors and generations. And according to Punch (2001) within a country all the children do not have the same childhood whether they are issued from a wealthier or poorer milieu. The concept of childhood cannot be understood outside its local and social context and not as global phenomenon. In some countries age is a reference for adulthood while in other countries such as Sub-Saharan Africa the transition from one state to another depends on rituals. We cannot deny that cultural factors influence the place of a child in society.

Each society considers differently a child; norms and traditions influence the perception of childhood. However, it is not a reason to justify the precocious working age of children in bringing the cultural argument. In several cases, economic considerations determine the child labour decision and not cultural factors. For proof, numbers of industrial countries have recently revised their legislation in a worrying way in reducing the minimum age to work. It is the case of France that has just lowered the age of work for apprenticeship from14 years to 13 years. If this measure aims to favour the insertion of young persons in the professional life, we have to consider the negative repercussions of this policy. It reduces for instance the professional trajectories of the young persons by "formatting" them too much early.

Moreover, some firms could find cheap, malleable and not unionized labour force, and from which they can part without any compensation. As stated earlier, childhood is a transition step towards a stable state of adulthood. However, if all the children do not have the same childhood, the convention gives a conceptual framework for reaching this aim. The question is what is the best mean to reach the state of adulthood? The UN considers that schooling is the best way to attain adulthood, which increases human capital and has a positive impact on growth and development. All the children must have the same childhood which consists in going to school and to endow their free time on leisure. It is necessary to acknowledge the apprenticeship as an intermediary form but it is also necessary to differentiate two aspects of the apprenticeship taken in the broad sense.

The first aspect is an effect of socialisation. It can be applied to younger children, since it concerns none dangerous activities and since it is limited to a low level of working hours. It can be quite in relation with some cultural traditions if they do not present danger for children. The second aspect is an effect of training in a professional perspective. Therefore, in this case, the age must be absolutely the highest as possible. Indeed, the aspect of training is not the same nature as the dimension of socialisation. It involves a defined trajectory of the child's activity for his future and in this sense restrains his space of future freedom.

The assimilation of these two effects without any precaution drives the defenders of cultural specificities to admit any type of activity in name of the respect of traditions. In reality, they refuse to accept economic constraints affecting child labour. This pressure is not only the prerogative of developing countries, as confirms it the legal measures taken recently by several industrialised countries in favour of a reduction of the age of apprenticeship which is viewed as a violation of the convention 138. Therefore, what is behind apprenticeship is not really in relation with the question of childhood.

In his recent works, Sen establishes a link between capability approach and human rights. In this approach, human rights are seen as the entitlements of capabilities. To underline the role played by this approach in the defence of human rights, Sen evokes the distinction between substantive opportunities and freedom of processes. This latter distinction is expressed by Sen through the example of a woman called Natasha. We suppose that Natasha is constrained by any authority to go out in the evening. This situation implies that she is not free to decide if she wants to go out or not. And even if she wants to go out, then the constraint is in correspondence with her choice, she has no freedom to make a choice. We are therefore in a situation of violation of freedom of choice, what Sen names a violation of the freedom of processes. Moreover, this situation underlines a lack of opportunities since precisely there is no choice. The capability approach focuses on the second aspect namely the absence of alternatives in the achieved choice and deals with the issue of substantive opportunities.

The capability approach seems over demanding since it involves the real possibility of alternative choices, which includes the possibility to evaluate freely the alternative choices. Hence, whereas the freedom of processes limits itself to the absence of freedom on a choice decided by another one, substantive opportunities is related to make something that has been chosen by another one and which would not be chosen if the freedom of choice has been given. However, as Sen (2005) underlines, if the capability approach allows to give a foundation to human rights by stressing on the aspect of "opportunity of freedom", it is hardly adapted to treat in an adequate manner the process of freedom.

The capability approach deals with the individual advantages and gives up partly the issues of equity or justice in the process of choice. In other words, it is interested in the alternatives of choice and not in the process which lead to achieve these choices. Thus, this approach can be used for instance as a way to defend democracy by stressing on the importance of the electoral choices, but does not allow to examine properly the democratic process in itself.

The Distinction for Child Labour and Child's Rights

The distinction between freedom of processes and substantive opportunities permits to reveal three very different aspects in the moral valuation of situations. The first aspect is the possibility to do, namely this is the means to accomplish actions. The capability approach examines the issue beyond means since it is necessary to take into account of the freedom of choice e.g. to consider the real presence of alternative opportunities. In this sense, the capability approach is an approach in term of freedom of choice. It is the second aspect there.

The third aspect concerns the process by which the choice is made or the procedural aspect of choice. It refers to the valuation of the importance of the freedom of processes. These three aspects have different implications in the debate on child labour and child's rights.

Concerning the distinction between the two first aspects, e.g. doing and the freedom to choose for doing, it is clear that the issue of choice between education and work is central regarding the freedom of choice and that child labour may be seen as a serious negative externality in the freedom of choice. But the freedom of choice has some implications beyond the dichotomy between work and education.

First, freedom does not limit itself to a dichotomic choice and it assumes to enlarge the choice to other alternatives for instance to apprenticeship. There is a list of questions relative to apprenticeship such as the minimum age at the beginning of apprenticeship, the conditions in which it is realised, etc. From this point of view, the capability approach can certainly be useful, for instance by establishing a link with health, but seems unsatisfactory.

It does not permit to answer on the whole to such questions. However, we can underline by emphasizing the freedom of choice (in terms we have defended earlier) that economic constraints determine essentially choices and then the capability approach becomes a strong argument to lay on the real absence of freedom of choice and to re-question about the diminution in the age of in apprenticeship. Then the freedom of choice repositions the distinction between child labour and child work.

In comparison with the first one, the second category is considered possible because it does not constitute an "aggression" against the moral and physical development of children. However, as the first one, it reveals an absence of freedom of choice.

Child work (even light activities) cannot be considered as a choice that they have made. Much worse, the longer hours of work affected to these working activities reduce seriously the future alternatives for children in terms of choice of life. In this perspective, the child work is also reprehensible. The tolerance of child work can certainly be recovering from a principle of reality but enters in spite of in contradiction with a vision of child's rights would give all its importance to the freedom of choice. If we now consider the distinction between freedom of choice and freedom of processes, it seems to us that the aspect of freedom of processes brings a complementary light but also a more over demanding argument in the field of child's rights.

Indeed, it is not only the question to know if the child's rights are respected on the basis of the freedom of choice, but to consider the process by which choices are made. Therefore this aspect is particularly important concerning children since it is often parents or tutors who decide for them. Even if these choices comply with children's expectations, the aspect of freedom of processes requires that children be involved in the choice and that they can reveal their preferences in a context of freedom of choice. Finally it comes to examine the power of decision within the family. Regarding the debate on child labour and the child's rights, there are some direct implications.

On one hand, education must be a freely approved choice and for which the child acts substantially. The educative rules must themselves be founded on voicing and the involvement of children must be encouraged in the definition of rules. On the other hand, if the choice is made for exercising an activity, the gains perceived have to be freely used by children. This perspective repositions completely the debate in the field of children's freedom in the definition of their own life and decisions involving them. This framework can appear over demanding but it is the price to pay for taking seriously in account the child's rights as a space of freedom regarding them. Then we can easily understand the decisive role played by the right to voice for children.

The Capabilities List Applied to Children

The capability approach made until now the object of fewer applications on questions linked to childhood. There are Klasen (2001) and Biggeri (2004) for a discussion on the importance of this approach for understanding children's wellbeing, Di Tommaso (2003) for a measure of wellbeing, Biggeri (2003) and Biggeri et al. (2005) for a first link with the child labour issue, Ballet et al. (2004) for an application on the children of streets. These two latter works are more directly inspired from the approach defended by Nussbaum (2000), from the list of ten capabilities established by Nussbaum. Biggeri et al. (2005), establish a list of capabilities revealed by children themselves during the First World Congress on Child Labour.

From an analysis of speeches and a set of more or less closed questions, they deduct a classification of capabilities according to age. On the one hand, some capabilities are often more revealed than others such as education, love and care, leisure and activity, physical health. On the other hand, the relevance of capabilities depends on age of children interviewed. Some capabilities are constantly considered for instance, physical health, freedom in opposition with exploitation, social relations. Others are given more value for some age categories: love and care diminish lightly slightly from the age of 15 years old; education is the object of a more important consideration from 6 years, religion and identity progress continuously according to age.

These results present a great interest because they give importance to what children consider as important and not what the adult in charge of children's wellbeing consider as important to them. Moreover, the study confirms clearly that education is the capability that is the most in consideration. Such a result seems to confirm the policies of development based on education as a cure of child labour. Biggeri et al. (2005), reveal five essential aspects of the capability approach dealing with children's wellbeing. First, the set of parents' capabilities affect directly or indirectly the set of children's capabilities. Thus, there would be a kind of intergenerational transfer of capabilities.

The first aspect presents a particular interest in the case of debt bondage performed by parents which is finally transferred to children. Secondly the possibility to convert the capabilities into functioning depends on the behaviour of parents and other adults because children being generally dependant to parents, they do not have an entire autonomy and their choice is more or less severely constrained by the parental decisions and parents attitude. The degree of autonomy increases in average with age. Thirdly, every capability has certainly an intrinsic value, but it has also, particularly in the case of children, an instrumental value for the development of autonomy and of freedom of choice. Fourth, the evolution of the life cycle and more specifically the age of children have to be linked with different capabilities. The importance of some capabilities then does not appear to be identical at every stage of the life cycle and for different age of childhood (child, teenager).

The relevance of every capability must be consequently examined according to age and stage of the life cycle. Fifth, children constitute the keystone of future changes. In other words, as being strongly influenced by the intergenerational transfers of capabilities from their parents, they are also considered as future parents, future transmitters of capabilities. Then, they play a very important role in changes and in the possibilities of conversion of capabilities with time.

Dynamic of Capabilities

The normative considerations we bring constitute a direct reaction to the approach proposed by Biggeri et al. (2005). In comparison with this approach we want to underline two critical points. On the one hand, it seems to us that the overlapping between the five aspects of the list of capabilities developed by these authors is more important than their distinction. Considering the overlapping dimension leads to modify the prominence of certain capabilities. However, the authors are essentially concentrated on the distinction aspect and not on the embedding structure. From a heuristic point of view, if the distinction between these aspects is appropriate, it raises some serious difficulties for understanding some issues such as children of streets. On the other hand, the authors finally lean essentially on the forth aspect of the capability.

This issue of the intergenerational transfer of capabilities is central in the debate on socially sustainable development; approach enunciated earlier, namely the relevance of capabilities in the life cycle and according to age. But several nuances can be enlightened. Firstly, the distinction between intrinsic value and instrumental value of capability is not emphasized. It is indeed possible that children give more importance and then give a better consideration during interviews for the intrinsic value of capabilities and minimise the instrumental value. That means they underestimate the importance of some capabilities for reaching those whose intrinsic value seems the most important to them. For instance, it raises the question on the necessary capabilities capable to develop the capability dealt with education. It means from a point of view of policies, that instrumental capabilities may be more important than others.

Moreover, the result underlined by the authors does not emphasize the link with the second aspect enunciated in the capability approach namely the role of parental attitude and constraints imposed by parents. This result refers partly to this link since children are be able to value either capabilities transferred by their parents or capabilities that children could not have been able to enhance because of constraints from their parents. But the difference between both aspects is worth being raised since the conditions of achievements are not always constant in terms of intergenerational transmission of capabilities. It seems to us that these difficulties are mostly related to the methodology chosen by the authors. It is a static method where children of different ages are interviewed for a given period of time. A diachronic method reflecting the trajectory of children would be more fruitful because it would permit to have the opinion of children themselves on the revaluation of the capabilities to which they had given an importance in a previous time. Let's take the example of a capability for which the relevance is judged very weak by children: religion and identity.

This capability can be underestimated because the moral development of children is insufficient and because they do not perceive the importance of such a capability. For instance the works of Kolhberg (1981) show particularly that the moral development of children followed different stages. Hence, to children, religion and identity can appear at different stages of childhood as a secondary matter and without having any intrinsic value compared to education. But taken over long period, beyond childhood, religion and identity can take a higher and substantial value whereas education will take also an instrumental value through its achievement.

A diachronic analysis could be able to capture precisely these changes. We apply now these considerations to the issue of children of streets. On the one hand, the attitude and the constraint imposed to children by their parents determine the phenomenon. The family violence is the main factor. Eradicating the phenomenon supposes to act on violent practices. But an interview of children at some point of time would give some results in favour of education. However, education is not the solution since some forms of education through the institutional violence are also at the origin of the phenomenon.

In terms of intergenerational transmission, violent practices reduce considerably the identity trajectory of children and restrain the freedom of future choice, affecting also a set of capabilities comprising those linked to social relationships. Hence, from a static point of view of children embedded in a given situation, the affective relationships may not be seen as the essential capability whereas it determines the other capabilities. Affective relations influence also educative performances and in the case of children of streets, it constitutes the main motor of the dynamics of the phenomenon. Children rights and the capabilities approach as capabilities processes of freedom introduce temporal aspects, their approach remains static through their methodology. Some works have however already attempted to make the approach dynamic. It appears that the aspect of freedom of processes constitutes an appropriate way to integrate dynamics in this approach. Hence, contrary to Sen, who puts in opposition the capability approach to the approach of freedom of processes; it seems to us that the latter could improve substantially the former.

Evoking freedom of choice, if this freedom precisely concerns only the choice and not the process by which the choice is done constitutes a restrictive view which is surely acceptable from a static point of view, but insufficient when it comes to include dynamic considerations in the analysis. Regarding children, the dynamic dimension is essential because if normative considerations are taken into account, it is certainly to consider their present situation but also in the perspective when they will be adults themselves. The freedom to achieve a valuable life of dignity, through a set of positive choices depends also on the capacity to express the choices in question. From a dynamic point of view, substantive opportunities cannot be opposed to the freedom of processes. They are both complementary. Choices have not to be only performed on actions to do or not, but also on rules permitting to achieve these choices.

This last aspect constitutes a meta-choice in relation with the choice of doing or not. We then name the approach as a capability approach of processes of freedom, in the sense that the processes of decision freely defined determine themselves the choices of actions among different opportunities. This approach has a major impact regarding the choice between education and work. It is not only a question of offering education as an alternative for work. The forms of education must permit to children to voice freely, assuming two conditions. On the one hand, within the family children have to be able to freely express their preferences. On the other hand, educative rules are themselves jointly defined between adults and children as well as within the family as at school.

These considerations imply to go beyond the Millennium objectives in terms of rate of enrolment. A higher rate of enrolment is indeed not significative because it does not mean necessarily a form of education freely accepted. A higher enrolment rate can be even compatible with some very violent forms of education. On the contrary, taking into account of children in the definition of procedures and rules of education themselves calls to a not violent form of education. Conclusion Acknowledging the children's rights and restricting their exploitation may remain voiceless if any financial support is not engaged by the richer countries in favour of the achievement of this objective in the poorer countries. On the contrary, rich countries tend to reduce the minimal age for working. Cultural and tradition arguments are not relevant to restrict these rights. It is especially necessary to accept that choices are made under economic considerations. But this point of view allows to focus on the central role played by the capability approach in terms of analysis of the freedom of choice.

This approach brings out a critical point of view important for debate, notably calling into question the distinction between child labour and child work. However, a central element must be held for the analysis beyond the capability approach: the freedom of processes. Then, the debate is more fruitful with regard to the power of decision and voices affecting directly children. The capability approach is enlarged to dynamic way and is seen as an approach in terms of capabilities processes of freedom in which the choice of rules and procedures are as important as the choice resulting from these rules and procedures. In terms of education, this framework requires a substantial participation of the children in the educative rules and campaigns in favor of a form of not violent education.

8

Child Labour and Health

Child labour is an important global issue associated with poverty, inadequate educational opportunities, gender inequality, and a range of health risks. Child labour is defined by the relevant international conventions (UNICEF's Convention on the Rights of the Child, International Labour Organization [ILO] Convention 138, and especially, 182) not by the activities performed by the child, but by the consequences of such activities (exceptions are the so-called unconditional worst forms of child labour such as prostitution and bondage). For instance, work affecting a child's health and schooling should, according to these conventions, be eliminated. Identifying the health effects of child labour is essential because it enables policymakers to decide which types of child labour to target for eradication.

The ILO estimates that there are approximately 250 million child labourers worldwide, with at least 120 million of them working under circumstances that have denied them a childhood and in conditions that jeopardize their health and even their lives. Most working children are ages 11 to 14 years old, but as many as 60 million are between the ages of 5 and 11. Although the exact numbers are not known, available statistics indicate that approximately 96% of child workers reside in developing countries in Africa, Asia, and Latin America; there are also pockets of child labour in many industrialized countries. In spite of a reported decline in child labour during the period 1995 to 2000, child labour remains a major concern. Most child labourers begin working at a very young age, are malnourished, and work long hours in hazardous occupations; frequently they do not attend school. They receive very low wages or are unpaid, and their income or help is usually essential for family survival.

They are mainly employed in the informal sector, with agriculture accounting for more children workers than any other sector. It is estimated that, in developing countries, at least 90% of economically active children in rural areas are employed in agriculture. Recent ILO statistics from 20 developing countries categorized the proportion of economically active children aged 5 to 14 years as employed in agriculture, animal husbandry, and related work at 74% (73.3% of boys and 78.8% of girls).

Short term, the most obvious economic impact of child labour at the family level is an increase in household income. Long term, the under accumulation of human capital caused by low school attendance and poor health is a serious negative consequence of child labour, representing a missed opportunity to enhance the productivity and future earnings capacity of the next generation.

Child labourers grow up to be low-wage–earning adults; as a result, their offspring will also be compelled to work to supplement the family's income. In this way, poverty and child labour is passed from generation to generation. Although child labour is recognized as a global health problem, research on its health impact on children has been limited and sometimes inconsistent. In 1998, Graitcer and Lerer published the first comprehensive review of the effect of child labour on children's health by extrapolating data from the Global Burden of Disease Study. The occupational mortality rate among children matched the adult occupational mortality rate, such that the occupational mortality rate indicates mortality associated with child labour. In another study, in 2000, Graitcer and Lerer did not find any differences in the health status of working and nonworking Egyptian children in the short run (the children were not followed to adulthood).

A 2003 report on children's work in Morocco, Yemen, and Guatemala, and a review developed under the aegis of Understanding Children's Work Project provide an overview of the nature and extent of child labour, its determinants, and its consequences for the health and education of children in these countries.

Several case–control and cohort studies have reported on the association of child labour, impaired growth, and malnutrition. The health effects of child labour on children and the correlation between current health and future health status are difficult to investigate and are compounded by short-term versus long-term health consequences. The situation is further complicated because work can contribute to an improvement in a poor child's nutritional status (a positive health effect). Finally, the anthropometric measurements that traditionally have been used to evaluate children's health status are of limited value for those who are age 10 years and older.

We provide evidence, garnered from a cross section of countries, on the relation between child labour and children's health. To our knowledge, this study represents the first use of cross-country data to examine the issue. The benefit of cross-country data is that they allow us to synthesize indicators, creating a set of indicators unavailable in micro- or individual-country data. The drawback to using different data sources is that the statistics may not be comparable. To avoid problems of comparability, we limited ourselves to data that were standardized by the institutions that collected or compiled them.

We analyzed the health effects of child labour on children by correlating existing health indicators and the prevalence of child labour in a large group of developing countries (Algeria, Angola, Bangladesh, Belize, Benin, Bolivia, Botswana, Brazil, Burkina Faso, Burundi, Cambodia, Cameroon, Chad, Chile, China, Congo, Colombia, Cote d'Ivoire, Costa Rica, Democratic Republic of Congo, Dominican Republic, Egypt, Ecuador, El Salvador, Eritrea, Gabon, Gambia, Ghana, Guatemala, Guinea, Guinea Bissau, Haiti, Honduras, India, Indonesia, Iran, Iraq, Jamaica, Jordan, Kenya, Laos, Liberia, Libya, Lesotho, Madagascar, Malaysia, Malawi, Mali, Mexico, Mongolia, Mozambique, Morocco, Myanmar, Namibia, Nepal, Nicaragua, Niger, Nigeria, Oman, Pakistan, Panama, Papua New Guinea, Paraguay, Peru, Philippines, Rwanda, Senegal, Sierra Leone, Solomon's Islands, Sri Lanka, Sudan, Swaziland, Syrian Arab Republic, Uganda, Uruguay, Tanzania, Venezuela, Vietnam, Thailand, Togo, Yemen, Zambia, Zimbabwe).

Methods

Data and Indicator Sources: We derived our estimates on the prevalence of child labour among children aged 10 to 14 years from only 1 data set - the World Bank's World Development Indicators.

This source limits its estimates of working children to the "economically active population," which means that children who are in non economic activities or are employed in hidden forms of work such as domestic service, prostitution, and armed conflict are not included. Health indicators, such as health status, and health determinant indicators, which give information about the health of a community or population relative to some criteria or in comparison with other communities or populations, were obtained from the World Development Indicators, the Global Burden of Disease Study, and the life tables for 191 countries (our study included only the 83 developing countries).

The following rates and per centages were obtained from the World Bank database: male and female adult mortality rates, fertility rates, the prevalence of undernourishment (per centage of population), the prevalence of HIV/AIDS among adults (per centage of population), and national poverty levels (per centage of population below the national poverty line, as determined using the World Bank's country poverty assessments). The World Bank's data set came from multitopic welfare surveys, such as the Living Standard Measurement Study (LSMS), which measure and analyzes poverty. Dozens of countries have implemented multitopic surveys, and many of them have conducted the same survey repeatedly, allowing for relevant comparisons across time. Multitopic surveys can also be used to measure the effect of public policies and programs on poverty. The LSMS—one of the best known and most useful of these surveys—has a questionnaire designed to study multiple aspects of household welfare and behaviour; it also incorporates extensive quality-control features.

The main objective of LSMS surveys is to collect household data that can be used to assess household welfare, understand household behaviour, and evaluate the effect of various government policies on the quality living conditions of the population. Accordingly, LSMS surveys collect information on employment, household income and expenditures; asset ownership, such as housing or land; health; education; fertility; nutrition; migration; and access to services and social programs. To minimize errors and delays in data processing, LSMS surveys are implemented with distinct procedures that resolve most inconsistencies in the raw data before the data reach the central statistical office. Data on HIV/AIDS infections, non-HIV infections, and malaria among children aged 5 to 14 years, associated with 4 major risk factors (malnutrition, poor water and lack of sanitation and hygiene, unsafe sex, and dangerous occupation), came from the Global Burden of Disease

Study. These indicators are expressed as disability-adjusted life years calculated as the sum of years of life lost because of disability and years of life lived with disability.

Mortality rates among children, both boys and girls, aged 10 to 14 years were obtained from these life tables. The data, all from the year 2000, were collected from 83 countries in 6 geographic regions, as defined by the Global Burden of Disease Study (sub-Saharan Africa, Latin America and the Caribbean, Asia and Pacific Islands, China, India, and North Africa/Middle East). Data Analysis The data on child labour (expressed as a per centage of children aged 10 to14 years who were workers) and health indicators were analyzed by multiple regression to ascertain the effect of child labour on the various health indicators. All data were aggregated at the national level. The strength of the association between the per centage of children who were workers and HIV/AIDS infections, non-HIV infections, and malaria as expressed by disability-adjusted life years were also correlated using SPSS version 10 for Windows.

The following were designated as dependent variables: the mortality rate among boys aged 10 to 14 years, the mortality rate among girls aged 10 to 14 years, and the per centage of the population aged 10 to 14 years undernourished. Mortality rate among children aged 10 to 14 years is an important health indicator, commonly related to accidents. We chose mortality rate among children as a dependent variable because we could test independent variables against it to determine which independent variables most influence mortality in this age range. For each of the first 2 dependent variables, 2 separate regression models were developed, 1 using only the adult mortality rate for women and the other using only the adult male mortality rate. This avoided possible colinearity between these 2 independent variables, a problem that could have occurred had we used a combined version of the adult mortality rate. We chose prevalence of malnutrition in the population as a dependent variable because it reflects the health environment of households and we wished to determine which variables were significantly related to it.

The independent (or predictor) variables used to predict the dependent variables were the following, in various combinations: adult mortality rate for men, adult mortality rate for women, per centage of the population below the poverty line, per centage of adults infected with HIV/AIDS, per centage of the population undernourished, per centage of children aged 10 to14 years who were workers (child labour prevalence).

This association could be caused by other factors affecting the population's health status that were also correlated with the per centage of children engaged in paid labour. Therefore, we included control variables such as the per centage of the population below the poverty line and the adult mortality rate in the regression.

The results of the regression confirmed that several variables played a determining role in the mortality rates of children aged 10 to 14 years and that 2 of these variables also affected the level of undernourishment. The prevalence of child labour was a significant predictor of undernourishment in a population and of the mortality rate for children aged 10 to 14 years (boys and girls), confirming that child labour affects children's health.

We also looked at the association between childhood morbidity, as measured by disability-adjusted life years, and the prevalence of child labour in the 6 regions we studied. In each of the regions with a high prevalence of child labour, there was a high correlation between child labour and childhood morbidity associated with HIV/AIDS, non-HIV infectious diseases, and malaria. Child labour remains one of the most provocative and controversial challenges facing the world at the beginning of the 21st century. Furthermore, child labour's close links to poverty, lack of education, poor health, and gender inequalities highlight the need for broad-based social and economic progress. By extrapolating data from the Global Burden of Disease Study, Graitcer and Lerer estimated mortality, morbidity, and disability associated with child labour.

Despite the limits of the Global Burden of Disease Study—for example, the health statistics were constrained by the age stratification used, and the injury data were not provided by occupation—Graitcer and Lerer were able to estimate work-related injury and mortality. They concluded that in all regions the occupational mortality rate among children matched the adult occupational mortality rate, indicating that children may be working in conditions that are as hazardous as, or even more hazardous than, those of adults. Burn injury estimates from the Global Burden of Disease Study show that work-related burns constituted more than one third of all burn injuries sustained among children aged 5 to 14 years. It is worth noting that this statistic did not take into account burns sustained during housework, the most common of which occur while cooking over an open fire.

Graitcer and Lerer did not find any health problems in working Egyptian children, but they argued that a child's exposure to poor working conditions and health hazards may result in health consequences much later in life.

In reports on child labour in Morocco, Yemen, and Guatemala, the researchers of the Understanding Children's Work project found few or no ill health effects resulting from work and suggested that this might be because the healthiest children are selected for work or because health consequences may not become apparent until a later stage in a child's life. They also showed that it is not work per se that is damaging to a child's health, but rather certain kinds of work. Studies with an ecological design have proven valuable in descriptive and etiological epidemiology, as well as in economics, social planning, and policy evaluation. Our study is the first to analyze the health effects of child labour with cross-sectional data, showing that some health indicators are affected by child labour.

Child labour, poverty, and adult mortality rates explain, at a significant level, the variance in adolescent mortality among boys and girls aged 10 to 14 years. The per centage of the population that is undernourished does not explain adolescent mortality rates for either boys or girls. For each 1 of the first 2 dependent variables (adolescent mortality rates for boys and girls aged 10 to14 years), we developed 2 regression models, one taking into account only the adult mortality rate for women and the other the combined adult mortality rate for men and women. We did this to avoid any colinearity between these 2 independent variables. The per centage of the population living below the poverty line was designated an independent variable because of its relevance to policy decisions on education, health, decentralization of resource management, and preventive measures.

As predictor variables, child labour and poverty both were significantly correlated with malnutrition (as measured by the per centage of population that was undernourished), whereas the per centage of HIV/AIDS among adults was not significantly related to malnutrition. Mortality rates for different age groups are important indicators of health status in a country. In the absence of incidence and prevalence rates for disease (morbidity data), they serve to identify vulnerable populations.

They are also among the indicators most frequently used to compare levels of socioeconomic development across countries. The finding that child labour prevalence is significantly correlated with adolescent mortality, a population's nutrition level, and the presence of infectious disease among children suggests that countries with high child labour prevalence have low health status. Work can limit a child's opportunities to obtain an education, especially for girls, whose educational attainment is a recognized determinant of child survival and health.

Work can expose children to physical and social environments conducive to high-risk sexual behaviour. Because child labour is significantly correlated with infectious diseases among children, including HIV/AIDS, interventions that reduce child labour rates could have a direct health benefit. We have identified a set of health indicators affected by child labour, and our data support the hypothesis that child labour affects children's health, particularly as measured by adolescent mortality rates. Given the nature of the available data, it is difficult to carry out a proper causality analysis. The methodological weakness of an ecological study is that estimates of effect at the ecological level cannot be extrapolated to individuals. The ecological design did not permit us to obtain direct estimates of the effect of child labour in exposed versus unexposed populations. Therefore, we could not be certain, for instance, that the children experiencing greater morbidity and mortality in a given population were actually child labourers.

Other drawbacks to the ecological method are that the method relies on existing data sources, which are often flawed and may involve confounding variables for which control may be difficult. Problems with the ecological approach, however, are minimized when measurement, analysis, and interpretation are all at the group level and the data sources are reliable. The ecological design lends itself to the study of structural or sociological effects on human behaviour and concomitant disease or injury. The principal characteristic of the ecological design—namely, that it examines differences between groups—makes it well suited to evaluating social and health policies, such as those related to injury prevention. Although our findings indicate that child labour may be affecting the health of children, more data are needed to develop a better understanding of the short- and long-term health problems associated with child labour.

Most important, longitudinal studies are required to understand the short- and long-term health effects of child labour on the individual child. Hazardous child labour In May 2002, the ILO issued a new Global report on Child labour that describes the extent of the problem. Almost 250 million children, about one in every six children aged 5 to 17 on the face of the globe, are involved in child labour. Of these, some 179 million (one in eight) are trapped in the "worst forms" of child labour. The worst form are those that endanger the child's physical, mental or moral well-being. Children can be found in almost any economic sector. However, at a global level, most of them are in agriculture (70%). Some hazards in agriculture are the exposure to pesticides, the use of dangerous machinery or tools (like knives), carrying heavy loads, the presence of snakes, and so on. Children working in agriculture are the ones suffering most injuries.

And one of the sad characteristics of child labour in agriculture are the few, if any opportunities for advance or change. For children working as domestic labourers, the hazards are sometimes not that obvious. Here, it can be the psychological hazards, like isolation, abuse, exploitation that make this form dangerous. Domestic labour is often called "hidden" and it is often difficult to find those children. Other sectors where children are working (although not in large proportion) are mining (1%) and construction (2%). The work done is generally very dangerous for children. Children are often "achievers", they want to perform well, go that extra mile, and are inexperienced and untrained in dealing with hazards. Tools are not made for them, and thus pose more hazards. There are no personal protection devices for children.

Additionally, they are also not organized and powerless. Girls are at special risk. They often begin to work at a younger age and have a double work burden (at home and in the fields). They frequently work longer hours, and in different cultural settings may get poorer nutrition. Occupational hazards cause not only short-term health effects (mainly injuries, skin problems, etc), but most effects are long-term and will only become evident in adulthood. Therefore, they are difficult to measure and to quantify. Cancer, infertility, chronic backpain and IQ reduction are some of the expected long-term outcomes. Health professionals are in a key position to identify children at risk, advise the parents on ways to reduce this risk and recommend action to policy-makers.

They should be able to recognize and assess the occupational and environmental health threats present in the places where children live, learn and play, and work, in the urban and rural communities. They should also know that these threats increase in low-income populations and minority communities, and in degraded environments. In combating hazardous child labour the most important challenge is the translation of knowledge and legislation into action, moving good intention and ideas into protecting the health of the children.

For this, the involvement of the relevant stakeholders like health and safety experts (they know about hazards and health outcomes), labour inspectors (they know how to enforce the law) and general health experts (they know about the vulnerability and health outcomes in the child and are the first-line care givers), is absolutely essential. The elimination of child labour is a long-term objective. However, in the meanwhile, we cannot allow that children are injured or harmed at work in their struggle for survival, especially when we have the knowledge and means to prevent this. Child labour remains a widespread problem in the world today.

There are at least 250 million working children between the ages of 5 and 14 in developing countries, but due to imprecision in the estimates some authors believe that this number could be much higher, reaching 500 million children. The majority of the child workers live in the developing countries of Latin America, Asia and Africa, but there are also pockets of child labour in many industrialized countries. There is a consensus that work can have positive effects on children such as the development of discipline, responsibility, self-confidence and independence; teaching children how to manage money; and providing valuable models to teach them work skills. On the other hand, it can also have a negative impact on health and development of the children.

The plain fact that the children are working is not a concern in itself, but it is the type of work they perform that will determine whether work is harmful to them. Child labour will be more harmful if it interferes with school, recreation and rest; the younger the child is; the worst the nature of the work schedule, the longer the hours or the frequency of the nocturnal work; the more hazardous the occupation and the lower the wage. Some child labour is clearly light, as the activity performed by a child delivering newspapers for two hours a day. This work is not likely to harm the child's health or development, or reduce his attendance in school. But even in this situation there is some level of exploitation in the fact that the child probably receives a lower wage than an adult would receive to perform the same job. There are also some socially or morally intolerable forms of exploitation, such as child prostitution, which most people would agree is necessary to eliminate.

Even so, it is very difficult to get consensus on how to address this problem. However, the majority of these occupations are not extreme situations like the ones above and in these cases it is necessary to balance their beneficial and harmful aspects to define which occupations are appropriate for children. In most countries of the world it is possible to find children working in very hazardous conditions, but is difficult to find good data about the impact of child labour on health to evaluate its harmful aspects. Some environmental epidemiologic studies and research on young workers suggest that children could have higher health risks than adults have when exposed to some hazards. Moreover, several theoretical concerns about the impact of occupational exposures on child health still need to be studied.

In this we intend to describe the child labour profile in developed and developing countries, to summarize the epidemiologic evidence of the greater impact of some occupational exposures in child health when compared to adults, and the theoretical concerns about the impact of child labour on health. Furthermore, we will describe the policies that have been used to combat harmful child labour. We consider child labour the activities performed by persons of less than 18 years of age that contribute to the production of a marketable product, good, or service, whether that activity is done for pay or not. This includes household work performed in the parents home, in situations where such work can be assimilated to an economic activity as, for example, when a child must devote his or her entire time to that work so that his or her parents can be employed outside home and is therefore deprived of the possibility of going to school. We are also using child work as a synonym of child labour.

The Child Labour Profile

It is very difficult to estimate the number of child workers in the world. The definition of child labour varies a lot in terms of the ages and activities covered by the statistics preventing comparisons. Moreover, child labour has a hidden nature, as great numbers of the children are working in the informal sector and some are in illegal situations, making very hard to generate reliable national statistics. (ILO, 1997) The available statistics indicate that around 96% of the child workers are in the developing countries of Africa, Asia and South America. It is important to consider that these regions have 87 per cent of the children under 18 years old of the world. Considering the child workers between the ages of 5 and 14, Asia makes up 61 per cent of child workers in developing countries, while Africa has 32 per cent, and Latin America 7 per cent.

Thus, while Asia has the highest number of child workers, Africa has the highest prevalence of child labour (40 per cent), and in Latin America, one child in five works. (OMS, 1987), (ILO, 1998), (UNICEF, 1997) Though primarily a developing country problem, child labour is emerging in many East European and Asian countries, which are in transition to a market economy. When considering all forms of child labour, the prevalence in developed countries is surprisingly high.

A study in United States found that 80 per cent of the high school students report that they hold jobs during the school year at some point during high school. Other research in the United Kingdom showed that between 15 and 26 per cent of the 11 years old and between 36 to 66 per cent of the15 years old were working.

It is known that some of these workers are engaged in hazardous jobs. Therefore, in addition to the differences in the size of the problem, there are also differences in the shape of child labour between developed and developing countries. In developing countries the children start to work at a very young age, some are malnourished, work for long hours in hazardous occupations, and frequently do not attend school. They receive very low wages or are unpaid workers and their income or help is usually essential for family survival.

They are mainly employed in the informal sector and bonded labour stills a problem in several places. Most part of the children works for jobs addressed to the internal markets. It is estimated that probably less than 5 per cent are employed in export industries. The developed countries were apparently able to eliminate bonded labour and street work; moreover, the informal sector is much smaller than in the developing countries, and child workers generally attend school. Some relatively wealthy children work for discretionary money. But child labour, including the hazardous form of it, can be found in most rich countries and very poor people, especially ethnic minorities and migrants, can face similar child labour conditions as in developing countries.

As it was convened in the ILO Convention 182, the worst forms of child labour should be prohibited and eliminated. The worst forms of child labour includes all forms of slavery or practices similar to slavery; the use, procuring or offering of a child for prostitution; the use, procuring or offering of a child for illicit activities and the work which is likely to harm the health, safety or morals of children. This will be a challenge for the governments that need to prepare themselves to offer a reasonable alternative to child labour. Some of the alternatives are discussed in the section "Interventions to Combat Child Labour".

Children's Activities and their Hazards

Many of the working children labour in very dangerous or hazardous occupations such as agriculture, manufacture, construction, retail and marginal activities. A quick overview on the characteristics and hazards of these activities are described in this section. Agriculture is the most common child occupation worldwide, and employs more working children than any other sector. This activity is consistently ranked among the most hazardous industry for mortality and morbidity. Moreover, most farms are not family units anymore where the children are helping their parents with the daily chores and learning their future job. There is an international trend for the introduction of mechanization, specialization (monoculture) and technological advances in the fields.

These process are followed by the decrease in the numbers of farms, especially small family farms, a decrease in the numbers of workers employed with an increase in the size of the farms and in productivity. Thus, there are fewer children and adolescents of the owners working on farms, and higher number of adolescents hired as farm-workers or farm-workers' children that are working alongside their parents in the fields. The children generally start to work in agriculture at a very young age and usually work for long hours for little or no payment. The seasonal characteristics of the work, the long hours required, the distance from school and the lack of schools with higher grades in the rural areas are some of the reasons that reduce school attendance.

In agricultural work children are exposed to dangerous farm machinery, which is a common cause of fatal and non-fatal injuries, whether they are operating it or working near these machines. Children are also exposed to strenuous labour, like carrying or lifting heavy loads and working in uncomfortable positions such as stooping in the same position or bending very frequently, which could affect the musculoskeletal development of the children.

Other hazards present in the fields are pesticides and the weather, especially the heat, which can be particularly dangerous for children. Poor field sanitation contains its own hazards facilitating the transmission of communicable diseases and worsening the pesticides and the heat hazard due to the lack of water. Migrant workers can be particularly at risk since their housing conditions are frequently inappropriate.

Very often manufacturing uses the child-labour workforce, but the types of industry vary widely from country to country. Most of these children are employed in small workshops or in home-based work. They seldom work in medium-size or large enterprises, but such establishments sometimes contribute indirectly to child labour by subcontracting out certain production tasks to small workshops and home-workers that make extensive use of child labour and generally are not covered by child labour national laws. Industry has specific hazards linked to each production process that are specific to the tasks performed.

On the other hand, there are some general hazards that arise not from the production process but from uncaring management. Examples of these problems are naked electric wires, lack of first aid facilities, poor ventilation, lack of sanitation, lack of sufficient light, heavy lifting, exposure to loud noise, proximity or operation of dangerous machines, and the lack of protective equipment. In some cases physical punishments are frequent. Specific hazards vary according to the industry type. Thus, child workers will be exposed to high temperatures, high risk of accidents caused by cuts and burns at the brassware and glass-bangle industry, to silica dust at the earthenware and porcelain factories, and to chemical hazards and risk of fire and explosion at the matches and firework workshops.

Child workers are also exposed to important hazards in the export sector. In the carpet industry in India the children are exposed to repetitive movements, chemical hazards, inhalation of wool dust contaminated with biological agents and inadequate working postures. In the production of soccer balls in Pakistan, children are exposed to inadequate working postures, and in the shoe industry in Portugal, Italy and Brazil, children are exposed to glue. Manufacturing is a very hazardous sector and the subcontracting practice is an issue of high concern. This practice discharges the medium-sized and large-enterprise industries of the hazardous activities, by out-sourcing this type of work to small workshops and home-based work that are frequently exempt from the existing legislation. Moreover, even if these establishments were covered by the law, they are much more difficult to monitor and have less economic capacity to work towards higher standards.

Even for adults, the construction sector is one of the most hazardous working environments with regard to the risk of accidents. Despite this fact, this sector employs a considerable number of children in several parts of the world. In Brazil, four per cent of the workers between the ages of 10 and 14 and eight per cent of those between 15 and 17 work in the construction sector. In the United States 2.5 per cent of teen workers are employed in construction although this sector is responsible for 22 per cent of the fatal work-related injuries in workers younger than 17 years. In addition to the risk of accident, there are exposures to noise, silica, asbestos, harmful dust, heavy loads, etc.

The retail sector employs half of the working teens in the United States for the most part in restaurants. Retail is responsible for half of the non-fatal injuries and twenty per cent of the fatal injuries. Although this type of work seems to be safe some tasks can be very hazardous and forbidden by law to be performed by teens such as working with hot grease and slicer machines. Since job titles may not reflect the nature of the tasks performed, it is difficult to divide the activities that are according to the law and the ones that are in violation. Also, these sectors often require long hours of work and changing schedules, which can be related with leave the work late at night and difficulties to combine work and school.

The informal and hidden nature of the domestic work makes it difficult to estimate the number of domestic workers around the world, but it is one of the most common forms of urban child labour in developing countries and employs mainly girls. In Brazil eight per cent of the workers between the ages of 10 and 14 were domestic workers. It is very difficult to study domestic workers since it is hard to contact them in order to get an interview. But it is known that domestic service does not need to be hazardous, although frequently it is. Workers often live at the workplace, are expected to work at all hours of the day with few days off, and are deprived of attending school. Far from their own families, they are very vulnerable and can receive harsh treatment from their employers, sometimes suffering physical, mental, and sexual abuse. In some cases they lack an appropriate place to sleep and do not receive sufficient food. They usually receive low or no wage; bonded labour is very common in some places.

Child prostitution has been defined as "the act of engaging or offering the services of a child to perform sexual acts for money or other consideration". This definition stresses that child prostitution is not committed by children but by the adults who engage in prostitution or offer a child's sexual services to others. NGOs estimate that at least 1 million girls worldwide are lured or forced into this scandalous form of child exploitation. Child prostitution is more frequent in developing countries such as Brazil where 200,000 children are exploited, but it can be found in developed countries such as the United States, which has at least 100,000 child prostitutes. Although girls are the most frequent targets, boys are also often exploited. There are documented cases of children as young as six or seven being exploited in Brazil. While this huge problem may be widely visible to child-prostitution exploiters, it remains virtually invisible to the people who could help these children.

Commercial sexual exploitation frequently involves trafficking of children whether they are kidnapped or sold by their parents. The children are often recruited under the false pretense of marriage or a good job in the city. While the main media focus is sex tourism, in which persons from developed countries travel to developing countries in search of sex with children, it is important to keep in mind that local persons also exploit these children. But the new face of exploitation is transnational, with criminal networks that take place not only in neighboring countries but also across the globe.

Child prostitutes suffer extreme physical and mental abuse, making this form of exploitation one of the most hazardous. They also risk drug addiction, early and unwanted pregnancies, and HIV and other sexually transmitted diseases.

The process of rescue and rehabilitation for these children is very complicated. They are frequently prosecuted by the system that should be protecting them. Even if they manage to return to their homes, they often face stigma and rejection by their families and communities.

With its high level of urbanization, Latin America has the largest number of street children. In the Russian Federation after the transition to a market economy, street child labour is a growing problem. Many of them are not street children in the strict sense since the majority of these street workers return home each night and provide critical financial support for their families.

These children shine shoes, wash and guard cars, carry luggage, sell goods at the traffic-light intersections and scavenge and pick up rags. They struggle to legitimize their work on the streets. Street workers are mainly exposed to street violence. Many are lured to drugs, prostitution and illegal work (thieving, trafficking drugs). They often need to defend their space on the street and can be prosecuted by the police (in Rio de Janeiro, Brazil, for example, three street children are killed every day, many by the police). They are also exposed to traffic accidents and extreme weather conditions and seldom attend school.

Scavenging is one example of a very hazardous street work. It adversely affects the child's self-esteem; moreover, it is very unhygienic. While working for their families, children can learn from a reasonable level of participation in the household chores that can develop a sense of self-worth. But sometimes, working for the family is essential to enable the parents to work outside the home. This is a hidden form of exploitation that affects mainly girls and it is often not even considered work. In Brazil four per cent of the children between the ages of 10 and 14 and nine per cent of the children between 15 and 17 perform exclusively household activities without attending school.

Work for the family can demand long hours, thus preventing the children from going to school or doing well in school, perpetuating the poverty cycle. It also includes some heavy chores as taking care of siblings and carrying heavy loads of firewood and buckets of water. Children are susceptible to all of the dangerous exposures faced by adults when placed in the same environment. However, children differ biologically from adults in their anatomical, physiological, and psychological characteristics because of their process of growth and development. Thus, exposure hazards that affect adults can affect children much more strongly.

In this section we examine the epidemiologic evidences and the theoretical concerns for exposures that could be particularly dangerous for children. The impact of child labour on injuries has been studied largely in the United States. These studies show that children have a higher risk of injuries than adults. In a study in the United States, teens between 15 and 17 have an injury rate of 4.9 per 100% full-time equivalent workers, while in the group of 16 years of age and older this rate was 2.8.

There is also evidence that heavy loads can be more dangerous for children the smaller they are. Parker et al. found that back injuries were more common in smaller workers than in larger workers. The other epidemiologic evidence that highlights dangerous exposures for children come mainly from studies of young workers and from environmental studies. These studies show that children have higher susceptibility to lead, silica and benzene. In addition, children are more susceptible to noise, heat and ionizing radiation.

The IOM report raises concerns that inappropriate assignments for children to perform tasks for which they are developmentally incapable of undertaking result in hazardous activities. The inappropriate structure of difficult work schedules (long hours, early/late hours with frequent changes) and the lack of supervision could increase the risk of work-related injuries and illnesses. Also, such characteristics of children and adolescents as inexperience, lack of physical and emotional maturity, adolescent sleep needs and the need to balance school and work would require work environments to structure and to minimize the risks to which young people are exposed.

The report also focuses upon the developmental factors that could put teens at a higher risk than adults. Childhood and adolescence are periods of rapid growth in a young person's life. Thus, they could be at particularly high risk of injuring ligaments and damaging bone-growth plates. Although little research has been done on the long-term consequences of premature exposure to heavy work and to repetitive back-straining movements, ergonomic factors, nevertheless, remain a concern.

Expert panels have hypothesized that children are particularly vulnerable to potential carcinogens due to their rapid cell growth. There are concerns that chemical exposures could have adverse effects on normal hormonal development of adolescents, altering the delicate balance of hormones and their feedback loops. Chemical exposures could result in devastating effects, given the importance of the endocrine system during this life period. Some authors also believe that exposures to toxic chemicals at a very young age could alter the body's response to future toxic exposures. Rapid cell growth could strengthen the exposure effects, thus shortening the latency period of some diseases. Even in situations where it does not happen, children have longer periods of exposure to cumulative hazards. Precocious exposure might predict that children become ill in young adulthood instead of at an older age.

Machines, tools, work furniture and personal protective equipment are not designed for children. Children using machines, tools and work furniture (seats, workbenches, etc.) designed for adults may develop musculoskeletal disorders such as chronic repetitive-strain injuries, repetitive-motion trauma, back problems, tenosynovitis, vibration-induced disorders and white-finger syndrome. They could also be at higher risk for injuries due to fatigue. Moreover, personal protective equipment frequently does not fit children. Thus, they often have to work without it or use alternative devices that do not provide real protection.

The appropriateness of permissible exposure limits for children established for adults since children respond differently than adults to physical and chemical exposures, the permissible exposure limits (PEL) established for adults might not be sufficiently protective for children. If they are allowed to work in places where these types of exposures exist, permissible exposure limits should be evaluated according to the child's age.

Although most people agree that harmful child labour should be eliminated, controversy nevertheless remains about the possibility of going in this direction without eliminating poverty. Of course, the reduction of poverty, one of the prominent causes of child labour, is a very important issue and should be addressed. But child labour can also perpetuate the poverty cycle, and children, however poor their families might be, should not be harmed by work. Thus, the goal must be the elimination of harmful child labour, realizing that it will not be eliminated overnight. In this process it is important to establish priorities and try to offer as much protection as possible to child workers.

The priorities also seem clear and they should include the removal of child workers from hazardous work and bonded labour and the prevention of child labour at a very young age. In this section we will discuss the main types of interventions that could be used to combat harmful child labour. Historically, an important response to child labour has been the adoption of legislation to regulate the admission of children to work and the conditions under which legislation is undertaken.

Legislation needs to be updated and it is necessary to develop efforts to enforce it. Otherwise, large child-worker concentrations in the informal sector and agriculture indicate that this initiative needs to be articulated with other mechanisms that can support and complement the law enforcement. Primary Education Schools can play a major role in the battle against child labour. Make primary education universal is still a challenge for developing countries, but reaching this goal can have an immediate impact on the reduction of child labour. A great majority of countries have laws establishing compulsory education. But the existence of this law is not sufficient. Many developing countries have a long way to go before they can provide enough schools within a reasonable traveling distance for all children, and free-of-charge for the poor.

Moreover, it is necessary to improve the quality of the public schools. To be attractive to working children, the schools need, at least, to make a difference in the chances to get a better-quality job. Also, it is necessary to remember that working children frequently are living in extreme poverty, often to the point that in many cases, schools will need to provide minimum conditions to make it possible for children to learn: books, meals, and flexibility in the school calendar in order to accommodate their seasonal work. As we have seen, children's income is very often essential to family survival. Thus, once enrolled in school, working children will need to work less or stop working. In many cases outside financial support will have to be provided for the family as for example scholarships.

Developed and developing countries need initiatives in the education of children, parents, teachers, physicians and employers about child labour and its hazards. Once enlightened about the problem, they can make a difference in the decision whether or not to start to work and in the type of job chosen. Knowing that there are hazards in most jobs, it is important to educate young workers on occupational safety and health. This initiative should raise awareness about workplace hazards and ways of preventing illnesses and injuries; raise awareness about their rights on the job and resources available to assist and encourage them to be active participants in creating and maintaining safe and healthful work environments.

School-to-Work Programs: Vocational education teaches knowledge and skills for employment in specific fields. This type of training can qualify the teen jobs and build a bridge between the school and the work environment, which sometimes appear to be very disconnected of the real world and future adult jobs.

The market-based initiatives had been playing an important rule in raising the public awareness particularly in developed countries and it is a strategy that can be explored in developing countries. These initiatives include a variety of product labeling schemes and/or corporate codes of conduct designed to inform consumers that the goods they are buying are not made or processed by children. However, to avoid the migration of the child labour to more hazardous, more hidden and worst paid jobs, these policies should be complemented by investments in schooling and the inclusion in the codes of conduct the payment of decent wages for adults, so that the need of the families to rely on child labour may be reduced.

Poverty alleviation programs that generating income and employment can also have a long-term impact in the reduction of child labour. Government's challenge, then, is to articulate different policies and to provide reasonable alternatives to child labour; meaning that, the primary education should be universal and should have good quality and, that for families who depend upon child labour to survive, other sources of income will need to be provided. Probably it is good to work, for teens, in a non-hazardous job, in low or medium intensity. It is better as higher the quality of work and as more related with the future career it is. But the child labour can have a major impact on health and development, so it is important to combat the child work in hazardous activities, the bonded labour and the work of the children in a very young age.

The information system on this subject is very rudimentary. Thus the system should be built in a way that it includes the agricultural sector and the informal sector the major child employers. Also, some research is necessary to evaluate the illegal child labour, as the work of the very young and the ones in illegal activities as prostitution and drug traffic. The impact of the child labour on health is an issue that needs further research. It is known that the children are exposed, at least, to the same exposures as the adults when performing the same activities. There are also epidemiological evidences that the children can be more susceptible to some exposures than adults are. But there is a lot to be known in this subject, many theoretical concerns about the higher child susceptibility to exposures need to be studied. The shape of child labour is very dynamic and changes in time. The new trends need to be examined to establish its impact on health.

Things that already happened in developed countries start to happen in the most developed areas of the developing countries. More and more the children combine school and work, so if on the one hand the work is not depriving the school attendance, on the other it can be creating a great burden in terms of the time consumed with both activities, reducing the time to rest and play. Another trend is the exclusion of the very poor from the market. It is already established that the very poor work in more hazardous jobs than advantaged children. Moreover as the markets become sophisticated, the very poor, which are the ones in most need, have difficulties finding a job, once they do not have the minimum necessary skills. This trend reinforces the importance of the primary education as a way to decrease the number of excluded people and minimizes social inequities.

Some advantaged children had been working for discretionary money. It is a relatively large amount of money to buy superfluous things without any familiar compromises or any savings addressed to future big expenses. Some authors have questioned whether it is beneficial to promote money management skills, since it could generate subsequent dissatisfaction with their living standards when they need to deal with general expenses of the real life. The developing countries have some particular subjects that need to be studied. Most of the child workers in these regions are very poor and an excessive number are malnourished. Thus it is important to evaluate the impact of work exposures on malnourished children as a way to support the need of policies addressed to the adequate food intake of workers in general and child workers in particular, as the meal provision at work.

Some activities that occur just in developing countries also need to be evaluated. The bonded labour is not justifiable in today's world and needs to be a priority in every place it exists. The huge informal sector is a phenomenon of current economies. In a small city in the south of Brazil 85 per cent of the child workers are in the informal sector. Thus despite the difficulties to access data on it, the informal sector with its more visible and more hidden child labour activity, street workers and domestic services, needs to be studied and covered by the policies to combat child labour.

Another hidden activity in developing countries that can not be forgotten is the exclusive household activities without attendance to school. Almost nothing is known on the impact of this type of work on health. The work at home usually has a poor status, is unpaid, often is not recognized as work and besides depriving children from education, mainly girls, could also have important health consequences. The policies to combat child labour should be as comprehensive and articulated as possible and great care should be taken to avoid undesired consequences, as the migration of child workers to the worst types of jobs. The priorities and the goals should be established according to the size and shape of the problem in each place. But it seems reasonable to say that, for the developing countries, the single most effective policy to combat child labour is the universalization of a good quality primary education. On the other hand, for developed and developing countries, the combat of the illegal child work and the promotion of good quality teen job, as apprenticeships for future careers are probably policies that should be appiied.

Bibliography

Abbott, Edith, (1910). *Women in Industry: A Study in American Economic History.* New York, 1910.

Adams, Thomas S., *Labour Problems: A Textbook.* New York, 1905.

Basu, Kaushik, (1999). "Child Labour: Cause, Consequence, and Cure, with Remarks on International Labour Standards." *Journal of Economic Literature,* XXXVII, September: 1083–1119

Benson, Ian, and John Lloyd, (1983). *New Technology and Industrial Change: The Impact of the Scientific-Technical Revolution on Labour and Industry.*

Berg, Maxine and Patricia Hudson, "Rehabilitating the Industrial Revolution." *Economic History Review,* XLV: 24–50

Berg, Maxine. "What Difference Did Women's Work Make to the Industrial Revolution?" *History Workshop* 1993 (35/spr) 22-44.

Berlanstein, Lenard R., ed. (1992). *The Industrial Revolution and Work in Nineteenth-Century Europe London.*

Bolin-Hort, Per. (1989). *Work, Family and the State: Child Labour and the Organization of Production in the British Cotton Industry, 1780–1920.* Lund: Lund University Press.

Bonnet, M. "Que penser du travail des enfants?" in *Etudes*. Paris: Assas Editions No. 3944 (avril2001).

Clopper, Edward, 1912. *Child Labour in City Streets.* New York.

Cohen, Marjorie, "Changing Perceptions of the Impact of the Industrial Revolution on Female Labour." *International Journal of Women's Studies*. 1984 (7) 291-305.

Crafts, N. F.R. (1985). *British Economic Growth during the Industrial Revolution*. Oxford: Clarendon

Cunningham, Hugh, "The Decline of Child Labour: Labour Markets and Family Economies in Europe and North America since 1830." *Economic History Review*, LIII, 3: 409–428.

Cunningham, Hugh, and Pier Paulo Viazzo, eds. (1996). *Child Labour in Historical Perspective 1800–1985*. Florence: UNICEF

Dorman, P. (2001). *"Child labour in the developed economies"*. Geneva: ILO-IPEC working paper.

Dunlop, O. Jocelyn. (1912). *English apprenticeship and Child Labour. A History*. London: T. Fisher Unwin

Fassa, A.G., et al. "Child labour and health, problems and perspectives" in *International Journal of Occupational and Environmental Health*, Vol 6, No 1, Jan-Mar 2000, Philadelphia.

Fleischman, Richard K. (1985). *Conditions of Life Among the Cotton Workers of Southeastern Lancashire During the Industrial Revolution, 1780-1850.*

Galbi, Douglas. (1997). "Child Labour and the Division of Labour in the Early English Cotton Mills." *Journal of Population Economics*, 10, 4: 1–32

Gatley, David. (1996). *Child Workers in Victorian Warrington: The Report of the Children's Commission into Child Labour*. Stafford: Staffordshire University Press

Glen, Robert. (1983). *Urban Workers in the Early Industrial Revolution.*

Gupta, M. R. "Wage determination of a child worker, a theoretical analysis", in *Review of development economics*, Vol 4, No 2 (June 2000), Oxford: Blackwell Publishers.

Haspels, N. and Michele Jankanish, editors. *Action against Child Labour*. Geneva: ILO,

Heesom, A. (1981). 'The Coal Mines Act of 1842, Social Reform, and Social Control', *Historical Journal*.

Hendrick, Harry. 1994. *Child Welfare. England 1872–1989.* London: Routledge.

Hill, C., 'Pottage for Freeborn Englishmen: Attitudes to Wage-Labour', in his *Change and Cobtinuity in 17th-century England* (1975), 219-238.

Hobbs, S., J. McKechnie and M. Lavalette. (1999). *Child Labour: A World History Companion*. Santa Barbara: ABC-Clio.

Hobsbawm, E. (1964). 'Custom, Wages and Work-Load', in his *Labouring Men*, 316-43.

Hopkins, Eric. (1982). "Working Hours and Conditions During the Industrial Revolution: A Re-Appraisal." *Economic History Review* (35) 52-66.

Horrell, Sara, Jane Humphries, and Hans-Joachim Voth. (1998). "Stature and Relative Deprivation: Fatherless Children in Early Industrial Britain", *Continuity and Change*, 13: 73–115.

Humphries, Jane. (1998). "Female-headed Households in Early Industrial Britain: The Vanguard of the Proletariat?" *Labour History Review*, 63(1): 31–65.

Hutchins, Grace, (1933). *Children Under Capitalism*. New York.

Jaiswal, P. (2000). *Child labour, a sociological study*. New Delhi: Shipra Publications.

Kumar, B. (2000). *Problems of working children*. New Delhi: A.P.H Publishing Corporation.

Laqueur, Thomas W. (1974). "Literacy and Social Mobility in the Industrial Revolution in England." *Past & Present* (64) 96-107.

Lavalette, M. ed. *A Thing of the Past? Child Labour in Britain in the Nineteenth and Twentieth Centuries.* Liverpool: Liverpool University Press.

Lee-Wright, P. (1990). *Child Slaves.* London: Earthscan Publications Ltd.

Lindert, Peter H., and Williamson, Jeffrey G. (1983). "English Workers' Living Standards During the Industrial Revolution: A New Look." *Economic History Review* (36) 1-25.

Mantoux, Paul. (1928). *The Industrial Revolution in the Eighteenth Century.* New York: Harper.

Marx, Karl. (1967). *Capital.* New York: International Publishers.

Nardinelli, Clark. (1988). "Were Children Exploited During the Industrial Revolution?" *Research in Economic History* (11) 243-276.

Nardinelli, Clark. (1990). *Child Labour and the Industrial Revolution.*

O'Brien, Patrick, and Quinault, Roland, eds. (1993). *The Industrial Revolution and British Society* Cambridge.

Raymond Fuller, (1922). *The Meaning of Child Labour.* Chicago.

Richards, P. 'State Formation and Class Struggle, 1832-48' in P. Corrigan, ed. (1980). *Capitalism, State Formation and Marxist Theory.*

Richards, P. (1979). 'The State and Early Industrial Capitalism: The Case of the Handloom Weavers', *Past and Present.*

Robinson, Keith. (1996). *What Became of the Quarry Bank Mill Apprentices?* Wilmslow: Quarry Bank Mill Trust.

Rodgers, G. and G. Standing. (1981). *Child work, poverty and underdevelopment.* Geneva: ILO.

Rose, Mary. (1989). "Social Policy and Business: Parish Apprentices and the Early Factory System 1750–1834." *Business History,* XXI: 5–32.

Sanderson, Michael. (1974). "Literacy and Social Mobility in the Industrial Revolution in England: A Rejoinder." *Past & Present* (64) 108-112.

Seabrook, J. (2000). *No hiding place, child sex tourism and the role of extraterritorial legislation.* London:Zed Books, ECPAT Europe Law Enforcement Group.

Stearns, Peter N., and Walkowitz, Daniel J., ed. (1974). *Workers in the Industrial Revolution.*

Taylor, Arthur J., ed. (1975). *The Standard of Living in Britain in the Industrial Revolution.*

Thomis, Malcolm Ian. (1974). *The Town Labourer and the Industrial Revolution.*

Thompson, E.P. (1963). *The Making of the English Working Class.* London: Victor Golancz.

Thompson, E.P., 'The Moral Economy of the English Crowd in the 18th-century', *Past & Present* 50 (1971), 76-136.

Thompson, E.P., 'Time, Work-Discipline and Industrial Capitalism', *Past & Present,* 38 (1967), 56-97.

Tuttle, Carolyn (1998). "A Revival of the Pessimist View: Child Labour and the Industrial Revolution", *Research in Economic History* 18: 53-82.

U.S. Department of Labour, *Prohibition of Night Work of Young Persons.* Washington, 1913.

United Nations Children's Fund. *Profiting from abuse: An investigation into the sexual exploitation of our children.* New York: UNICEF, 2001.

Vincent, David. (1981). *Bread, Knowledge and Freedom: a Study of Nineteenth Century Working Class Autobiography.* London: Methuen.

Winstanley, Michael. ed. (1995). *Working Children in Nineteenth-Century Lancashire.* Preston: Lancashire County Books.

Woolfson, C.A. and Matthias Beck. "Child Labour", in *International Journal of Occupational and Environmental Health,* Vol 6, No 1 (Jan-Mar 2000), Philadelphia.

Index

N

O

P

R

S

T

V

W

Y